Managing the Evolving Corporation

MANAGING THE EVOLVING CORPORATION

Langdon Morris

VAN NOSTRAND REINHOLD
ITP A Division of International Thomson Publishing Inc.

New York • Albany • Bonn • Boston • Detroit • London • Madrid • Melbourne
Mexico City • Paris • San Francisco • Singapore • Tokyo • Toronto

Printed in the United States of America
For more information, contact:

Van Nostrand Reinhold
115 Fifth Avenue
New York, NY 10003

International Thomson Publishing GmbH
Königswinterer Strasse 418
53227 Bonn
Germany

International Thomson Publishing Europe
Berkshire House 168-173
High Holborn
London WCIV 7AA
England

International Thomson Publishing Asia
221 Henderson Road #05-10
Henderson Building
Singapore 0315

Thomas Nelson Australia
102 Dodds Street
South Melbourne, 3205
Victoria, Australia

International Thomson Publishing Japan
Hirakawacho Kyowa Building, 3F
2-2-1 Hirakawacho
Chiyoda-ku, 102 Tokyo
Japan

Nelson Canada
1120 Birchmount Road
Scarborough, Ontario
Canada M1K 5G4

International Thomson Editores
Campos Eliseos 385, Piso 7
Col. Polanco
11560 Mexico D.F. Mexico

1 2 3 4 5 6 7 8 9 QEBFF 01 00 99 98 97 96 95 94

Library of Congress Cataloging-in-Publication Data

Morris, Langdon.
    Managing the evolving corporation / by Langdon Morris.
        p.   cm.
    Includes bibliographical references and index.
    ISBN 0-442-01906-8
    1. Organizational change—Management.   2. Strategic planning.
3. Leadership.   I. Title.
    HD58.8.M654   1994
    658.4'062—dc20

94-41472
CIP

To Elizabeth

Technical Credits

This book was drafted on Macintosh computers using Microsoft Word 5.0 software. Figures were prepared by the author using Deneba Canvas 3.01 software, except as noted.

Contents

Introduction

Between 1991 and 1993, 16 CEOs of major American corporations were fired. This unprecedented phenomenon reflects a fundamental change that is occurring throughout the globe: The shift from an industrial economy to an information economy. To survive amid these new conditions, leaders must define compelling visions for the future of their organizations. The future will not be like the past.

October, 1993: In the past year and a half, we have witnessed a remarkable failure of leadership of many American companies[1]*—David Nadler*

During one astonishing week in January 1993, three of America's largest corporations fired their CEOs: John Akers of IBM, James Robinson of American Express, and Paul Lego of Westinghouse were all pushed aside. But they were not the only CEOs of major corporations to lose their jobs recently. Between 1991 and 1993, 13 other CEOs of *Fortune* 500 corporations were also fired (Figure I.1).

This upheaval calls attention to unprecedented change in the global economy, and its powerful echoes still resound through the marketplace. Something fundamental is happening, and these firings are only symptoms: Although these men were well educated and carefully selected for top jobs in American enterprises, their corporations did not perform up to expectations. What went wrong?

The premise of this book is that these CEOs were removed precisely because they were not prepared for the changes that are occurring throughout the economy, and they did not understand the patterns underlying the changes. They may not even have recognized them.

In failing to understand, they certainly were not alone, for as we approach the dawn of a new century and a new millennium, we are a global

American Express	James Robinson III	January 1993
Ames Department Stores	Stephen L. Pistner	December 1992
Apple	John Sculley	July 1993
Compac	Rod Canion	October 1991
Cyprus Minerals	Chester B. Stone	February 1992
Digital	Kenneth Olsen	October 1992
GM	Robert Stempel	October 1992
Goodyear	Tom Barrett	June 1991
Hartmarx	Harvey A. Weinberg	July 1992
Imcera Group	M. Blakeman Ingle	December 1992
IBM	John Akers	January 1993
Kodak	Kay Whitmore	October 1993
R.H. Macy	Edward S. Finkelstein	April 1992
Sunbeam/Oster	Paul B. Kazarian	January 1993
TenNeco	James B. Ketelson	May 1992
Westinghouse	Paul Lego	January 1993

Figure I.1   **Fired CEOs of Major American Corporations 1991–1993**
The third column indicates the month and year they were fired.

society immersed in a process of change the likes of which has been seen only a few times in the entirety of human history. Suddenly, within the span of a single generation, the structure and character of the economy is fundamentally different—with stunning and often devastating consequences.

Just as the Renaissance once dawned across Europe, and industrialism exploded throughout the Northern Hemisphere, a new era is again upon us. Small businesses, large corporations, and entire industries struggle to adapt to these unfamiliar conditions. In so doing they are forced to reconsider their identities, their strategies, and all aspects of their operations.

*   *   *

In today's economy, major events occur with breathtaking frequency, and there is little time to respond to one before the impact of another is upon us. Surrounded by these events, we seek the underlying patterns that will help us to make sense of our times. The predominant pattern is the rate of change itself, for throughout the world change is now accelerating *exponentially*. Responding to change itself presents a significant challenge.

Another important pattern is the unprecedented decline in both income and wealth in the average American family since the 1970s. In a startling reversal of the postwar trend, the average family lost 15 percent of its accumulated wealth between 1984 and 1991.[2] During the same period, real wages for the average American man declined 10 percent.[3] We have suddenly become poorer, but why?

The answer is linked to the resource that powers our economy: oil. Since the birth of the oil industry in the 1860s, oil has been the critical source of energy for the industrial economy throughout the globe, and it remains so today. Five of the 20 largest American corporations are oil companies (Exxon, Mobil, Texaco, Chevron, and Amoco), while four others manufacture products that are directly dependent on oil-burning engines (GM, Ford, Chrysler, and Boeing).[4]

In the early decades of the 20th century, oil-powered machines replaced human labor in industry after industry, and combined with the newly developed practice of professional management, the result was a steady rise in productivity. With increasing productivity came increasing wealth and higher wages,[5] but through all of this economic growth, the price of oil remained remarkably stable.

However, the first Oil Shock of 1973 was a decisive event, for it marked the end of low oil prices. Since then, the energy that drives the industrial economy has become much more expensive, and therefore the cost of many other basic commodities has also increased along with the cost of living in the industrialized world (Figure I.2). This has led, of course, to an overall decline in productivity, and, inevitably, to lower wages.

Unaware of this larger pattern and perhaps unwilling to adjust their lifestyles, millions of American families consumed in excess of their incomes during the 1980s and literally became poorer. Some were so devastated by these events that they became economic refugees, homeless people sadly prowling the city streets in search of food.

Struggling with reduced incomes and diminished wealth in the 1990s, consumers no longer try to evade reality, but instead they search for value. 'Value' is the key issue in the marketplace today, and companies that are adept at providing value have become market leaders. As General Electric

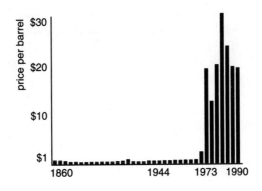

Figure I.2 **Oil Prices, 1860–1990**
As the Oil Shock of 1973 was a *cause* of inflation rather than a *consequence* of inflation, prices on this graph are indicated in nominal dollars.[6]

CEO Jack Welch comments, "If you can't sell a top-quality product at the world's lowest price, you're going to be out of the game."[7]

To create value in a marketplace where the cost of energy and material goods is increasing, economist and entrepreneur Paul Hawken points out that the dynamics of competition has shifted the focus to substituting intangible 'intelligence' for costly 'mass.'[8] Through careful design and the application of advancing technology, products are made from lighter-weight materials rather than heavier and more expensive ones; they are designed to function more effectively and to reduce the user's time and effort; and they are more durable. Overall, they do more with less.

Digitally controlled machines produce parts to ever-increasing standards of precision with less waste, while computer integrated manufacturing systems optimize the flow of materials through factories, reducing inventories. Bar coding and point-of-sale computing further reduces inventory costs, and even customer service makes a difference by making it easier for consumers to get exactly what they want without wasting time.

But hidden beneath the linked patterns of higher energy prices, increasing product intelligence, and the demand for consumer value is another, more subtle one that is also a consequence of the increasing cost of energy. This pattern concerns the issue of 'complexity.'

If we were to use a single word to describe our society, surely the word 'complex' would be a good choice, for even as complexity surrounds us, we have come to consider it a normal aspect of everyday life. There are abundant manifestations of its impact, from the tax code to the intricacies of the advanced technology that we use every day, to airplanes and space travel. Even the food we eat reflects this complexity, for it is grown on factory farms and delivered to stores thousands of miles away.

With each passing month, life seems to become more complex, and although this complexity can contribute to the richness of our experience, we also wonder if the continued advance of complexity throughout our civilization can be sustained, or if we will follow the Romans, the Mayans, and many others into irreversible decline. As archaeologist Joseph Tainter observed, "The image of lost civilizations is compelling: cities buried by drifting sands or tangled jungle, ruin and desolation where once there were people and abundance."[9]

After carefully reviewing the explanations that centuries of historians and archaeologists proposed, Tainter concluded that complexity itself may be the real root cause of collapse. He showed that the costs associated with complexity eventually (inevitably?) result in a situation in which the return on the investment in complexity no longer achieves the expected benefits.

When a society reaches that point in its development, it expends still more resources but does not receive the results that it wants or needs, for a pattern of 'declining marginal returns' has set in (Figure I.3).

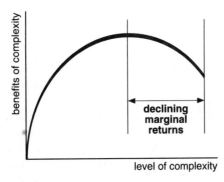

Figure I.3 **Declining Marginal Returns**
Based on Figure 19, *The Collapse of Complex Societies* by Joseph A. Tainter.

Tainter points out that "complexity is a problem-solving strategy," and certainly we have chosen this strategy through our dependence on high technology. "The problems with which the universe can confront any society are, for practical purposes, infinite in number and endless in variety. As stresses necessarily arise, new organizational and economic solutions must be developed, typically at increasing cost and declining marginal return."[10]

The development and use of advanced technology creates complexity, and in response to this complexity we make things more complex still. Each year there are more laws and regulations, more taxes and fees, more congestion, more constraints and more stress.

Complexity certainly carries with it a high social cost, for there is 'future shock,' and 'sticker shock'; and there are uncounted deaths from pollution, conflict, and industrial accidents. Ecosystems are destroyed and species made extinct. Millions of people are packed into society's prisons, and millions more live in crowded and filthy slums.

All of these phenomena are consequences of our complex way of life, and with each there is a cost. In fact, social complexity adds real cost to every product and service in the marketplace, and thus impacts productivity.

From this perspective, it is clear that the events of 1973 which resulted in higher oil prices have pushed the industrial economy into a pattern of declining marginal returns: We have passed the peak of industrialism (Figure I.4).

Amid the increasing stress, economic activity continues, but it is not guided by any grand plan. It is simply the aggregate of choices and actions taken by individuals, who do the best that they can. All over the world, consumers have adopted a potent strategy to deal with these difficult times,

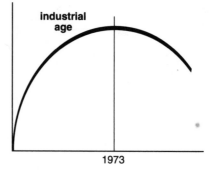

Figure I.4 **Declining Marginal Returns in the Industrial Economy**
The Oil Shock of 1973 marked the peak of the industrial economy. Since then, the pattern of declining marginal returns has affected all aspects of the economy.

the strategy of gathering information that helps them make the best possible choices, the strategy of *learning*. Learning is thoroughly decisive in today's economy, for confronted with the abundance of variety in the marketplace, consumers choose to learn in order to determine which are the best values. *Learning is the strategy through which people cope with complexity.*

Taken together, the aggregate of all individual learning is the phenomenon of *evolution* of society as a whole. As a result of individual learning and individual choice in the marketplace, we have begun the transition from an economy that was driven fundamentally by oil-powered industrial machines to one that depends on the process of learning and its artifact, *information.* This transition from an industrial economy to an information economy is a subtle, though decisive shift in human affairs, one that has been driven entirely from within the process itself. The very success of industrialism created conditions in which industrialism was no longer a sufficient economic model (Figure I.5).

Bioeconomist Michael Rothschild points out that to understand this new economy, we must learn to *think* about it differently than we have in the past.[11] The industrial economy was based on the productivity of machines, and the metaphors that were used to describe it were mechanistic. Unfortunately, that language is still in use today, and our habit of speaking as though we could 'overhaul' and 'fine-tune' the economy inhibits us from recognizing the important patterns of the information economy.

Slowed by old thinking habits and outdated economic models, most business leaders have not adjusted to the emphasis on learning, and they attempt to maintain control as their predecessors did for so many decades. Their tool for doing so has been the traditional command and control

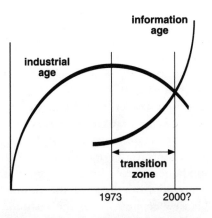

***Figure I.5* The Transition from the Industrial Economy to the Information Economy**
During the industrial economy, the primary economic force was the substitution of machines for labor. Since 1973, this economic pattern has been in decline, while the information economy has been developing rapidly. The information economy is characterized by the substitution of information for mass. During this transition from one economy to the next, society experiences extreme turbulence and uncertainty, as we observe today throughout the world.

organizational hierarchy that was once a source of strength, but now its very rigidity hinders their efforts.

If their organizations are to survive into the next century, leaders must abandon their futile quest for control and reach beyond the hierarchy. They must realize that their organizations will be successful only when they *evolve* in parallel with the technologies that they depend upon and the markets in which they compete. Such evolution will only occur through the application of learning, and it will occur systematically only in organizations that are *designed* for it to occur.

THE ORGANIZATION OF THIS BOOK

This book is for leaders of organizations, whether they are CEOs, senior managers, middle managers, or line workers, for the leaders are the ones who need to understand today's changes, and more importantly, the patterns that underlie them. Only when they thoroughly understand these patterns can they create organizations that are successful and enduring.[12]

Part One, "The 21st Century Organization," deals with the design of organizations, presenting new models that are already replacing the command and control paradigm in leading corporations worldwide. Chapter 1 describes the key issue for organization designers, the shift from structure-oriented thinking to process thinking. Chapter 2 describes five diverse process-oriented organizational models, and Chapter 3 synthesizes the five process-oriented models into a new approach to organization called 'recognition and response' (Figure I.6).

Part Two presents theory describing the new economic conditions in terms of key *Patterns of Change* that are occurring throughout the world. Chapter 4 deals with today's exponential rate of change and the significant consequences that it presents for all organizations. Chapter 5 discusses information and its fundamental role for all organizations, and Chapter 6 describes the difficult relationship between the knowledgeable individual, the key agent in this new economy, and the institutions through which individuals join together to accomplish their shared purposes.

Between Parts Two and Three is an Interlude that presents a model of the universal *Design Process,* a systematic approach to complex problems such as large-scale organizational change.

Part Three shifts to the *practical* perspective, describing key elements of the *Knowledge Infrastructure* that will enable organizations to operate effectively in the new milieu of information and learning. Chapter 8 presents the key elements of the information and communications systems that quicken the 'nervous system' of the recognition and response organization. Chapter 9 presents techniques to facilitate effective collaboration among the many individuals whose unique knowledge must come together to compose an organization's products and services, while Chapter 10 describes the design of the work place itself.

Finally, Part Four describes the *practice* of *Transformation* from command and control models to models based on recognition and response, through the application of the design process and a variety of transformation strategies. Transformation can be a difficult process for the corporation, but those that accomplish it will likely become the leaders in the

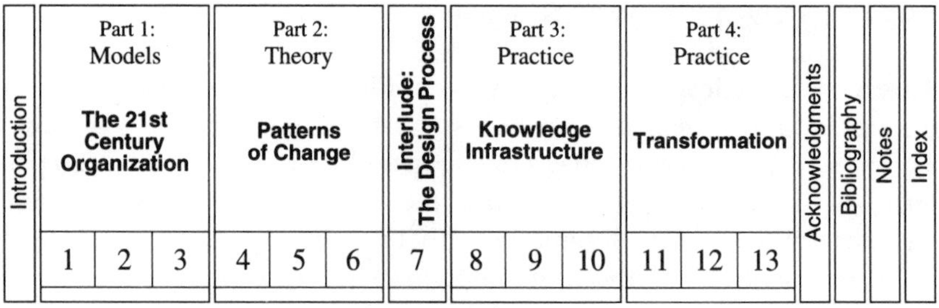

Introduction	Part 1: Models			Part 2: Theory			Interlude: The Design Process	Part 3: Practice			Part 4: Practice			Acknowledgments	Bibliography	Notes	Index
	The 21st Century Organization			Patterns of Change				Knowledge Infrastructure			Transformation						
	1	2	3	4	5	6	7	8	9	10	11	12	13				

Figure I.6 Contents of *Beyond Hierarchy: The Evolving Corporation*

decades ahead. They will also be the survivors, for it is likely that *only* these corporations will become 21st century organizations.

FIGHTING THE NEXT WAR

The 16 fired CEOs achieved tremendous success in their careers, but perhaps their problems came about precisely because of their successes, for perhaps they believed that their successes had prepared them for challenges of the 1990s.

The military is familiar with this problem. Historian Arnold Toynbee called it 'preparing to fight the last war.'[13] Thus did the French, responding to the horrors of the trench warfare of World War I, erect the monumental Maginot Line to protect them forever from German aggression. However, when the next war came only 20 years later, it was not a war of attrition in the trenches but a war of mobility. The Germans raced around the end of the Maginot Line and easily captured it from behind. The enormous guns of the Maginot Line faced in one direction only, towards the past.[14]

The issue is the same for the corporation: Leaders must understand that the present is not merely a linear extension of the trends of the past. Today's economy is not moving in a straight line, it is accelerating off the top of the scale and displaying previously unimagined possibilities which present unprecedented challenges.

To survive, corporations must adapt to these conditions, and as author M. Mitchell Waldrop points out, "adaptation requires changing an internal model."[15] If John Akers and James Robinson and Paul Lego were distracted by their prior successes, they may not have clearly understood the economic challenges of the 1990s and the need for adaptation. Lacking this vital context, they then *could not* have presented compelling visions to their employees and to their customers. Thus, their failures would have been inevitable.

In these demanding times, even CEOs get fired—and not just for outright incompetence or ethical lapses. Far more dangerous to the corporation is the leader who lacks a clear and inspiring vision, a subtle but decisive shortcoming. Leaders must be prepared to fight the next war, not the prior one, and to do so they must be visionaries. As adaptation to the new economy requires new models, surely now is the time.

PART ONE

MODELS
The 21st Century Organization

The neglected leadership role is the designer of the ship. No one has a more sweeping influence than the designer. What good does it do for the captain to say, 'Turn starboard thirty degrees,' when the designer has built the rudder that will turn only to port, or which takes six hours to turn to starboard? It's fruitless to be the leader in an organization that is poorly designed.[1]—Peter Senge

The design of most of today's organizations is based on a model of layered hierarchy and the concept of 'command and control.' Since the beginning of commerce, command and control has been the predominant organizational model for businesses throughout the world, and it was undoubtedly fundamental to the rapid expansion and tremendous successes of the industrial economy.

During the rapid change of the last two decades, however, its inherent limitations have supplanted its advantages, for today's command and control organizations tend to be rigid, inflexible, and slow to adapt. The very organizational structures that were so well suited to the business conditions of 1901 will render command and control organizations nearly incapable of functioning in 2001.

Part One explores the key issues of organization design and describes new organizational models that are suited to the demands of the 21st century.

1

Structure Becomes Process

The command and control organizational model, the pyramid, is based on the idea that an organization should be a structure. But structures tend to be rigid and to resist change. In today's rapidly changing world, organizations must be flexible and responsive to change. Rather than using organizational concepts based on structures, designers must apply concepts of 'process.' The shift from structure-oriented thinking to process-oriented thinking reframes the practice of organization design.

Give up control to get something better.[1]—*Gilbert Amelio*

. . . in an organism, processes are not organized around energy in the physicist's meaning of the term. They are organized around information.[2]—*Peter Drucker*

There are laws that govern many aspects of a corporation's existence, but by far the majority of the decisions that are made in the process of creating one are a matter of choice. A corporation is something which is *designed,* with all of the opportunities and risks inherent in this uniquely human process.

For the last one hundred years, however, it has been widely assumed that the design of a corporation must be based on the model of the command and control hierarchy. Designing this organization has simply been a matter of naming the required departments and arranging boxes in a pyramid. This hardly qualifies as a process of design at all, any more than drawing a mustache on a copy of the Mona Lisa constitutes making a new work of art (Figure 1.1). Yet this very practice has passed as organization design for many decades, and a standard hierarchical model has been taught to and implemented by generations of executives.

Figure 1.1 **The Mona Lisa?**
Drawing a mustache on Leonardo's *Mona Lisa* does not constitute designing a new work of art. (Mustache by Ernest Sid.)

STRUCTURE

The corporate pyramid is described as an organizational structure, and one of the most important attributes of this structure, as with all structures, is its durability. It is valued for its strength and rigidity, its ability to resist change and to stand unscathed by the passage of time and the most powerful of storms (Figure 1.2).

A command and control structure is meant to be as rigid as a building and to resist change by defining behavior patterns through which authority and responsibility are allocated. The patterns that are perhaps most pervasive are rewards for success and punishment for failure. Since these two kinds of feedback are also the most powerful, their continuing influence sustains the corporate structure.

Because these rewards and punishments come from within, they do not necessarily pertain to anything that an individual might have accomplished in the marketplace: Organizational structure is designed to minimize the impact of whatever happens outside. Former GE board member Walter Wriston commented about salaries in the company: "It didn't make a hell of a lot of difference if the guy had just screwed up or invented Lexan. You'd take the size of the guy's shirt collar and divide it by the Gregorian calendar and multiply it by the square root of pi, and you'd come out with a number that was totally meaningless."[3]

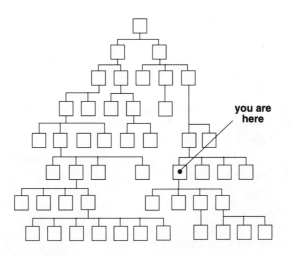

Figure 1.2 **The Pyramid**

Although this pattern of ignoring external reality has the benefit of protecting the organization from ephemeral shifts in the wind, it also isolates people from real feedback about whatever they're doing. Since the important feedback that they do get is from higher corporate authorities, their responses are conditioned according to the needs and perceptions of those in the hierarchy itself. Events in the marketplace are discounted, while events in the hierarchy are amplified.

For this reason, command and control hierarchies lose their focus on the market and begin to confuse their own perceptions of the world with reality: "Many of GE's best managers devoted far more energy to internal matters than to their customers' needs. As GEers sometimes expressed it, theirs was a company that operated, 'with its face to the CEO and its ass to the customer.' "[4]

The pattern of relationships that leads to this kind of behavior is known as 'corporate culture,' and it is the very embodiment of an organization's resistance to change. After all, a culture *is* a culture precisely because it resists change in order to reproduce itself ad infinitum, maintaining its cohesiveness and its identity despite all challenges.

This is inherently problematic in a changing marketplace, because a corporation's very rigidity suppresses its ability to adapt. Eventually, when the forces of calamitous change finally do overwhelm a structure, it does not fail gracefully or gently, but catastrophically, collapsing into a pile of rubble.

Modifications to rigid structures are complicated, time-consuming, and very expensive: "Hoping to cure itself with one last, huge gulp of bitter medicine, IBM yesterday announced an $8 billion second-quarter loss and the elimination of another 35,000 jobs by the end of 1994. IBM's loss . . . arises mainly from $8.9 billion in extraordinary charges to cover layoffs, plant closings, and other current and future efforts to shrink the struggling company."[5]

Unfortunately for IBM and so many other corporations, the real problem isn't the old structure or the new structure. The problem with the command and control model is its reliance on the very *concept* of structure itself. We are trapped in a mindset of 'structure' that prevents organizations from adapting to the reality of the marketplace.

ANOTHER VIEW OF COMPLEXITY

The belief that organizations must be structures, and that structures must be rigid, is a remnant of the Newtonian universe of cause and effect, the mechanistic thinking that was the intellectual foundation of the industrial economy.

However, as advancing technology has produced machines of ever-increasing capability and precision, those working in fields as diverse as physics, biology, chemistry, and economics have identified important principles beyond the familiar world of cause and effect. Some of these principles suggest new ways of thinking about the economy and its relationship with the organizations that compose it.

Economist Brian Arthur describes the shift as a matter of how people think about the world: "Nonscientists tend to think that science works by deduction. But actually, science works mainly by metaphor. And what's happening is that the kinds of metaphor people have in mind are changing."[6]

Arthur is among those who are developing a model of the economy that is the subject of a discipline called 'complexity.' Author M. Mitchell Waldrop describes complexity this way: "Instead of relying on the Newtonian metaphor of clockwork predictability, complexity seems to be based on metaphors more closely akin to the growth of a plant from a tiny seed, or the unfolding of a computer program from a few lines of code, or perhaps even the organic, self-organized flocking of simpleminded birds."[7]

Complexity offers explanations of an entire class of phenomena that, because of their very complexity, have remained at the periphery of scientific competence for many centuries. These are systems that ". . . have somehow acquired the ability to bring order and chaos into a special kind of balance. This balance point—often called *the edge of chaos*—is where the

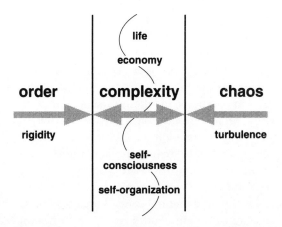

Figure 1.3 **Complexity**
'Complexity' exists in the narrow border between order and chaos, for it is here that processes such as life, the economy, self-consciousness, and self-organization can be found.

components of a system never quite lock into place, and yet never quite dissolve into turbulence either. The edge of chaos is where life has enough stability to sustain itself and enough creativity to deserve the name of life. The edge of chaos is where new ideas and innovative genotypes are forever nibbling away at the edges of the status quo . . . ."[8] (Figure 1.3).

Balance between lifeless order and lifeless chaos is an apt description of the economy itself, which consists of countless individual actions in the marketplace that together compose a dynamic yet coherent system. The concept of complexity is itself perhaps the best description of the economy that has ever been offered, and it is for this reason that complexity is fundamentally important to organization designers. If complexity is the reality of the marketplace, then this same notion of complexity is what organizations must be designed to accommodate.

At one extreme, rigid structures are too orderly to be responsive to the dynamic character of the complex market. At the other extreme, nothing will be accomplished by an 'organization' that is mired in turbulent anarchy. Complexity suggests that in between these two is a narrow bandwidth in which the corporation can function effectively amid the rapid changes of the marketplace, and this is where the new organization must be created.

SELF-ORGANIZATION

Complex systems are characterized by abundant interactions among their parts: "Think of the quadrillions of chemically reacting proteins, lipids, and nucleic acids that make up a living cell, or the billions of interconnected neurons that make up the brain, or the millions of mutually interdependent individuals who make up human society."[9]

In all of these systems, there is no central, controlling authority. Instead, the capacity to endure emerges in the context of shared purposes as a consequence of interactions, for the interactions themselves can lead to the phenomenon of *self-organization*. That the capacity to organize can come from the very process of interactions within the system itself is a compelling idea, and when we realize that ten billion neurons is not a self-conscious brain *unless* the neurons relate to each other in a very particular way, we see its essence.

This addresses the fundamental issue of organization design, for it tells us that the capacity to organize does not have to be imposed from the outside as it is in the command and control model.

As it is apparent that organizations using command and control are generally unable to respond quickly enough to the complex and changing marketplace of today, it may be that the very practice of command and control actually suppresses higher levels of organization from emerging. Tainter's model suggests, and experience verifies, that complexity is overwhelming to many organizations, and the pattern of declining marginal returns may have already set in. After all, the concept of declining marginal returns is a compelling explanation for the $8 billion that IBM lost in the process of reorganizing itself.

Companies like IBM repeatedly attempt to establish their organizational structures *a priori,* but because the marketplace environment is changing more quickly than they can respond, their structures are obsolete sooner rather than later. In the coming decades, those corporations that persist in organizing themselves around *a priori* concepts of structure will find that they cannot compete successfully, and many of them will cease to exist.

PROCESS

The complex realm between order and chaos is the realm of 'process,' for the focus there is not on the structures themselves, but on relationships and interactions. In fact, there must be virtually no emphasis on structure at all: *Structure becomes process.*

This critical distinction is described by scientist Erich Jantsch:

> this new understanding may be characterized as process-oriented, in contrast to the emphasis on 'solid' system components and structures composed of

them. . . . whereas a given spatial structure, such as a machine, determines to a large extent the processes by which it can accommodate, the interplay of processes may lead to the open evolution of structures. Emphasis is then on the becoming. . . . a system now appears as a set of coherent, evolving, interactive processes which temporarily manifest in globally stable structures that have nothing to do with the equilibrium and solidity of technological structures. Caterpillar and butterfly, for example, are two temporarily stabilized structures in the coherent evolution of one and the same system. . . . Not only the evolution of a system, but also its existence in a specific structure becomes dissolved into processes.[10]

In the corporation, these interactions are the basis of self-organization in response to the ever-changing marketplace. Among today's organizations as in most complex systems, the predominant medium of interaction is *information,* the uniquely powerful phenomenon that is fundamental to all economic activity. Information is also fundamental to all living systems, and therefore the processes which constitute an organization must be formulated around information.

Peter Drucker expresses this shift from mechanistic thinking to the prevalence of information:

Three hundred years of technology came to an end after World War II. During those three centuries the model for technology was a mechanical one. . . . Since the end of World War II, however, the model of technology has become the biological process, the events inside an organism. And in an organism, processes are not organized around energy in the physicist's meaning of the term. They are organized around information.[11]

Information is the prize, and it is the method as well. In the words of Gilbert Amelio, CEO of National Semiconductor, "The purpose of information is not to impose control, but to enable 10,000 people to make appropriate decisions that are just what I would have decided. Give up control to get something better."[12] Says Jack Welch, "Everybody has to know everything, so they can make the right decisions by themselves."[13]

The shift from structure thinking to process thinking reframes the concept of organization design and enables important new principles to be integrated into its practice, principles such as complexity and self-organization. Designing corporations around information and the interactions that it fosters is a radical departure from the practices of the last century. It offers the possibility that corporations can be organized on the lively edge between order and chaos, with the capacity that today's rigid hierarchies lack—to adapt to the rapidly changing marketplace of the information economy.

2

Beyond Hierarchy

The command and control hierarchy was developed as a model of corporate organization for the slowly changing economy of 1900. It was based on four key assumptions, and though all four are invalid in today's rapidly changing economy, command and control remains the predominant organizational model. Nevertheless, process-oriented models that go beyond the hierarchy to enable organizations to readily adapt are being developed and implemented by pioneering thinkers and managers throughout the world. Five of these approaches to the process orientation are presented here.

Most businesses today are still organized much the same way they were in 1663, with stultifying top-down management, close and distrustful supervision, and little room for creativity. The conflict between advanced technology and archaic mentality is, I believe, a major reason why the modern workplace is characterized by dissatisfaction, frustration, inflexibility, and stress.[1]—Ricardo Semler

The old organization was built on control, but the world has changed. The world is moving at such a pace that control is a limitation. It slows you down. You've got to balance freedom with some control, but you've got to have more freedom than you ever dreamed of.[2]—Jack Welch

The process of evolution has incorporated billions of years of testing and refinement into the design of all humans. Organization designers, however, have but a few thousand years of civilization to draw upon, and since our current situation is unprecedented, most of what has been done throughout human history no longer works. It is clear that new organizational models will be invented in our times.

These models will not be the traditional command and control pyramid, for it is obsolete as a model for organizing the corporation. Although the pyramid is easy to understand, its very simplicity is also its biggest draw-back, for in its modern application it is simplistic.

THE ASSUMPTIONS OF COMMAND AND CONTROL

The command and control hierarchy as a system of administration was perfected by the Chinese during many centuries of empire, and by the Roman army during centuries of conquest and administration. Later, the hierarchical model was adopted by the Catholic Church, and spread by it throughout the world. The very word 'hierarch' is Greek for 'high priest'; a 'hierarchy' is 'the graded ranking of church administrators.'[3]

The command and control model was developed in American business by the early railroads and by the industrial magnates such as John D. Rock-efeller, who created the vast Standard Oil empire.[4]

Rockefeller entered the oil business in 1863, and by 1870 he and his four partners had established Standard Oil and dominated the kerosene market. They chose the name 'Standard' to express their commitment to providing their customers with a consistent quality of kerosene that could be relied upon not to explode when lit, a troublesome problem in the days of kerosene lamps.[5] In addition to a standard formula for kerosene, Rock-efeller also developed a standard organizational formula, and in retrospect, there seem to be four primary factors that shaped Standard's organizational model (Figure 2.1):

1. Stability.

2. Hierarchy.

3. Command.

4. Control.

1. Stability

For three-quarters of a century, between 1863 and 1939, the world's oil market (for kerosene and later for gasoline) changed very slowly. Prices were remarkably stable. The lag inherent in the slow communications sys-tems of those days gave all organizations time to carefully plot and imple-ment their own business strategies.

The assumption of stability leads to the belief that the future will be like the past was, but clearly this is not the case today, now that the mar-ketplace is changing exponentially. Mass production and mass consump-tion are being replaced by the much different process of 'mass customi-

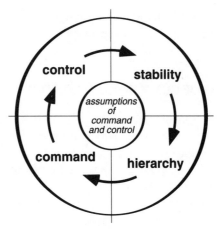

Figure 2.1 **The Assumptions of Command and Control**

zation,' while today's breadth of competition is far greater and the pace of innovation much faster. This rapid advance of technology shows no sign of slowing, and the stable conditions of 1900 will not return in our lifetimes.

2. Hierarchy

When Rockefeller began refining oil, the cost of coordinating a large enterprise was high because it took a long time to move information. To control this cost, people at each layer of hierarchy collected and filtered information, passing to the next layer only what was believed to be essential. The information that eventually reached Rockefeller at the top of the hierarchy made him the most knowledgeable man in the company.

The cost of coordination, of moving information, has steadily declined throughout the 20th century, particularly since computers have been applied to communications. Today, the cost of sending a message throughout a global organization is negligible. CNN broadcasts live from anywhere on the globe to everywhere on the globe, and individuals have immediate access to information whether they are in Siberia or at headquarters. Technology has made the hierarchy irrelevant as a tool for filtering information.

There are other aspects of the hierarchy, however, that cannot be dismissed. These will be explored below in "The Viable System Model" and in Chapter 3 in "Hierarchy, Redux."

3. Command

Positioned at the pinnacle and receiving information from throughout the company, Rockefeller knew more about the business than anyone else, and therefore he made decisions for the entire organization. Those working at successive organizational layers knew more than their subordinates and gave commands to those below them.

In the 1990s, the quantity of information available and the complexity of the marketplace is incomparably greater than it was 100 years ago. There is simply too much for any individual to comprehend, and in today's specialized and complex decision-making environment, collaboration has replaced command. The need to command is an anachronism, a remnant of a simpler time.

4. Control

With a stable marketplace, the benefit of lag throughout the economy, centralization of information, and the command approach to management, Rockefeller and his partners were able to maintain control over their vast, global empire.

Today, however, with so much happening so quickly, it is impossible for anyone to comprehend what everyone else should be doing, or even to provide detailed guidance. Technical specialization has advanced so far that no one other than the specialist knows what he or she ought to be doing, or if what has been done has been done well, until long after the event. The hope of control has become an illusion, and the exercise of power in quest of control has led in practice to overly constrained organizations rife with social conflict and inept at managing change.

*   *   *

For Rockefeller, the assumptions underlying the organizational model were probably explicit, and together they composed a system that fit the realities of the market. Today, command and control remains *the* accepted model of corporate structure even though the four underlying factors are decidedly invalid.

For managers, the promise of control is certainly a seductive prospect, partially accounting for the wide popularity of command and control. But operating on a basis of invalid assumptions, command and control companies have tremendous difficulties adapting to today's exponentially changing marketplace.

FIVE PROCESS MODELS

In the absence of stability, the shift to process thinking is a necessity, for it is clear that structural models cannot succeed amid rapid change. As specific process models emerge in response to existing conditions, whatever they may be, the process approach transcends the limits inherent in the command and control structure.

There are many different ways of designing the process-oriented organization, and to provide a sense of the wide range of possibilities, five models that are very different from each other are presented here. Of the five, two are based on natural systems (the viable system model and managerial bionomics), two are models of learning (the Deming model and core competencies), and one is based on a normative model of human relations that places high value on trust (Semco).

1. Semco: Trust.

2. Deming: An Organization as a System.

3. Managerial Bionomics.

4. The Viable System Model.

5. Core Competencies.

1. Semco: Trust

Ricardo Semler took over the management of Semco, his family's company, in the midst of a crisis that threatened to put the small Brazilian manufacturing firm out of business. On his first day as CEO, at age 21, he fired the entire senior executive team and started anew, guided by a philosophy of management and a commitment to realizing that philosophy in the operations of the company.

During the course of the 1980s, Semco abandoned the pyramidal organizational model, eliminated the corporate policy manual, set up a system for managers to set their own salaries, set up a system for workers to set production quotas and work hours, and saw productivity per worker increase from $10,800 to $92,000 (adjusted for inflation) between 1980 and 1987.

Employees vote on issues such as proposed corporate acquisitions, while potential employees are interviewed and accepted not by managers, but by their future coworkers.

Meanwhile, Semler himself became a celebrity in Brazil by writing a book, *Turning the Tables,* which sold more than 460,000 copies to become the best-selling nonfiction book in the history of the country.

The principle underlying the transformation of Semco is trust. Semler chose to trust the company's employees and to create an organization in which that trust was the foundation of the company's operations.

In this environment, trust replaced power, and consequently the middle of the organizational pyramid proved to be unnecessary and unproductive:

> The organizational pyramid is the cause of much corporate evil, because the tip is too far from the base. Pyramids emphasize power, promote insecurity, distort communications, hobble interaction, and make it very difficult for the people who plan and the people who execute to move in the same direction. So Semco designed an organizational circle. Its greatest advantage is to reduce management levels to three—one corporate level and two operating levels at the manufacturing units. It consists of three concentric circles. One tiny, central circle contains the five people who integrate the company's movements. These are the counselors. I'm one of them, and except for a couple of legal documents that call me president, counselor is the only title I use. A second, larger circle contains the heads of the eight divisions—we call them partners. Finally, a huge circle holds all the other employees [approximately 200]. Most of them are people we call associates; they do the research, design, sales, and manufacturing work and have no one reporting to them on a regular basis. But some of them are the permanent and temporary team and task leaders we call coordinators. Counselors, partners, coordinators, and associates. Four titles. Three management layers[6] (Figure 2.2).

Semco's approach to structure is minimal, based on the expectation, and now the practice, that workers will organize themselves in response to the demands of the work. Semler makes it clear that over the years, the composition of work teams has changed significantly, as products and product lines have come and gone with the trends of the marketplace.

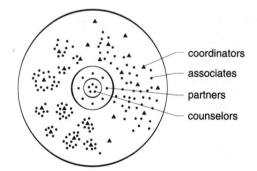

Figure 2.2 **The Semco Organizational Model**
Based on the description in "Managing Without Managers," *Harvard Business Review,* September–October 1989, by Ricardo Semler.

2. Deming: An Organization as a System

Another approach to modeling the corporation as a process is described by W. Edwards Deming. Dr. Deming defines a corporation as a system which is "a network of interdependent components" that work together to accomplish an aim.[7]

Rather than visualizing this organization as a fixed structure, Dr. Deming shows it as a process of developing and delivering products and services (Figure 2.3). It is a flow of materials from suppliers through production to customers, according to a design. The information that is used to manage the process itself also flows through the system along with materials. From consumers comes feedback, which is used to redesign and thereby improve products, services, and the processes themselves:

> [The model] is actually an organization chart. It generates improvement and adaptation. It is a process for learning. It shows people what their jobs are, how they should interact with one another as part of a system. Anybody can see from this chart what his job is, and how his work fits in with the work of others in the system. He may now engage his mind as well as his labor. He may now take joy in his work. This diagram as an organization chart, is far more meaningful than the usual pyramid. The pyramid only shows responsibilities for reporting, who reports to whom. It shows the chain of command and accountability. A pyramid does not describe the system of production. It does not tell anybody how his work fits into the work of other people in the company. If a pyramid conveys any message at all, it is that anybody should first and foremost try to satisfy his boss. The customer is not in the pyramid. A pyramid, as an organization chart, thus destroys the system.[8]

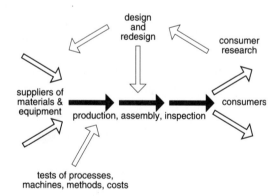

Figure 2.3 **The Deming Model**
Based on Figure 6, *The New Economics for Industry, Government, Education* by W. Edwards Deming.

Individuals understand their function within the overall process and can locate where they are in relation to others. They can work to improve the process by improving their relationships with others who are located before and after them in the process, for Deming suggests that, "The secret is cooperation between components toward the aim of the organization."[9]

In addition to Dr. Deming's books, there are now dozens of others that describe his concepts and their application. This model is being successfully applied throughout the world in all kinds of organizations, which shows that the movement from structure thinking to process thinking is already quite advanced.

3. Managerial Bionomics

Traditional economic theory is based on the static, Newtonian world view, and is unable to account for such fundamental economic factors as 'learning' and 'innovation.' Thus, it is of limited use to today's managers: "When it came to world financial markets, [Citibank CEO John] Reed had decided that professional economists were off with the fairies. Under Reed's predecessor, Walter Wriston, Citicorp had just taken a bath in the Third World debt crisis. The bank had lost $1 billion in profits in one year, and was still sitting on $13 billion of bad loans that might never be paid back. And not only had the in-house economists not predicted it, their advice had made matters worse."[10]

In response to the limitations of the traditional models, researchers and theorists such as economist Brian Arthur and bioeconomist Michael Rothschild have developed new models to account for the complex realities that we observe and experience. Rothschild studied economics and biology as separate disciplines, until one day he understood that both deal with problems that are essentially the same, though they operate at vastly different time scales.[11] He realized that information plays a fundamental role in natural systems and in human culture, and based on this observation he developed 'bionomics,' which models the economy as an ecosystem. Rothschild describes bionomics this way:

A capitalist economy can best be comprehended as a living ecosystem. Key phenomena observed in nature—competition, specialization, co-operation, exploitation, learning, growth, and several others—are also central to business life. Moreover, the evolution of the global ecosystem and the emergence of modern industrial society are studded with striking parallels. Briefly stated, information is the essence of both systems. In the biologic environment, genetic information, recorded in the DNA molecule, is the basis of all life. In the economic environment, technological information captured in books, blueprints, scientific journals, databases, and the know-how of millions of individuals, is the ultimate source of all economic life. As mankind's ability to copy and exchange information improved, first with the invention of the printing press and more recently with the creation of the computer, the accumulation of scientific knowledge quickened and then accelerated again. Today, a staggering profusion of companies—from fast-food chains to microchip makers to international airlines—convert fragments of this vast body of knowledge into goods and services that satisfy human needs and desires. Each organization strives to survive in its niche of the economic ecosystem. Though the pace of economic change is amazingly fast, its basic mechanics are remarkably similar to those found in nature.''[12]

Using this model, Rothschild analyzes issues such as economic competition, global trade, the tax code, regulated monopolies, marketplace competition, public education, and the economics of pollution. In each case, and in considerable detail, he shows that bionomics is a cogent tool for analysis, as well as the means to develop normative responses to current economic situations.

An ecosystem is characterized by geographic boundaries and constraints pertaining to climate, competitors, and resources, and these factors influence the evolution of the species within it. An economy has constraints and resources within which businesses adapt. Genetic mutations create new living structures with new possibilities and new forms of behavior just as new technologies similarly alter the economy. Change and competition are the ongoing realities of the ecosystem, with predators and prey involved in a constant interadaptive process, just as they are also the foundations of economic competition.

Since the 1990 publication of *Bionomics: Economy as Ecosystem,* Rothschild has established The Bionomics Institute to promote the bionomic model through conferences, seminars, consulting, and publications. Support for bionomics is growing among business leaders, academics, and public officials.

'Managerial bionomics' is the application of bionomic principles to the management of an individual corporation, just as managerial economics is the application of traditional models in the managerial context. In particular, bionomics offers for the organization designer a new way of understanding how the economy functions and how an individual firm can better position itself to be successful. It presents a much better picture of economic competition and the critical role that learning plays in all economic activity. In Rothschild's words, "What bionomics does is fundamentally alter the mental map."[13]

Bionomics shows that organizational capabilities which enhance learning and adaptation are most important because they lead to innovation and flexibility, which in turn leads to marketplace advantage and the capacity to respond to new conditions whenever they occur. Such occurrences are totally unpredictable and also completely inevitable.

4. The Viable System Model

Over a lifetime of work as a manager, cybernetician, and consultant to corporations and nations, Stafford Beer has developed a comprehensive and profound approach to the issues of organization design. Beer is a leader in the field of cybernetics, the discipline that he calls 'the science of effective organization.' Cybernetics describes a set of scientifically verifiable principles that are fundamental to the design of organizations. Applying these principles, Beer developed a model of the anatomy and physiology of the human nervous system, which he then developed into a model of organization design. In 1972, he published *Brain of the Firm*[14] to present these models.

The human system, like the corporation, seeks perhaps above all to continue its own existence—to survive. To do so, it must maintain viability in a changing environment. Hence, Beer calls his approach the 'viable system model.' In addition to *Brain of the Firm*, now in its second edition, Beer has also written two companion volumes, *The Heart of Enterprise*[15] and *Diagnosing the System for Organizations*,[16] and this trio offers much for organization designers to consider.

Variety. One foundation of Beer's model is the fundamental cybernetic concept of 'variety.' The environment in which the corporation functions, the marketplace, offers an increasing variety of products and services among which consumers are able to choose: There are red ones, yellow ones, blue ones, and green ones. There are big ones, little ones, slow ones, and fast ones. There is advertising to get the attention of consumers amid this noise, and all kinds of shops (including, now, mail order catalogs and home shopping on TV) where consumers can select exactly what they want.

If everyone buys blue and green ones, a company that makes only red and yellow ones offers a variety that doesn't match the variety that the market is (for the moment) choosing. Why didn't the company correctly predict that blue and green would be the preferred colors? Or later, when it no longer requires prediction, but merely observation, why doesn't the company rush its own super-duper blue and green models into stores? Perhaps its manufacturing plant cannot produce blue or green at all. Cyberneticians call such a mismatch a problem of 'requisite variety.'

Responding appropriately to the marketplace requires matching an organization's variety of products and services with the market's desired variety. Accomplishing this successfully and repeatedly over the long term supports the continued survival of a firm, and hence its viability.

A manager might ask, "What do we need to do to stay in business?" while the cybernetician asks, "How can the firm be organized to achieve requisite variety?" These are, superficially, the same question, but because the manager and the cybernetician are likely use to dramatically different approaches to these problems, they may also reach vastly different conclusions.

The cybernetician's approach to dealing with the infinitely complex environment is to define how an organization can reduce the environment's variety to something more manageable. This is done by filtering out the superfluous and selecting only that which it *must* know to survive, exactly as the individual organism does in the face of this same environment. Each individual organism perceives enormous quantities of information, (billions of bits each minute), filters most of it out automatically, and responds to what captures its attention (which, it hopes, is also what really matters).

Necessary Context. Beer shows that the problems of variety filtering, communication, and decision making are handled in individual organisms by balancing local autonomy with centralized control, according to a pattern of rules through which it distinguishes between different contexts that naturally occur.

For example, neural nodes throughout the body control local action, largely without the participation of the central authority, the brain, which is informed only after the fact. We are familiar with these as our 'reflexes.' At another level of context, the heart, lungs, and diaphragm are coordinated as a system according to the level of metabolic activity, and at yet another level, our conscious mind decides whether to turn left or right at the corner.

The pattern of rules that defines the various contexts must be systematic and logical, or else the system simply would not be viable over the long term. Beer observes that the human nervous system is organized into five contextual levels corresponding to five neural structures, each of which is responsible for processing a different kind of information.

These different kinds of information are distinguishable because they pertain to progressive levels of context for organization within the organism. Thus, each organism consists of very small parts, atoms and molecules, organized into larger parts, cells, which are themselves organized into still larger organs. Organs are organized into systems, which together compose an organism (Figure 2.4). Cell, organ, system, organism, as well as present and future are inherent differences of context that are built into the very

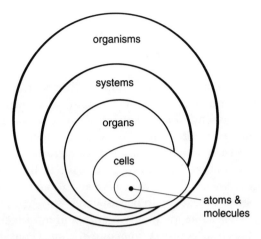

Figure 2.4 **Five Levels of Context**
Each of these five circles represents a different level of context, or 'logical type.' In this example, 'cells' is shown differently because there are organisms that are single-celled, and thus members of (at least) two classes.

design of life as we know it. These differences are the overriding logic of our world: This is 'reality.' The 'management' issues pertaining to the cell are different from the issues pertaining to the organ, and from those pertaining to the organism as a whole, for these are entirely different contexts.

To survive, to function coherently in this real world, an organism must sustain itself in the narrow space between rigidity and chaos, and its nervous system must be competent to clearly distinguish between these different contexts in the here and now.[17] For example, while individual cells are busy at their metabolic functions, they are not aware of, and cannot be concerned about, the bus that will run over the organism if it doesn't cross the street in time. Getting out of the way is the responsibility of the conscious mind. If the cell were to attempt to make such a decision, chaos would result and the fine edge of complexity would be lost. The cell would be operating 'out of context.'

Gregory Bateson has pointed out that just as the distinction between contexts is necessary for the functioning of the nervous system, it is also necessary for the functioning of consciousness.[18] Some actions and messages between individuals define the appropriate context in which other actions and messages are intelligible. For example, fighting war and playing war involve similar actions, but in significantly different contexts. How do the participants know if it's a 'real' war or a 'play' war that they are engaged in?

By defining context, people are able to communicate effectively (more or less). The word 'context' comes from the Latin, meaning 'to weave together.' By differentiating between contexts, we can weave a reality in which we can function coherently.

In the viable system model, the notions of appropriate context in nature and in human consciousness lead to a model of management decision making that is a hierarchy, but not one based on power or seniority. (How interesting it would be to differentiate between this neuron, older than that one, and thus receiving a higher salary!) It is a hierarchy in that it is based only on necessary context: Each of the five logics in Beer's model has its own *unique competence within its appropriate context,* and all must function together as a system for viability to be sustained.

By analogy, while someone in an organization must focus on fabricating today's product (one context), someone else must consider what products will be marketable next year and five years hence (another context).

Five Systems of the Viable System Model. The viable system model maps the five-layer model onto the organization by identifying five particular kinds of organizational context. Beer calls these 'Systems One through Five':

- *System One.* Production and delivery processes that provide products and services for the marketplace and that are managed with *local autonomy* are, in Beer's term, 'System One.'

- *System Two.* When an organization consists of many independent divisions or business units, each is a System One, and *coordination* among them ensures that the actions of one do not adversely impact the others. This is a function of 'System Two.'

- *System Three.* A corporation's *resources* must be *allocated* among its Systems One, and their performance regulated in the here and now. This is the responsibility of 'System Three.'

- *System Four.* *Preparation for the future* is the result of a thinking process much different from the focus on the here and now, and it is the responsibility of 'System Four.' This is the part of our mind that is wondering where we ought to go on vacation, quite separate from that part which guides the fork from the plate to the mouth.

- *System Five.* The ultimate decision makers define the *identity* of the firm as a whole, just as the self-conscious mind defines and expresses the identity of the individual through consciously directed action. This is 'System Five.'

Beer's visual representation of the model suggests a wiring diagram, indicating that the coherence of the organization comes through interactions among its parts (Figure 2.5). The connections between Systems One through Five are communications channels through which messages are sent and received, just as nerves are the communications pathways in the organism. Beer identifies specific kinds of communications that the organization must sustain to support the differentiation of contexts. By so doing, the organization increases the likelihood that clear and necessary communication can occur.

Another aspect of Beer's model is the idea that it is recursive, that the same five levels of context necessarily function at each level of organization. Thus, a factory must organize itself to ensure that all five levels of management are operative. At the division level, which manages many factories, the same five levels will be present, and each of the factories will be represented there as a separate System One. This nesting at each subsequent recursion can continue until an entire organization is represented, and even continue beyond one organization to show the relationships among competitors in an entire industry.

At each level of recursion, the same communications channels are established, and they are linked across recursions to facilitate communication between those at all levels of recursion. As they operate at different levels of recursion, their contexts will be different; but as they function at the same role in different recursions, they will surely have a lot to discuss.

Both the defining of appropriate context and the emphasis on communications distinguish this model from structural models that it superficially resembles. Although there is a structure represented here, its design

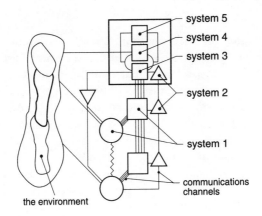

system 5
system 4
system 3
system 2
system 1
communications channels
the environment

Figure 2.5 **The Viable System Model**
Based on Chart One, *Diagnosing the System for Organizations* by Stafford Beer.

has been derived from an understanding of contexts and communications that the laws of cybernetics insist *must* be represented. In the viable system model, the process of communications precedes organizational structure.

The viable system model's approach to contextual logic and communication transcends the command and control's approach to power politics, and in this regard, the command and control model appears naive and simplistic. Some would surely counter, however, that to imagine any group of people abandoning power politics for a scientific approach to organization design may be even more naive. Nevertheless, the model offers invaluable insight into the principles underlying the organizations that are so important to our society.

5. Core Competencies

The concept of 'core competencies' was described by C. K. Prahalad and Gary Hamel in a 1990 *Harvard Business Review* article and in their recent book. This concept takes on greater relevance as global competition increases and companies find themselves working to maintain their presence in diverse markets:

> In the short run, a company's competitiveness derives from the price/performance attributes of current products. But the survivors of the first wave of global competition, Western and Japanese alike, are all converging on similar and formidable standards for product cost and quality—minimum hurdles for continued competition, but less and less important as sources of differential advantage. In the long run, competitiveness derives from an ability to build, at lower cost and more speedily than competitors, the core competencies that spawn unanticipated products.[19]

As technologies have become more complex and more specialized, it simply has become too expensive to maintain state-of-the-art competencies in all of the technical specialties that make up a modern product line. Consequently, a corporation must identify competencies that are core to its present and future knowledge, and central to the products and services that it offers or intends to offer. Prahalad and Hamel suggest that no more than five or six competencies can truly be core.

They cite the example of Canon, whose core competencies in precision mechanics, fine optics, and microelectronics are combined into a wide array of products, including cameras, printers, and copiers, each of which requires two or all three competencies. Investment is channeled into maintaining and advancing a firm's core competencies, for they are the critical capacities from which products and services are derived.

Other competencies will not be considered 'core,' but are nevertheless critical to the firm's ability to create successful products and services. Access to noncore competencies must be obtained through joint ventures, alliances, partnerships, vendor relationships, and subcontracting. Confirming the applicability of this model in the real world, recent years have seen alliances established between companies that are also direct competitors. IBM and Apple, for example, established joint ventures in two distinct competency areas (in operating systems, Taligent; in multimedia systems, Kaleida) in which their needs and capabilities were complementary, joint ventures that would have been unthinkable five years before.

As the necessity for focused application of limited resources is clear, such joint ventures enable companies to address markets that they could not afford to address alone.

The core competence model is a process-oriented approach that also has implications for organization design and management. Clearly, its fundamental concern is learning and the strategic application of that learning.

The model also explores the idea that new combinations of core competencies are the fertile soil of innovation and marketplace differentiation. Because the command and control approach encourages specialization and separation, it is wholly unsuited to a world in which combinations of core competencies make the fundamental difference.

*   *   *

These five models show that there is tremendous diversity of approaches even within the domain of process-oriented thinking. Although there do not appear to be outright contradictions among them, the differences suggest that there are many ways to consider these issues.

While Beer emphasizes the necessity of a logical distinctions between contexts as an analog of the structure and function of the nervous system, Deming focuses on organizing the production process. The idea of core competencies is aligned with managerial bionomics in stressing the strategic importance of technical knowledge, while the central principle at Semco is trust.

It is notable that there are many similarities as well. Semco's four-layer model, derived from experience, is not so different from Beer's five-layer model, derived from cybernetics and experience. The main difference seems to be Semco's lack of an explicit System Four, and surely this role is handled by one or more of the company's counselors. We should note, however, that this may not be cybernetically valid in Beer's terms, for the viable system model calls for System Four to filter the messages that System Five receives, and this filter is not present at Semco.

Prahalad and Hamel point out that, "top management's real responsibility is a strategic architecture that guides competence building,"[20] an idea that is entirely consistent with Beer's concept of System Five and its focus on identity.

Although one or another of these models may provide an appropriate framework that can be readily applied to a specific corporation in a specific situation, far more powerful would be a set of generalized practices that together would constitute a complete approach to the process-oriented organization. The development of this synthesis is the subject of Chapter 3.

3

Recognition and Response

The synthesis of the five process-oriented approaches described in Chapter 2 is a new model of organization design, 'recognition and response.' In the process-oriented organization, the capacity to recognize the essence of the changes that are happening in the marketplace is fundamental to survival and to success. Thus 'recognition' replaces 'command.' Once a situation is understood, what matters is that appropriate action be taken, and so 'response' replaces 'control.' The implementation of recognition and response relies on a set of eight practices that together compose the key capabilities for process-oriented organizations.

The basic themes are always the same. They may be summarized by notions such as self-determination, self-organization and self-renewal . . . . Science is about to recognize these principles as general laws of the dynamics of nature.[1]—*Erich Jantsch*

The exponentially changing marketplace, which is characterized by nearly infinite variety and overwhelming complexity, is the milieu in which a corporation must be able to function effectively. Since a corporation is made up of individuals who are (presumably) working together by choice, the fundamental issue that organization designers have dealt with for many decades is the design of organizational structures that balance the 'autonomy' of these individuals who make up the corporation, with the 'control' of the central authority, whose aim is to provide cohesiveness to guide the actions of these individuals. The essence of the structure orientation is the assumption that those who exercise control know more, *a priori*, than others.

The process orientation takes a different approach. The concept of self-organization suggests that a capacity for self-control can emerge as a *consequence* of interactions between the individuals themselves, and that appropriate structure will then result. Since these interactions will inevitably be concerned with the marketplace, the structure that emerges from them will remain current with marketplace conditions as those conditions change. This reframes the issue of organization design as primarily a matter of *information and communications,* from which self-control can arise.

It must be noted that this possibility of emergent organizational structure is achievable in an organization due to a key distinction between an individual organism and an organization comprising individuals. For the individual organism, structure is indeed imposed *a priori* in the form of a physical body, a structure that defines absolute limitations on performance. In contrast, organizations are composed of many individuals and are not subject to such limitations. While an individual inevitably faces death, organizations can persist through many generations by passing on accumulated information. They can operate without interruption for hundreds of years, as indeed many organizations have done throughout history.

In this regard, an organization is more like a species and less like an individual.

On the other hand, organizations have purposes that are very much like those of individuals. Thus, an organization has some qualities of the species and some qualities of the individual. For this reason, great care must be taken to select appropriate metaphors to describe the organization. As Michael Rothschild suggests, when we select the wrong metaphors, our thinking often gets muddled and we reach dramatically inappropriate conclusions.[2]

Bionomics shows that a process orientation is consistent with both the species and the individual perspectives, for at root they share a reliance on information and communications. In the individual, coordination among the many parts of the body is certainly dependent on its capacity to exchange information internally, as exemplified by the brain itself: Its 10 billion neurons exist to constantly exchange information with each other, and when that exchange stops, so does life. In the species, the transmission of life from one generation to the next is dependent upon information encoded in DNA and communicated via the reproductive process, which succeeds only when the information is protected.

THE NEW PARADIGM: RECOGNITION AND RESPONSE

In the industrial economy, a coherent set of models coalesced into an overall paradigm that expressed the spirit of the times. Among the factors that constituted the industrial paradigm were the Newtonian science of cause and effect, which led to a mechanistic approach to economics. These, combined with the psychological approach to conditioned behavior led to the command and control approach in repetitive industrial settings (Figure 3.1).

In contrast, the information economy originates in the rapid change that has come about due to advanced technology. Its science is based on relativity, complexity, and biology. The last two are reflected in its economics, which is bionomics (Figure 3.2).

Because the flow of information is the key to the information economy, all organizations must become competent to function in an information-rich milieu. What is necessary for survival is the ability to comprehend what is going on, to recognize precisely what is unique about any particular situation. Of course, an organization cannot do this, for organizations are abstract entities without eyes or ears, or any other physical properties for that matter. Organizations have individual members, and these individuals have eyes and ears and intelligence, which they use to perceive and comprehend the marketplace. Hence, the psychology of the information paradigm is learning.

As agents acting on behalf of an organization, individuals must gather information that is relevant to the aims and operations of the organization. Individuals recognize important information in the marketplace and communicate it to others who need to know.

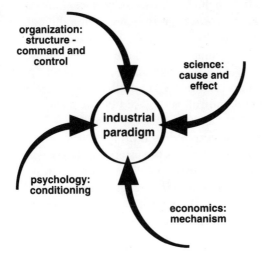

Figure 3.1   **The Industrial Paradigm**

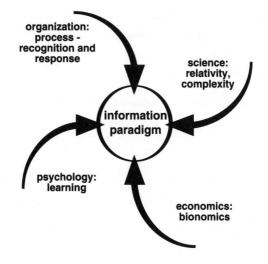

Figure 3.2 **The Information Paradigm**

The capacity to recognize change is so utterly fundamental to survival and to success that in the vocabulary of organization design, *recognition* replaces command.

Once a situation is understood, what matters is that appropriate action be taken. Since a corporation is incapable of taking action itself because it is only an abstract entity, whatever action is to be taken must be taken by individuals on its behalf. Thus, *response* replaces control.

Because the acts of recognizing and responding are accomplished by individuals, and only by individuals, individuals are poised between the customer and the company, in relationship with both, and representing the company by forging the agreements that match its capabilities to the needs of customers (Figure 3.3). Overall, the industrial economy paradigm of 'command and control' is replaced by the information economy paradigm of 'recognition and response' (Figure 3.2).

Recognizing and responding is precisely what living things do in order to continue to live: The first is the essence of perceiving the environment; the second is the action that is its direct consequence.

In the new paradigm, then, recognition and response are the fundamental processes in the short term, and they are processes that only individuals perform. The aggregate of these actions may lead to adaptation and evolution, or they may not, but we can never be sure in advance. All we can do is take the next step forward in the hopes that the path ultimately leads where we want to go.

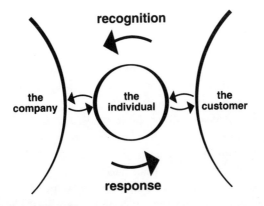

Figure 3.3 **Recognition and Response**
Since a corporation is not a tangible thing that is capable of taking any action in and of itself, individuals represent the company in all of its interactions with the marketplace and with the community.

Whereas evolution in the natural world is a matter of genetics and natural selection from generation to generation, evolution in the economic world is a matter of shared information, knowledge, innovation, and invention that may change from moment to moment. Recognition and response organizations depend on mastery of these four elements, elusive as they may be, for they are essential to the information economy. While the intent may be to evolve in conjunction with the marketplace, the best that the individual firm can do is to take action (respond) according to its best guess about what is going to happen, and then to respond to the feedback that comes from its actions. Evolution will happen, if it does, beyond the control of any organization because it occurs as the aggregate of all actions. Conscious action and evolution are thus of different logical types.

HIERARCHY, REDUX

Just as it is clear that the structure-oriented thinking of the corporate pyramid inhibits individuals from taking appropriate actions, it is also clear that nature has solved the problem of how to organize billions of living cells into coherent entities by using hierarchies of logical types of context. Thus, we must reconcile the phenomenon of self-organization with the necessity of distinguishing between logical types.

To some extent, this is a question of boundaries. There are existing social constraints that demand some form of hierarchy, including the law itself, which requires that a corporation have officers and directors who accept legal responsibility for its acts. Capital markets also demand this level of accountability.

The Semco model shows that self-organization can occur within these constraints. Semler points out that on legal documents he is referred to as the company president, but otherwise he is one among five counselors. Presumably his legal responsibilities influence his role as a counselor.

Management professor Elliott Jaques has suggested that the appropriate distinction between hierarchical layers of an organization concerns the time spans that those at each layer are responsible for managing: "Real management and hierarchical boundaries occur at time spans of three months, one year, two years, five years, ten years, and twenty years."[3]

In this model, individuals at successive layers deal with greater complexity than those below and must dispose a comparably greater capacity to understand and to devise appropriate responses.

This is also a structure of logical context, rather than one of politics, a self-organizing system in which issues are handled in the context of the uniform and logical scale of perspective towards the future. We return again to the logical type, distinguished in this case in the context of time and as a matter of complexity and capacity to respond to the emerging future.

This is notable, for here amid the issues of organization design we have encountered the phenomenon of 'vision,' the critical capacity to define the future and to organize resources to achieve it. In our fast-moving world, those who expect the future to be like the past are trapped in illusion, and as it was suggested in the Introduction, no complex organization can persist for long in a complex milieu without a compelling vision.

Those who can clearly see the future and can realize their visions thereby bring the future into the present, and they are the ones who will have authority in the organization as a consequence of that very capacity. In the self-organizing system, the existence of hierarchy is a consequence not of the past, nor of seniority, but of the future.

This, then, is the critical distinction between the structure orientation and the process orientation. Whereas 'structure' looks necessarily to the past and the history of events and is therefore limited by what has been known and done before, *'process' looks toward the future and what could and should be done*. Fittingly, the very word 'process' comes from the Latin *procedere*, meaning 'to go forward.'

This distinction further explains the long list of fired CEOs: American businesses are in the process of sorting between those who look to the future and those who look to the past. Surely there will be more CEOs pushed aside in the coming years, for changing conditions will continue to expose those who lack the vision necessary to go forward successfully amid complexity and rapid change. More will be said about vision in Chapter 7.

Inasmuch as hierarchies are natural and logical, and the accountability which accompanies them is demanded by society, they will surely remain with us. But just as surely they cannot continue in their present form.

It is the application of the hierarchy as a social weapon that must be abandoned. As it is presently practiced, hierarchical command and control is used by those above to bludgeon those below into reluctant submission. This practice leads to numerous pathologies, some of which have already been discussed, and more of which will be presented in Chapter 6.

The need for the hierarchy must be reframed from the perspective of the future and the process orientation rather than as an implementation of backwards-looking, structure-oriented thinking. This can come about as a result of organizational practices that support a rich environment of information and communications in the pursuit of the unknown future.

THE PRACTICES OF RECOGNITION AND RESPONSE

The five organizational models presented in Chapter 2 are quite diverse. The choice between these five models, or any others that may be best suited to a particular organization can only be made in the context of the purposes that the organization aims to achieve and the specific conditions that it faces. But no matter what approach to process is taken, there will certainly be practices that are common to all approaches.

Together, these practices would constitute a metaprocess, a synthesis that is not inherent in any particular organizational model, but rather is a generalized set of practices that are inherent to the process orientation itself, and coherent with the overall paradigm of the information economy (Figure 3.4).

An organization design using this metaprocess must be a means of achieving short-term and long-term viability within a rapidly changing environment, and as such it will be focused on achieving *coordination*. Beer notes that the coordinating functions within organizations are "almost totally misunderstood and under-represented in contemporary management technique."[4] Appropriately, then, implementation of the recognition and response approach is largely a matter of practices, or 'rules', that support such coordination among the many individuals whose actions create a corporation.

It is worth pointing out here that all systems are based on rules, and the efforts of scientists are put forth in the attempt to discern them. The

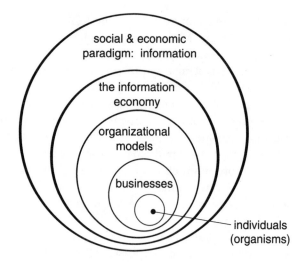

Figure 3.4 **The Context of Recognition and Response**
These five circles show the levels of context in which organizational models, including recognition and response, must fit. Compare with Figure 2.4, page 21.

challenge is always to discern the rules as precisely as possible. As science advances to a more thorough understanding of the universe, it is primarily our understanding of the rules that advances: The shift from Newton's models to Einstein's is the shift from one set of rules to a more useful set.

Thus, the idea of a set of specific coordinating practices is compelling, particularly when by this we mean *explicit* practices. After all, command and control organizations also have underlying practices, but some of them are unconscious, some of them are unspoken, and many of them are tremendously counterproductive.

Bringing a set of practices to the forefront also creates an environment of openness and exploration. It provides the possibility that all practices can be changed, deleted, or amended as necessary, which seems likely given the changing character of the marketplace.

Introduced here, then, are eight organizing practices that together enable a corporation to implement a tremendous variety of specific approaches to the process-oriented, recognition and response organization (Figure 3.5):

1. Commercial and Social Purposes.

2. Self-Organization.

3. Learning.

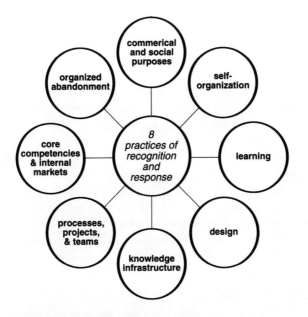

Figure 3.5 **Eight Practices of Recognition and Response**

4. Design.

5. Knowledge Infrastructure.

6. Processes, Projects, and Teams.

7. Core Competencies and Internal Markets.

8. Organized Abandonment.

These eight practices have been derived from a great many sources, including, of course, the process models presented in Chapter 2. In addition to some key theoretical material that has already been noted, including particularly the sciences of complexity and cybernetics, contemporary business literature is rich with concepts, examples, and models. The selection of these eight is based on the synthesis of theory, information, and practical experience that has come from dealing with real issues and real problems in many organizations over many years, both as an executive and a consultant.

Practice 1: Commercial and Social Purposes

A corporation is composed of individual people, and their aggregate capacity to do meaningful work is the basis upon which it exists. What makes work meaningful is the purposes for which it is done, and the expectation of the results that it will achieve. The work that is done to create an organization is the expression of what one might call shared 'commercial purposes.'

Some would also add the expectation that the work be done in a humane way, a way which supports everyone with whom the organization comes into contact—its employees, customers, shareholders, suppliers, and the community as a whole. This requirement concerns an organization's 'social purposes,' which exist side by side with its commercial ones.

These purposes are the context through which each individual participates in the creation and continuation of an organization's existence. Purposes that are powerfully composed can inspire action and can also lead to a compelling vision. Without such purposes, however, there can be no point to the existence of an organization, and surely it would disappear from utter neglect.

Practice 2:   Self-Organization

As the basis of organization shifts from preestablished authority that is derived from the past, towards information and the capacity to create the future, the focus of organization shifts away from command and control toward recognition and response. A rich flow of information among all participants enables a corporation to become a self-organizing system, through which the actions of its individual agents aggregate into coherence.

Since information flows freely, the practice of the hierarchy is applied as a consequence of the meaning of information, rather than as a technique of intimidation or privilege. Individuals make decisions based on their competence—based, that is, on the information that they have and their capacity to utilize it. Perception (recognition) is demonstrably useful when it leads to appropriate action (response). Whether the individual happens to be a sales clerk or the CEO is of little consequence.

Practice 3:   Learning

Learning is fundamental, for it is the activity through which each individual gains competence and capacity to understand and use information, and therefore to more fully participate in the life of an organization. Through learning, individuals become capable of making finer distinctions concerning the behavior of the marketplace, and thus of recognizing ever more subtle patterns. Likewise, it is through learning that individuals become capable of devising and implementing more subtle actions that will better represent their organizations. Thus, learning is fundamental to the organization that exists in the information economy, and the methods by which learning is fostered are fundamental.

It is worth noting here the critical distinction between learning and education, for these are sometimes confused. Learning occurs within an individual, and it is motivated by an individual's own quest for knowledge, for greater capacity. In contrast, education originates in external requirements and expectations that are imposed by others. While learning is self-compelled, education can be a matter of disinterested compliance. Of these two, clearly learning is the more powerful. More will be discussed about learning in Chapters 5 and 7.

Practice 4: Design

Design is a uniquely human undertaking: It is the application of conscious thought to the process of defining the way something ought to be, and then making it so. As an act of expression, design is the corollary of learning, for as learning is the transformation of information in the process of personal growth, design is the expression of the self through ideas, events, and artifacts.

Design is also a discipline in and of itself, a coherent model that guides the process of transforming a vision from that which could be, or should be, into that which is. It is a fundamental practice, a process map to get from whatever the current condition is to the envisioned state.

A more complete description of the design process is the subject of Chapter 7, and an application of the design process to organizational transformation is presented in Chapter 11.

Practice 5: Knowledge Infrastructure

Since information and communications are absolutely vital to the coordination functions of recognition and response organizations, the methods by which they are created, augmented, recorded, transmitted, shared, and managed are critical to long-term success. Together, these methods constitute a corporation's 'knowledge infrastructure,' the set of tools that facilitates all aspects of work by individuals, teams, and the organization as a whole.

In particular, the knowledge infrastructure consists of information and communication systems, but it is not just technology, for it includes the very processes by which people work together face to face and the work place itself. These are the subjects of Chapters 8, 9, and 10.

The implementation of the knowledge infrastructure is an important aspect of the transformation from command and control organizational models to recognition and response models, because this infrastructure supports the shift from structure thinking to process thinking.

Practice 6: Processes, Projects, and Teams

Much of the work in the recognition and response organization is self-organized by the individuals who do it. Since we now understand that process must precede structure, it makes no sense to devise' organizational models based on the fragmentation of the work according to departmental structures or last year's products. Instead, the work is organized to meet the current and future needs of customers as they are currently understood.

Work processes exist to accomplish particular purposes, and they are changed when the purposes change or the methods change. This is, of course, the central theme of Work Process Reengineering, as defined by Michael Hammer and James Champy,[5] which is further described in Chapters 9, 11, and 12.

In addition to the focus on processes, much of the specific work that needs to be done can be organized into projects that have specific objectives that can be fulfilled in specific time frames: projects have purposes, beginnings, and, perhaps most importantly, endings.

The work of doing processes and projects can be readily accomplished by individuals who organize themselves into teams. These teams are not fixed and permanent, but rather they change as the work itself changes, or as the ideas and preferences of the team members themselves change. The fluidity of individuals to move throughout an organization to find the work for which they are best suited and to which they can make the strongest contribution is the subject of Practice 7, described below.

Practice 7: Core Competencies and Internal Markets

As there are limited resources with which to work, the products and services that a corporation offers in the marketplace are based on the core competencies which have been selected to provide competitive advantage. These competencies also provide a context in which many of the learning and design activities of the members of the organization are focused.

The choice of core competencies is one of the most important strategic decisions that will be made, for it will influence every aspect of an organization's future.

Since information is recognized as the key strategic asset, each person who is knowledgeable (which is everyone) is unmistakably important, and their efforts must be coordinated according to the strategic needs of the corporation. To facilitate the process of fitting individual capabilities with the corporation's needs at any given time, an internal marketplace is an extraordinarily effective means of allocating an organization's resources. The corresponding external marketplace is, after all, how most of society's resources are allocated.

With an appropriate set of rules to provide continuity, people move between projects as the *work* requires. Since projects, teams, and internal markets are driven by external markets, there may be few fixed departments in the corporation and few individuals who stay in one role more than a few years.

Practice 8: Organized Abandonment

Peter Drucker has pointed out that to ensure that your competitors do not make your products and services obsolete, it is best to make them obsolete yourself. The way to do this is to systematically abandon them, and to replace them with better ones before others do.[6] This practice recognizes the prevalence of change and organizes the firm in conjunction with its flow.

The same concept is applicable to the organization itself, for as the marketplace evolves, an organization must abandon its outdated practices and replace them with new ones that fit contemporary needs and capabilities. Rather than letting competition make the organization itself obsolete, the organization, too, can be systematically replaced from within.

By practicing organized abandonment, an organization has the opportunity to achieve a longevity that is beyond the capability of individuals. Although individuals are stuck with whatever body they arrive in, the corporation can remake itself from scratch and persevere through countless generations. Surely this is the evolving corporation.

*   *   *

These eight practices address key issues that arise for organizations that adopt a process orientation. Each could be the subject of a book, or even a few books. Some have been the subject of dozens. There may be other key practices that are not described here, and some of the ones here may be found to be less fundamental than they now appear to be. Whether the list should include nine or seven practices is not as important as the idea that there *are* fundamental practices of process-oriented organizations, and that through an open-ended process of inquiry and experimentation, leaders will reach operationally valid conclusions about what is appropriate for them. The proof will be in the pudding—and nowhere else.

VISUALIZING RECOGNITION AND RESPONSE

One of the enduring strengths of the command and control model is the fact that the pyramidal organization chart is so *specific*. It shows everyone exactly where he or she is, and exactly what every individual has to do. As Deming says, the chart shows that one must please the persons above.

Process models are rarely so specific, and although this ambiguity does reflect reality, it also presents a challenge that encapsulates the difficulty of making the shift from structure thinking to process thinking.

Nevertheless, the objective of process thinking is to create the conditions through which self-organization can emerge as a stronger while more flexible way of binding an organization together than can be accomplished with command and control. It is therefore the *idea* of recognition and response, and then the application of it through whatever practices seem relevant that is important. Ultimately, this must be compelling enough to

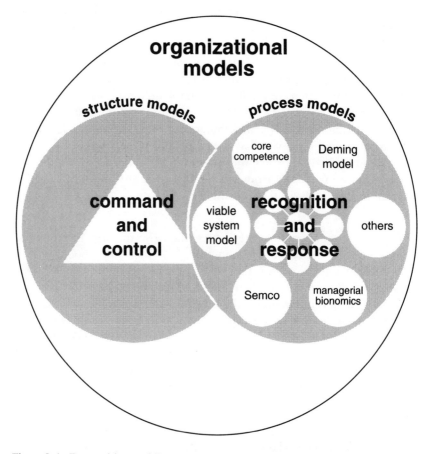

Figure 3.6 **Recognition and Response**
Within the domain of all organizational models, structure models are generally distinct from process models, and the 'command and control' model is the predominant approach to structure. Among process models, five specific ones are indicated, along with a circle representing others not described here. 'Recognition and response' is a synthesis of all of the process models.

inspire the transition from the illusory certainty of structure to the sometimes unsettling ambiguity of the process milieu. For just as the unifying idea of structure leads to the stifling rigidity of the pyramid and the pathologies of command and control, so the unifying idea of process leads to recognition and response and the capacity to evolve (Figure 3.6).

The extent to which the hierarchy will be expressed in recognition and response will vary. In some industries, such as medicine and insurance, strict regulation will require significant hierarchical accountability. In industries that are undergoing rapid change, however, hierarchical practices will generally obstruct progress because the demands of extreme competition will make old knowledge obsolete so quickly.

Even more important than these eight practices and the concept of recognition and response is the transition from structure thinking to process thinking, and the transition from power politics to information and communication. Making these transitions requires the willingness to question, to imagine, to envision, and to design. From these acts the new organization, *your* new organization, will emerge.

ABOUT THE REMAINDER OF THIS BOOK

Throughout the rest of the book, the eight practices will be discussed in more detail and in the context of how they can be specifically implemented.

What follows in Part Two concerns the key Patterns of Change occurring throughout the information economy and provides additional theory to support the recognition and response model.

After Part Two is a brief interlude that describes the design process, which is subsequently used as a model of large-scale organizational change.

Parts Three and Four describe the *implementation* of recognition and response, including specific initiatives and strategies for the transformation from command and control organizational models to process models.

PART TWO

THEORY
Patterns of Change

Here we are only 23 years after the invention of the microprocessor, and all of us who have thought even fleetingly about these issues are absolutely stunned by the pace of change we've experienced in the 1980s and early '90s. And look what's ahead in the next few years. It's not . . . Alvin Toffler's "future shock"; it's "now shock."[1]*—Michael Rothschild*

Exponential change occurs because of the rapid development of new technologies. The inevitable emphasis on technology in the marketplace means that exponential change will continue to be the dominant pattern of the information economy. Because exponential change is so fundamentally important for all organizations, it must be thoroughly understood. In addition, the specific nature of information itself and of the corporation must also be well understood, for these are essential elements of the new economy. They are the subjects of Part Two.

4

The Rate of Change

The rate of change is the most significant overall pattern in today's economy. It is unlike anything that humanity has ever experienced, and it has significant consequences for all aspects of the organization. Amid this rapid change, leaders must learn to see the patterns of events rather than focusing on the events themselves. The shift from 'event thinking' to 'pattern thinking' parallels the shift from structure-oriented organizations to process-oriented organizations.

December 1992: IBM executives admit that they missed the boat. At a news conference yesterday in New York, they described an industry that is changing so rapidly that the company has been unable to keep up. They said the move by customers from highly profitable mainframes to smaller and more efficient minicomputers and workstations took them by surprise.[1]—Ken Siegmann

On January 26, 1993, five weeks after this news conference, IBM chairman John Akers was fired. During his last year as chairman, 1992, IBM lost the tremendous sum of $5 billion.[2] The company struggled, unsuccessfully, to adapt to the changing computer marketplace, and by the second quarter of 1993, IBM had lost an additional $8 billion, most of which as a consequence of its intent to eliminate 70,000 jobs.[3] A comparable number of jobs had already been eliminated in 1991 and 1992, and while all of this was going on, IBM's stock plummeted to a value of $56, a mere one-third of its 1987 high of $168. In less than five years, IBM went from being among the most highly regarded companies to one in severe distress. What happened?

When we look only at the events themselves, we are not likely to find a satisfying explanation, but if we find the *patterns* that unify these events, we may come to understand what happened to IBM, and what has happened to many other companies as well.[4]

Many of the problems that have impacted IBM are attributable to a pattern concerning the development of computer technology that was first identified in 1963 by Gordon Moore, one of the inventors of the computer chip. Moore observed that the number of components on a chip was doubling every two years.[5] Five years later, Moore cofounded Intel corporation, which quickly became a leader in the design and manufacture of these chips.

In 1976 Moore realized that the development cycle was shortening even more. He revised his forecast to predict that each doubling would henceforth take only 18 months to accomplish. In the 30 years since Moore first made his observation, now known as 'Moore's Law,' this remarkable miniaturization trend has meant astonishing advances in the performance of computer chips, in the advanced technology that is used to make them, and in the computers that use them. In the history of commerce, no industry has achieved systematic increases in performance that compare with the computer industry (Figure 4.1).

Moore's Law is not a secret in the industry, and certainly many people at IBM are aware of it. In fact, many of the scientific and engineering innovations that sustained the trend were made by the leading computer company for most of the 20th century, IBM. Computer researcher Hans Moravec comments: "Integrated circuit manufacturers have been aware of the trend since Gordon Moore, one of the inventors of the integrated cir-

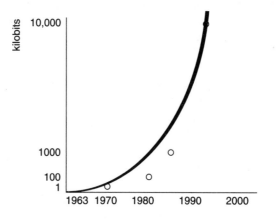

Figure 4.1 **Moore's Law**
Moore's Law predicts the number of kilobits that will be achieved by the best-performing computer chip in any given year. First described by Gordon Moore in 1963, Moore's Law has been a remarkably accurate technology forecast for 30 years.

cuit, noted [it] in 1963. . . . Computer makers have made similar observations, and new products in both of these related fields are designed with the trend in mind. Established manufacturers design and price products to stay on the curve, to maximize profit; new companies aim above the curve, to gain competitive edge."[6]

By 1980, powerful chips enabled computer manufacturers to provide many of the capabilities of larger mainframe computers in smaller and less expensive minicomputers and personal computers (PCs). The PC market grew explosively throughout the 1980s, largely because of IBM itself. In an astounding expression of its marketing power, IBM *established* the market simply by *entering* the market, thereby legitimizing a new product category.

By 1985, a PC on a desktop could do work that had once only been done on mainframes. Today, despite the astonishing engineering that goes into it, the PC has become so inexpensive to build that it is a global commodity, its components bought and sold in mass quantities in an intensely competitive market that beautifully exemplifies the shift from mass to intelligence.

Throughout the 1980s, even while it dominated the PC marketplace, IBM resisted the opportunity to take full advantage of the PC's capabilities, choosing instead to limit its development of the PC in order to protect its decades-old and very profitable mainframe business.

Other computer companies saw the opening and stepped in to develop the products and services that IBM did not offer, and so IBM's deference to its mainframe business drove many customers away. IBM's efforts to sustain its mainframe business ran counter to the trend of advancing technology, counter to the needs of its customers, and counter even to the company's own long-term best interests: "Customers used to tell me, 'I have a mainframe, so go away,' " said Glenn Osaka, general manager of the commercial systems division of Hewlett Packard. "Now they say, 'I want to get rid of this mainframe. Can you help me?' "[7]

If the leaders of IBM had understood the pattern of evolving chip technology and what it meant for their customers, they could have seen that the decline of mainframes was a likely consequence. Whereas mainframes are tools for large-scale, centralized data processing and storage, an extension of industrial-age thinking, PCs are powerful tools that help individuals to *learn* in ways that were never possible before. As such, they have become indispensable in the information economy. Linked via networks, PCs enable people to access the massive databases that can be stored only on mainframes, thereby making appropriate use of both kinds of computers.

IBM could have prepared itself by developing its products and its marketing plans in harmony with the advancing technology that drove the market, but instead the company was blinded by its past success and its dependence on the mainframe.

It's not so difficult to point out IBM's shortcomings in hindsight, now that the outcomes are so clear. But many understood these trends when the outcomes were far less obvious than they are today. These were the founders of the companies that exploited IBM's weaknesses, for they saw patterns and opportunities where IBM's leaders saw only events. One such company is Sun Microsystems, founded in 1983.

The founders of Sun clearly understood both the technical and the market implications that the leaders of IBM apparently did not. They understood the technical aspects so well, in fact, that in 1984, one of them, William Joy, developed what is now called 'Joy's Law,' a formula that predicts exponential increases in the processing speed of computer chips from year to year.[8] Joy's Law complements Moore's Law, and the two together have predicted the development of chip technology with remarkable accuracy (Figure 4.2).

By 1991, in only its ninth year in business, Sun's share of the PC workstation marketplace was 29%, while IBM had only 16%.[9]

Perhaps the leaders of IBM misunderstood this market because they never recognized the significance of the larger trend. This is a common failure of those who focus on events and crises rather than patterns. In these times of rapid change, *those who focus just on events are doomed to a downward spiral of reactions to the changing marketplace. In contrast, those who*

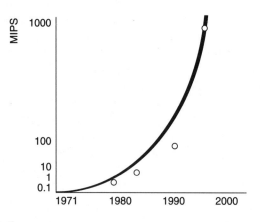

Figure 4.2 **Joy's Law**
Joy's Law predicts the top speed in MIPS (millions of instructions per second) that will be achieved by the best-performing computer chip in any given year. It was first described by William Joy in 1984.

recognize the underlying patterns can anticipate the marketplace and become market leaders.[10]

LIFE CYCLES

For decades, business analysts have tracked the developmental patterns of products and services in the marketplace using the product life cycle model. Starting with the introduction of a product or service, sales grow, eventually reaching maturity, a peak of profitability, and then they decline. The graph of this curve often looks like the letter 'S,' and is often called the 'S-curve' (Figure 4.3).

S-curves can describe the development of individual companies or entire industries. They are also applicable to individual people (we're born, we grow up, we pay taxes, and then we die) and, as Joseph Tainter shows, to entire civilizations[11] (see the Introduction, pages ix–xvii).

The simplicity of the model is one of its appealing virtues, for it can help one to focus on the broadest and most informative patterns.

If IBM's leaders had charted the life cycle of its mainframes with reliable data, they may have had a clearer picture of what was going on in the overall market and might have developed an appropriate strategic response. The overall mainframe life cycle curve can be seen as a component of a larger curve showing the entire computer industry (Figure 4.4). This approach could also be applied to an analysis of generations of computer chips[12] (Figure 4.5).

These examples suggest that accelerating change throughout the computer industry shortens the life of each product, and this is the case, to varying degrees, in all other industries. Acceleration is the norm. One rea-

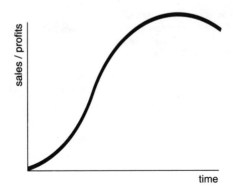

Figure 4.3 **The S-Curve**

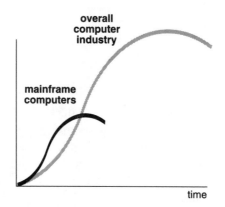

Figure 4.4 **Mainframe Computers**
A conceptual S-curve of the mainframe computer market is shown in conjunction with an S-curve showing the computer industry as whole. If the real data supported the concept shown here, mainframe manufacturers that plotted the curve would have been forewarned of the likely trend in their industry.

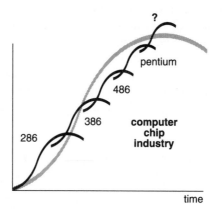

Figure 4.5 **Generations of Computer Chips**
The introduction of successive computer chips makes the prior generations of chips obsolete. Competition in the marketplace means that each successive generation has a shorter overall life span than the previous ones.

son for the shorter cycle times is increasing competition, which drives companies to search for competitive advantage by introducing new products more frequently.

When the sales of a product begin to decline, the challenge is to introduce its replacement at just the right time so that the profit of both old and new is maximized. If the timing is off, however, a company can find that its biggest competitor is itself. This also happened to IBM: "Despite IBM's efforts to the contrary, minicomputers have been eating into mainframe sales. 'The number one company that's cannibalizing IBM is IBM.' "[13]

The model of the product life cycle and the problem of timing new product generations is a microcosm of the larger processes of social change. We experience fear, risk, and expectation in the transition from the old and comfortable ways to the new and unknown: Change itself has come to dominate the character of our times.

CHANGE AND TECHNOLOGY

The word 'change' comes from the Latin *cambire*, meaning to exchange or barter. That meaning is still with us today. When you need bus fare and you give someone a dollar bill, the quarters that you get back are your 'change.'

This original meaning has evolved in our usage to describe a more general process of exchanging one entire state of affairs for another, life becoming somehow different than it was before. Our lives are different than they were 10 or 20 years ago because we have matured as we have grown older, but our lives are significantly different from the lives of our parents and grandparents 50 or 100 years ago because society as a whole has changed, and changed significantly. This broader change is largely a consequence of the technology that we have come to rely so heavily on, technology that didn't exist one or two generations ago.

Technology enhances our lives by fulfilling material needs, and for many, by providing aesthetic pleasures. Technology influences every aspect of society, and we rely on it to sustain our urban lifestyle with food, clothing, and shelter, as well as entertainment. Our dependence is so thorough that many of us would not know how to survive without it. Do you know how to grow your own food? Could you find safe drinking water?

This dependence has a deep impact on how we perceive the world and how we understand it, both literally and figuratively. We look through eyeglasses and microscopes and telescopes that make fuzzy things clearer, small things larger, and distant things closer. We listen to the radio, and we talk on the telephone, exchanging messages with others who are nearby and far away. We watch and listen to hours of television. We travel in autos and airplanes, whether it is to the store to buy milk or halfway around the world to visit a friend or climb a fabled mountain. Some travel to the moon or send robots to distant planets to take pictures. Technology extends the reach of our hands and our minds farther into the universe, making it more accessible and more understandable.

The word technology comes from the Greek root *technē,* referring to art and the skill and ingenuity of making things. We have built a society based on making things that have become part of who we are, *extensions* of our very selves.[14] We identify so closely with the cars we drive that our cars are us, and so are the neighborhoods we live in, the clothes we wear, the jobs we do, the flags we wave, the products we make and sell, and especially the products we buy.

It is said that when you're holding a hammer, everything looks like a nail. Select a different tool, a drill perhaps, and the way that you look at the world is then recontextualized by the possibilities inherent in that tool. "Where do I need a hole?" you ask.

This happens with companies, too. IBM identified itself with mainframe computers and saw the mainframe as *the* tool for the ages. The company came to be called "Big Blue" because blue was the color of its mainframe boxes.

We depend so totally on technology that our understanding of it even has a great impact on our philosophies. As new techniques are developed through the work of artists and scientists and engineers, new technology is brought into existence that impacts how we live. As technology changes, we change; many of us have been persuaded by this dependence to see technology, by and large, as a good and beneficial thing. We envision a future filled with more and better technology for everyone and for everyone's children, a world of *The Jetsons* and *Star Trek.* We welcome the sign that says, "Yield to Progress!"

But as technology becomes more and more powerful, we also see that its application has other consequences. We have learned that there is an important difference between what is feasible and what is desirable, although in our haste to use new toys we often neglect to distinguish between the two.

Nevertheless, the creation of technology is also the creation of new economic potential. Its use results in new experiences, new behaviors, and new ideas, which lead to reexamination of social values. This often results in changes in the beliefs and in the behavior of people, which then lead to the understanding of new possibilities that are then expressed in new technology—which leads to further exploration of values. Thus, as machine labor replaced human labor, the notion of human slavery became unacceptable.

The interaction between values and technology, and their coevolution, has resulted in a momentum that has driven society through change after change over many centuries.

Most of the scientists who have ever lived are still alive (as are most of the people) and still working today, and the effort that is put into science and technology increases steadily year after year. Since the information scientists work with is encoded and stored, they don't have to recreate humanity's knowledge. Instead, they can study the work that has been done in the past and extend it through their individual efforts. Universities throughout the world continue to train generations of scientists, and as these scientists work at the advancement of technology, they introduce still more change into our lives. The activities of billions of people has become a momentum that compels society forward like a river in flood.

THE RATE OF CHANGE

Whereas each drop of water in a river corresponds to a single change in the marketplace, a new idea, a new technology, the flow of water corresponds to the aggregate of all ideas and technologies. The faster the flow, the faster the pace of change. But whereas the flow of a river may be seasonal, rising and falling during the year, the pace of change throughout human history has been increasing steadily since the advent of agriculture and urbanism some 10,000 years ago.

A graph of social change during prehistory would probably be a nearly straight line, perhaps ascending ever so slightly as knowledge slowly accumulated, a *linear* series (Figure 4.6).

The development of agriculture resulted in increasing specialization and a much greater need for commercial exchange. Trading posts evolved into cities that became regional trading centers, and many cities still reflect these origins. 'Copenhagen', the capital of Denmark, for example, is a combination of two Danish words, '*købe*,' to buy or bargain, and '*havn*,' a port.

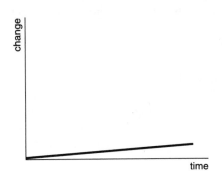

Figure 4.6   **Linear Change**

Writing seems to have originated as a consequence of trade, for the first known documents were written in Sumeria to record promises made and fulfilled, trade agreements and their accounting. Thousands of years later double-entry bookkeeping was invented to more accurately monitor increasing trade throughout the world.[15]

As agriculture became more efficient, people were able to pursue other work, and they gathered to build cities where they made and traded their wares in markets. During the last thousand years, and particularly the last one hundred, the efficiency of farming has advanced so much that the world's population has gone from being predominantly agrarian to predominantly urban.

Urban culture stimulates economic specialization, as manufacturers and traders strive to find economic niches where there is no competition. With a concentration of intellectual activity and driven by economic necessity, cities produce technological advances at a fast rate. In addition, because innovations build on prior innovations, change is cumulative. The time increment between significant changes is reduced, and each decade sees more innovation than the one prior.

Much more new technology was produced during the 19th century than during the 18th century. As the accelerating progression became apparent to scholars and philosophers of the early industrial revolution, the notions of continuous progress and economic growth became ideals of Western thought. Public schools became mandatory, and the young were taught the philosophy of progress to prepare them for life in the factories of modern society.

Competition between nations focused on industrial capacity and its consequent military capacity, with the winners gaining shares of the global markets for industrial goods and raw materials. The ebb and flow of economic advantage accompanied important industrial innovations. Overall, the gradual acceleration of change during the industrial revolution is described in mathematics as a *geometric* rate of change (Figure 4.7).

EXPONENTIAL CHANGE

The trend of accelerating change continues toward the 21st century, but now the rate of change has accelerated so much that it can no longer be understood as merely geometric. We are living during a time in which changes occur so frequently that the *rate* of change doubles and doubles again. Mathematicians call this is a kind of change *exponential* (Figure 4.8): "Suppose you own a pond on which a water lily is growing. The lily plant

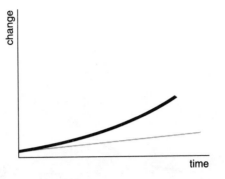

Figure 4.7 **Geometric Change**

doubles in size each day. If the plant were allowed to grow unchecked, it would completely cover the pond in 30 days, choking off other life forms in the water. For a long time the lily plant seems small, so you decide not to worry about it until it covers half the pond. On what day will that be?''[16]

Change accelerates when information moves faster, and with today's computers, information moves faster than it ever has before. Unable to respond to rapid change resulting from the use of its own products, IBM is hoisted with its own petard.

Exponential change tends to be uncontrollable, fast, and discontinuous. There is no lead time in which to master the impact of one event before another is upon you, and events pile up before there is time to respond (Figure 4.9).

For many decades the growth of the world's human population has been accelerating, and now doubling takes only 40 years, an exponential

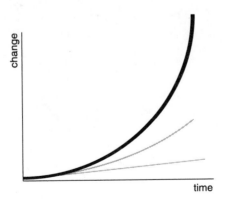

Figure 4.8 **Exponential Change**

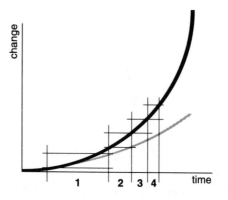

Figure 4.9 **Diminishing Response Time**
As change accelerates along the exponential curve, successive events of the same magnitude are of shorter durations and are more frequent. Event 1 is nearly three times longer than event 2, while events 3 and 4 are shorter still. The times between significant changes are progressively shorter, making it progressively more difficult to respond appropriately.

phenomenon with significant impact on the earth and all its inhabitants[17] (Figure 4.10). With the increasing population comes growth in economic activity—increasing industrial production, increasing consumption of resources, and increased tons of the by-products of economic activity, mountains of trash, and polluted soil, air, and water: "As population increases, the resources that support it are decreasing: the soil is eroding; the minerals are being mined out; ground water tables are sinking; plant and animal species are being eradicated at a pace probably unprecedented since the

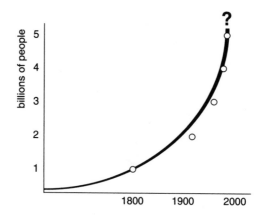

Figure 4.10 **World Human Population**

extinction of the dinosaurs. More and more people drawing on fewer and fewer resources—we appear to be on a collision course.''[18]

Exponential processes in nature are limited, eventually, by environmental constraints, and the human population will eventually approach such limits. The convergence of exponential population growth and the consequent consumption of resources portends a scarcity unlike anything in the past, because the scale of the industrial economy is far larger than it has ever been. Human economic activity is now so vast that it has consequences for many aspects of the world that have never been impacted before. Industrialism once stripped entire islands bare of trees, but now entire continental tropical forests are being destroyed, with unknown impact on the global climate.

Already, water is becoming a scarce resource in places where it was once abundant, particularly in exploding cities throughout the world. Mexico City, for example, is expected to have more than 25 million residents by the year 2000, and many millions of them will live in polluted slums that will lack basic water and sewage treatment facilities. Humans have never before lived in cities of this size or in urban conditions such as these.

Through billions of years on earth, the anatomy and physiology of all living species evolved in response to the immediate demands of the 'natural' world. For early humans, staying warm and finding food and water were decisively important. Survival meant responding to the sudden, day-to-day issues of life in what we today call the 'wilderness.' Human anatomy and physiology have not changed much for over one hundred thousand years, and so the survival habits that developed during the course of evolution remain the unchanged basis for thinking and decision making in today's much more complex urban culture. Although we have left the natural wilderness for the urban jungle, we retain our wilderness mind and our wilderness habits.

In the industrialized nations, however, most physical needs are met through commerce and the medium of urban culture, and survival depends upon one's ability to adapt to human culture. The natural world of one hundred thousand years ago is nearly irrelevant.

Compared with the millions of years of human evolution in the natural world, today's urban culture and all of the events of this century are insignificant and have yet to even make a mark on human evolution. Human 'hardware' is designed to deal with seasonal change in the natural environment, but the focus of our lives is a fast-changing, complex culture, from which we have worked to *remove* the impact of natural forces. Today's systemic threats come primarily from slow and gradual cultural and environmental processes such as global warming and the growth of the human population, but these processes are quite unlike the events that our ancestors faced.[19]

This mismatch between today's culture and our evolutionary heritage underlies the difficulties we have in managing cultural complexity. Our evolutionary process simply did not give us the tools for it. Jay Forrester noted this discontinuity in 1971: "It is my basic theme that the human mind is not adapted to interpreting how social systems behave. . . . In the long history of evolution it has not been necessary for man to understand these systems until very recent historical times. Evolutionary processes have not given us the mental skill needed to properly interpret the dynamic behavior of these systems of which we have now become a part."[20]

We have created a culture that we are unable, in fundamental ways, to comprehend. We lack the innate skill to understand the increasing complexity deriving from the exponential rate of change in a world that is fundamentally different from a world of linear or geometric change. In the words of scientists Robert Ornstein and Paul Ehrlich, "the human mental system is failing to comprehend the modern world."[21] Somehow we must make the shift from 'event thinking' to 'pattern thinking.'

DISEQUILIBRIUM AND LAG

The consequences of exponential change lie not simply with the impact of specific events, of course, but with larger patterns caused by multiple changes that occur simultaneously.

Every change that impacts an organization requires a response. The more appropriate the response, the better it will be positioned in the subsequent activity of the marketplace. But it takes time to understand the consequences of an event, to prepare a response, and then to implement the response. It can take months, or even years, to design and introduce a product to compete with the latest innovation from a competitor.

While we are busy getting our new product ready to challenge our competitor's existing product, what are they doing? Working on their next product, of course. And by the time we catch up with where they were, they won't be there any more.

The time between an event and awareness of the event is lag; the time between the awareness and the response is also lag. The time between the response and its impact is yet a third instance of lag (Figure 4.11). The longer these three instances, the more likely it becomes that change will overwhelm the individual firm. With each change, the firm is worse off than before, weakened. Subsequent changes pound it even harder. Soon

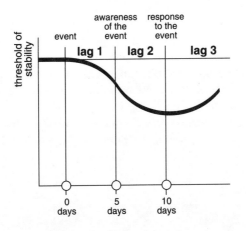

Figure 4.11   **Lag**
There are three instances of lag associated with each major event. First, there is the lag between the event and awareness of the event; second, the lag between awareness and the preparation and implementation of a response; and third, the lag between the response and its results. While all this is occurring, the organization is operating below its threshold of stability.

comes retrenching and downsizing. As its products and services get further behind market demand, it gets harder and harder to catch up.

Chrysler Corporation, for example, got so far behind the auto market of the 1970s that it needed a guarantee of loan repayment from the federal government in order to obtain capital to survive long enough to develop competitive products. During the years leading up to the loan guarantees, the company had become so embedded in crisis that it simply became paralyzed and couldn't respond effectively.

Scientists have observed a similar phenomenon in natural systems that seek equilibrium. To establish equilibrium, any system must deal with the impacts of environmental events which it does not control. When there is an event that impacts the company or the market, it takes time, say 10 days, to respond to the event, and thus to return to the state of balance.

Suppose, however, that on the sixth day, there is another external event which also impacts the system. This is the beginning of trouble, for the time interval between impacts is now *less* than the time required to adapt to a single impact. If the pattern persists, the system will be *permanently* unable to regain its equilibrium. Each subsequent impact will arrive before the prior impact has been accommodated, and thus the system will go into what is called 'chronic disequilibrium.' It will oscillate out of control and never achieve balance[22] (Figure 4.12).

This tendency to imbalance is what exponential change brings to the whole of society because the impacts of additional complexity are not merely additive. Some changes amplify the impacts from others, driving many systems into chaos that they simply cannot escape. They struggle and fail to achieve stability, repeatedly overshooting and undershooting their targets (Figure 4.13).

This turmoil is quite evident in many traumas of the modern world. Governments oscillate between the policies of the left and the right, with

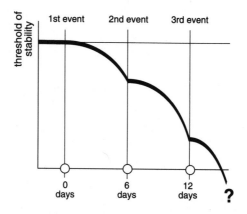

Figure 4.12 Chronic Disequilibrium
If a second event occurs before the appropriate response has ameliorated the impact from the first event, an organization is pushed further below the threshold of stability. If events consistently occur more rapidly than an organization can respond to them, the organization will be pushed into a pattern of chronic disequilibrium, as we observe in many organizations and governments in the world today.

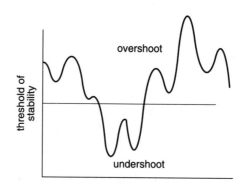

Figure 4.13 Chronic Disequilibrium, Redux
Because of today's exponential rate of change, most organizations seem to oscillate wildly without ever achieving stability.

Democrats and Republicans posturing for their constituents while shouting at each other across the halls of the legislature, making little attempt to find common ground. Economies oscillate between inflation and recession, rarely experiencing the desired middle ground of stable growth. Companies expand into new markets, downsize, and then repeat. Real estate markets in which there is sustained demand stimulate building booms that turn into overbuilding, leaving developers in bankruptcy and banks owning unwanted properties that they cannot sell.

Instability that is caused by exponential change is a phenomenon that we ourselves have created, and it is a permanent aspect of our culture. It is driven by the use of technology by an ever-growing number of humans. Our inability to cope with it is forcing our institutions deeper into disequilibrium, amplifying the sense of malaise as we come to recognize that we face global problems of unprecedented complexity.

Even the CIA has noticed that something new is happening. In 1989, Director William Webster established a fifth CIA directorate, one focused on strategic planning, to identify "changing requirements for intelligence in a changing world."[23]

So, here we are in an exponentially changing world, and just as exponentially changing chip technology is fundamental to IBM and the entire computer industry, exponentially changing technology in aggregate is fundamental to the future of our culture *and* to the future of each company. Its importance cannot be overstated: *The exponential rate of change is the most important pattern.*

5

The Flow of Information

Information is fundamental to the new economy, but the explosion of computers threatens to overwhelm all organizations under mountains of useless data. Data must be filtered to find the information that is hidden within. When information is then combined with theory and experience, it becomes knowledge, and the processes of creating information and knowledge are the processes of learning.

April 1993: Hughes Information Technology has recently won a ten-year, $766 million contract from NASA to build and operate a database storage system for environmental information relayed from NASA's satellites. The data will be made available to scientists around the world. The amount of data to be received every three days is expected to equal the entire holdings of the Library of Congress.[1]

As exponential change causes chronic disequilibrium and overwhelming complexity, conditions become more difficult to comprehend, and the task of decision making becomes more difficult throughout the enterprise (Figure 5.1).

Every aspect of this pattern is driven by a single phenomenon, a phenomenon of unique importance throughout our exponentially changing society. This phenomenon is *information*, which underlies the creation of technology, its commercialization, and its use.

Information is an outcome of interactions between individuals and between institutions, for when individuals interact, there is an exchange that results in new understanding, new information. When institutions interact, the volume of information that is exchanged is likely to be much greater, and the consequences more extensive, because the greater economic scope of institutions magnifies their every action. A corporate or governmental action can immediately impact thousands or millions of individuals.

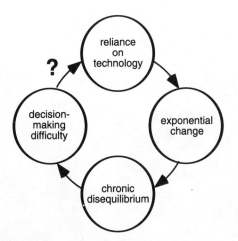

Figure 5.1 **The Difficulty of Decision Making**

These interactions create relationships that extend over time and space, leading to a web of products and services, of rules and regulations and laws, of competition and cooperation, opportunity and constraint that make up the immense and immensely complex global marketplace. More individuals interacting with more institutions means . . . more information, and more complexity.

Increasing complexity affects the implementation of initiatives such as government programs, which often have undesirable consequences that are not foreseen. More complex programs may have adverse consequences that are, indeed, utterly *unforeseeable* due to the very nature of complexity itself.

Who expected that a high-rise housing project built for low-income families would be considered uninhabitable and demolished within 20 years? When it was clear in 1972 that Pruitt-Igoe was a failure, millions of dollars of public investment was blown into a huge pile of rubble and dust. More than 20 years later, still more of these projects have met the same fate (Figure 5.2), and the government has finally proposed to demolish nearly all of them.[2] Here we see a prominent example of the failure to understand the modern world.

Working amid such complexity, managers must make decisions while events are happening, long before the outcomes of long-term trends are clear. It is difficult to predict what information will prove to be significant, and what is ephemeral, but nevertheless decisions must be made quickly because delays may be more costly than mistakes. Comments Jack Welch,

Figure 5.2 **Demolition of Christopher Columbus Homes, Trenton, New Jersey, March 6, 1994**
The actual social results of high-rise public housing were opposite the desires and expectations of their builders, illustrating that our social systems often behave counterintuitively to our expectations. Jay Forrester points out that this is because of the very complexity of today's society. Photo by AP/Wide World Photos.

During the global expansion of the 1980s, companies responded to rising demand by building new factories and facilities in computers, airplanes, medical equipment—almost everything you can think of. Then, when the world economy stopped growing, everybody ended up with too much capacity. The worldwide capacity overhang, coming at a time when everybody feels poor, is forcing ferocious price competition. As it intensifies, the margin pressure on all corporations is going to be enormous. Only the most productive companies are going to win.[3]

Marketplace competition is driving companies to increase specialization through the development and application of new technology, fostering the constant commitment to innovation. Thus, technology is both a consequence of *and* a stimulator of exponential change. This self-reinforcing process is a positive feedback loop, which means that the rate of change can *only* accelerate (Figure 5.3).

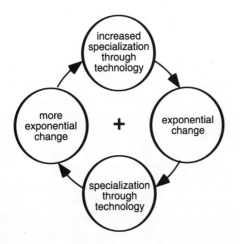

Figure 5.3 **The Acceleration of Change**
Exponential change leads to specialization through technology, which itself contributes to further exponential change, which leads to increasing specialization, which leads to . . . . Thus, exponential change is both a cause and a result of advancing technology. There is no graceful way to exit the loop.

Being an innovator means taking risks, and with risk comes the possibility of being wrong. It requires learning from failures *and* successes, and applying the learning as quickly as possible.[4] However, in the distorted command and control environment, many managers have been trained that failures threaten their own futures and are thus conditioned to avoid risk. Trapped in the aversion to mistakes, many have not grasped the intimate connections between risk-taking, learning, innovation, and market leadership.

One company that has is General Electric. When Jack Welch became chairman of GE in 1981, he realized that the company could not afford to participate in any market in which it could not be a leader, and he therefore insisted that all GE subsidiaries be first or second in their markets.

Implementing this strategy during the 1980s, GE sold 19 of its major subsidiaries that were not market leaders and acquired 23 others that were already leaders or could be combined with companies that GE already owned to achieve leadership positions.[5]

GE's determination to carry out its straightforward but difficult strategy shows how a clear understanding of an important pattern becomes the basis for coherent action. However, the very complexity of an organization itself presents many obstacles to the process of discerning the important patterns. One of the most prevalent obstacles is the difficulty of keeping track of the data that an organization accumulates.

DATABASES: THE NASA EXPERIENCE

The experience of NASA illustrates the challenges that institutions face as they struggle with complexity. NASA is a scientific research and development organization, and one of its most important products is technical data. The NASA Charter specifies that it shall, "provide for the widest practicable and appropriate dissemination of information concerning its activities and the results thereof."[6]

Between 1964 and 1989, NASA accumulated a database of 6 trillion bytes of data, the equivalent of 3 billion printed pages. This huge database documented the work of thousands of NASA scientists and engineers and technicians and designers, including, of course, the data from NASA's space missions. Although such raw data are useful to NASA and to others, it is the *information* that may be hidden in the data, and the consequences for the present and future action, that is even more compelling. But such information becomes available only after the data are filtered (Figure 5.4). It is an understatement to say that finding the information hidden in mountains of data is difficult. Filter data well, and you may find information that contributes to success. Filter it poorly, and the potential benefit is probably lost.

Among the 6 trillion bytes there are surely data with little or no potential value, data that no one will ever care about knowing, data collected long ago and no longer relevant. There may also be dozens or hundreds of valuable or important ideas that may never be found. And somewhere in the database, there is apparently a document, or even more than one, that discusses the affect of temperature on the performance of space shuttle O-rings. Sadly the people at NASA who needed to know this did not know it in 1986, and the Challenger exploded.[7]

The critical resilience of O-rings depends on their temperature, and the launch was on an unusually cold day. This temperature dependence had been a con-

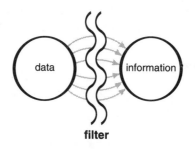

Figure 5.4 **Data Filtered into Information**

cern of engineers during the development of the booster and had been communicated to company managers and NASA officials. In fact, an engineer had attempted to have the Challenger launch delayed because of this low temperature but had been unsuccessful.[8]

Without appropriate filters, it is impossible to distinguish the valuable ideas (music) from the mountains of trivia (noise). Note, however, that the difference between music and noise depends *entirely* on the specific situation at hand, so data filters must be 'tunable' to fit any situation, and this makes the filtering problem even more difficult.[9]

Meanwhile, NASA's own forecast suggests that more such problems may lie ahead, for the agency predicted in 1989 that its 25-year-old database would double in size in only three more years, by 1992. It further predicted that the database would then double again in only two additional years, and that it would double yet again before 1996, consisting by then of an overwhelming 48 trillion bytes, or 24 billion pages of data[10] (Figure 5.5). This is a perplexing management problem.

As of 1990, NASA had stored, "at least 1.2 million reels of information beeped back to earth from orbiting satellites and lunar and planetary probes. Yet NASA 'does not have an agency-wide inventory of its data' and 'does not know what is being retained and where it is located,' endangering critical information that could be vital to future scientific ventures."[11]

Science magazine has reported that data from the Landsat earth satellite surveillance system was virtually inaccessible: "The system is so bogged down even now that people call the data centers 'data cemeteries.' "[12]

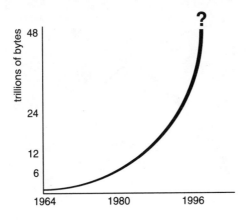

Figure 5.5   **The NASA Database**
Can NASA manage 48 trillion bytes (48 terabytes) of data effectively? What will it cost just to maintain the database? Is this cost socially justifiable?

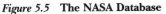

It would, of course, be impossible to collect so much data without computers, and this is a conundrum of computer technology. The exponential miniaturization of computer chip technology makes possible the exponential growth of computer databases and severely exacerbates the problem of managing the data. The cost of obtaining a new bit of data has declined exponentially, and since one can store ever more data at ever less cost, the amount of data is increasing exponentially just as the cost of storing it is comparably decreasing. The cost per byte declines, but the overall cost increases steadily. Managing these intertwined exponential phenomena is an enormous, and often expensive, challenge (Figure 5.6) that raises many questions:

- How much of NASA's budget is allocated to managing its database?

- How many computers will be fully occupied in storing, sorting, indexing, and printing out data?

- How many people will be required to program, and then to maintain these computers?

- Can this work be done in a way that makes the data accessible, and thus useful, to those who have a use for it?

There are not likely to be simple answers to these questions, nor to the questions that will inevitably arise concerning the current or future value

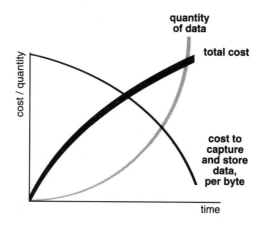

Figure 5.6 Parallel Phenomena
As it gets progressively less expensive to create and store a byte of data, the quantity of data increases reciprocally. If this were not the case, the enormous databases of organizations like NASA would not exist. Nevertheless, the total cost rises inexorably.

of the data, particularly in the context of the federal government budget deficit.

NASA's database is an exponential phenomenon occurring within a single government agency, and nearly all federal agencies and most large companies face the same problems. More and more resources are absorbed in assembling and maintaining growing databases. The risk of *not* sustaining the effort is too great for most organizations to even consider.[13]

DEFINING INFORMATION

In the industrial economy, those who knew what to do with machines were successful. Today, however, there is an information economy precisely because knowing how to use information is the key distinction between those who are successful and those who are not. Information has not replaced industrialism, but it has changed everything about how industrialism is carried out.

Data, and data filtered into information, are the raw materials of the economy, which is why database management is such an important pattern for the 1990s. While some are good at sorting the music from the noise, others are inept beyond the reasonable limits of patience. The inept are those who are absorbed in events, fixated on the tasks at hand, and oblivious to larger patterns.

In addition to collecting data and information, another important aspect of this technological pattern has to do with sending it from one place to another. As recently as 200 years ago, long distance communication required the writing and posting of a letter, which would then take weeks or even months to reach its destination. The cost of coordinating large and widely disbursed government and business enterprises was high, and response times were long.

Because of computer chips, the cost of sending messages has reached unprecedented lows. Numerous technologies, including satellite communications, fiber optics, cable TV, cellular telephones, pagers, fax machines, computer modems, electronic mail, networking, and video conferencing all add to the expanding flood of information that roars down the nascent 'information superhighway.'

It seems that every day there are advances that enable people to communicate with one another more directly at less cost. On June 2, 1993, the newspaper reported that President Clinton began receiving electronic mail at the White House through Internet, the international computer network of networks. One no longer needs to use a postage stamp (or a postal service) to send a message to the President.[14] The cost of communications is going down while the speed of communication is increasing.

The underlying marketplace phenomenon that drives this entire process is, of course, the fact that information is economically useful. Each subsequent information technology increases society's reliance on information, and thereby our reliance on information technology. An ever-growing proportion of humanity's resources are directed into the development and deployment of computers and databases, and as a result, researcher Hans Moravec has forecast that by the end of this century, developing computers "is likely to be the main occupation of the human race."[15] Michael Rothschild suggests that future generations will consider the computer chip to be the most significant invention of the last 500 years.[16]

Interestingly, as information technology gets less expensive, the value of information has become more distinct from the medium of its transfer. Books once represented the pinnacle of learning, and only scholars and the wealthy owned them. Erasmus commented, "When I get a little money I buy books. If any is left, I buy food and clothes."[17]

Today paper money (itself entirely symbolic) is being replaced by an even more ephemeral form of information, electronic bits of worthless computer code that represents the ownership of tangible assets all around the globe. Electrons that represent money, which itself just represents buying power, zip around the globe from continent to continent, a process so abstract that no one ever sees or touches the electrons or the money.

Available in such abundance and transmitted so cheaply, information has become a commodity. It is bought and sold, mined, refined, and traded, just like physical commodities such as oil and iron ore. But information has different properties than material commodities, for although it has no mass and no size, its consequences are economically decisive. Information is purely potential, a unique energy that motivates every aspect of human culture.

Another reason that information is unlike other commodities is that it isn't necessarily *used up* when it's used. More than one person can use the same information, and each can receive unique value. Sharing information may actually increase its value, as the purpose of collaboration is to make information more useful by combining the informed intelligence of many individuals into . . . new information.

Some information is most valuable when it is a secret—that's why we have the CIA. Companies are intent on protecting their secrets, mostly consisting of technical information that has been accumulated at great cost and which may be used to create new distinctions, and thus advantage in the marketplace.

Sometimes, however, a secret that was valuable yesterday isn't worth anything today. As the rate of change increases, the likelihood increases that a particular piece of information will quickly become irrelevant. New technical information replaces older technical information overnight, particularly in the most rapidly changing marketplaces such as that for computers. Last month's breakthroughs may not be unique for very long.

The value of information, the cost of sharing it or keeping it secret, and the danger of its obsolescence, are issues that organizations must understand and master to deal successfully with exponential change. To do this requires an understanding of the essential character of information.

The root of the word information is 'inform,' from Latin *informare* meaning 'to give form to.' Information is that which provides shape or character, as a potter gives shape to clay or a sculptor to stone. But information gives form in a deeper way, for it is not so much an external shape that information affects, but a more subtle essence.

This essence is foremost the *meaning* of words and phrases, for in their meaning lies the greatest interest and the most importance. 'Meaning' has to do with the deep and fundamental issues of existence, with the source of commitment, of caring, and of the capacity to affect the future. It is the source of *motive*, the energy to pursue visions, to change the world and so to make it more as we think it ought to be. Information has tremendous power and profound impact on our lives and our journey through the world. We receive new information, and we ask, "What does this mean?"

"Information is that which changes us,"[18] suggests Stafford Beer, because by simply knowing some information our actions are shaped. A lack of information also shapes our actions, although we discover the lack only in hindsight: *"If only I had known!"*

Anthropologist Gregory Bateson proposed a definition of information that expresses the same sensibility, but with a different and illuminating choice of words. He wrote that "Information consists of differences that make a difference."[19] By the time the existence of information has been recognized, information has *already* made things different, precisely because having information causes us to *perceive* the world differently than before. Without being recognized or acknowledged, of course, it isn't information—yet. But once it is seen or heard or read or felt, information is the 'difference' whose meaning has already resulted in changes in our perception. How we perceive the world has everything to do with how we behave in the world, so a change in our perception is utterly decisive.

Both definitions express the powerful relationship between information and action. The recognition that information exists leads immediately to action: Information "changes," and information "makes." Inasmuch as 'making' is the essence of exchange in our technological society, and inasmuch as 'change' now dominates every aspect of society, the power of information is literally compelling us into the future. And it is precisely this power that the corporation must master if it is to survive.

A THEORY OF KNOWLEDGE

The ultimate payoff that justifies an investment in data collection comes when data are filtered into information that is useful. Information, in turn, can then be applied to the accomplishment of useful work as that immensely valuable phenomenon of the information economy: the *knowledge* of how to actually accomplish something. But knowledge comes about only under specific conditions, only when information is integrated with *theory* and with *experience* (Figure 5.7). W. Edwards Deming observes:

> Theory is a window into the world. Without theory, experience has no meaning. Without theory, one has no questions to ask. Hence without theory there is no learning. . . . To put it another way, information, no matter how complete and speedy, is not knowledge. Knowledge has temporal spread. Knowledge comes from theory. Without theory, there is no way to use the information that comes to us on the instant. [20]

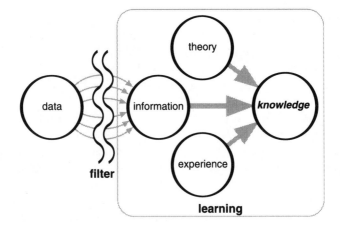

Figure 5.7 **Learning & Knowledge**
Knowledge is the result of learning, the process of integrating information, theory, and experience into meaningful wholes. Learning is done only by individuals.

In the words of Peter Drucker:

> Only when a [person] applies information to doing something does it become knowledge. Knowledge, like electricity or money, is a form of energy that exists only when doing work. The emergence of the knowledge economy is not, in other words, part of 'intellectual history' as it is normally conceived. It is part of the 'history of technology,' which recounts how man puts tools to work.[21]

The integration of theory, information, and experience creates knowledge, and this integration is the process of *learning*, a process that is fundamental to all successful organizations. It is also, as we saw in the Introduction, the strategy by which individuals deal with increasing complexity.

From these distinctions we can see more clearly the difference between education and learning that was discussed in Chapter 3, Practice 3 of the recognition and response model (page 36). As education comes from without, it can be sure only to convey descriptions that are encoded and expressed through numerous media, including speaking, writing, drawing, and computer code.

Learning is much different. It is the very personal process of integrating theory, information, and experience into knowledge, and it can occur only within the individual's consciousness. Such an integration cannot be forced to happen, which makes it apparent that learning leads to competence that is far beyond what education can hope to accomplish.

When someone questions us, we say, "I *know* what I'm doing." Such knowledge always and necessarily concerns the past. Because experience is an integral component of knowledge, knowledge exists only as a consequence of what has *already* been done. Those who accept things as they are may have the knowledge to maintain the status quo, but their knowledge may not be sufficient to deal with the constant novelty of a rapidly changing environment. As important as knowledge is, it does not advance unless it is accompanied by the vision that looks toward the future and defines how things *ought* to be. More often than not, the view forward is stimulated by the asking of questions. This is discussed in more detail in Chapter 8.

Professor Russell Ackoff points out that beyond knowledge lie *understanding* and *wisdom*, which are even more fundamental to the responsibilities of management (Figure 5.8). Whereas information, knowledge, and understanding are concerned with doing things right, wisdom is concerned with doing the right things. It is only from wisdom that compelling visions can come.[22]

Interestingly, when knowledge, understanding, or wisdom are shared, they can be shared only as information. One person's knowledge reverts to information for its recipients, until they reintegrate it in the context of their own experiences and their own theories, thereby making it knowledge, understanding, or wisdom once again.

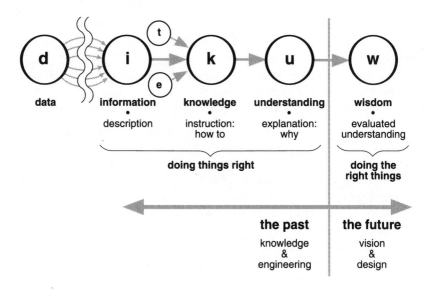

Figure 5.8 **Russell Ackoff's Theory of Wisdom**
The progression from data to information to knowledge to understanding to wisdom is described by Russell Ackoff, who observes that the distinction between doing things right and doing the right things is the difference between understanding and wisdom. This distinction, which he attributes to Peter Drucker, is crucial for our society in these times of rapid change. Adding to Ackoff's theory, we observe that this distinction divides the past from the future: Knowledge comes only from what already exists and what has been done; wisdom concerns the future and what *could* and *should* be done.

It was the capacity to encode information in the form of computerized messages that propelled society from the industrial economy to the information economy. This capacity enabled people to share information with each other at an unprecedented scale, leading to the creation of new knowledge at an unprecedented scale. Now that we are surrounded by information, we are forced by our own economy to distinguish information from knowledge, understanding, and wisdom. We will become adept at distinguishing 'doing things right' from 'doing the right things' as we become more proficient at recognizing the important patterns, and at using models to understand the long-term consequences of our present-day choices.

PATTERNS AND MODELS

The problem with the huge NASA database is finding the data that can make a difference, which occurs long before issues concerning knowledge even arise. This problem of data filtering is an issue for all organizations, and it is fundamental to all organisms, including humans. In fact, data filtering is an issue that is encountered by all *systems*, living and nonliving. Systems exist in the context of environments to which they must adapt, and the precise nature of their efforts to adapt depend on the data that they gather about their environments, how they interpret the data, and how they then respond.

Our very existence is evidence that evolution has indeed solved the filtering problem. Our senses receive enormous quantities of data, billions of bits each minute especially through our eyes, and also through our ears and noses and skin and taste buds. Transmitted as electrical impulses, the brain is able to make sense out of it all without being overwhelmed, enabling us to walk down a busy street without running into every person we pass, or every signpost, and all the while our conscious mind is thinking about some abstract problem in physics or philosophy, or about what's for dinner.

The brain uses patterns to filter the stream of data it receives, to assemble it into coherent models of us-in-the-environment. Many of these patterns are developed through conscious learning: We learn to read, write, walk, and sing. Learning and creating the patterns of conscious behavior occupies a large portion of our awareness, beginning at birth and continuing throughout our lives.

At the same time that we are looking forward to the next good meal and some relaxing conversation, the brain is also actively engaged in filtering data that are sent from receptors located throughout the body. These receptors constantly measure the quantities of dozens of chemicals that perform metabolic functions. Oxygen and carbon dioxide in the lungs and blood must be calibrated with the heart rate, while digestion proceeds on that big lunch we had hours ago, and numerous hormones circulate throughout the body delivering messages to cells of various organs. We don't have to learn these patterns consciously (which would be impossible) because we receive them as part of our preprogrammed genetic heritage.

All metabolic data must be assimilated and interpreted immediately, because if any aspect of our metabolic functioning goes out of control, we are likely to die. Three to five minutes without oxygen, for example, is about all the brain can tolerate. When all metabolic variables thus operate within the parameters that constitute 'health,' we are healthy. When they deviate from those parameters, un-health results, which often threatens the survival of the system. How does the body know exactly how much of which chemical is the right amount? For this it must refer to a pattern, a model value that it has already established.

Science has discovered that it is not possible to regulate any system without using a model of that system, because regulation is fundamentally about comparisons between what 'is' and what 'needs to be.' Whether it is a human body or a business or the economy of a nation, regulation can only occur when regulatory parameters have been defined in a model that is *outside* the system that is being regulated. This invariant reality pertains to all systems: "A regulator [of a system] contains a model of that which it regulates."[23]

If there is no model, then there can be no regulation, for lacking a frame of reference through which data can be interpreted, there can be no way to discern if events are happening as they should, or as they shouldn't. And thus no possibility of taking precise and appropriate corrective action (other than by guesswork) and no way to assure that the system will continue to be viable.

Such a model can exist only at a different logical level from the system itself because the model is a description of the system and is necessarily a different logical type. The model must include reference to the purposes of a system as well as to the modes of its operation, purposes that are the expression of doing the right thing. This is why the definition of commercial and social purposes are the first practice of the recognition and response organization, for this is the attempt to embody the wisdom to do the right thing from the very beginning.

The distinction of logical types between a system and its model underlies Einstein's comment that "The world we have made as a result of a level of thinking we have done thus far creates problems we cannot solve at the same level at which we created them."[24]

THE PROCESS OF REGULATION

Since a system is likely to consist of many parts, the relationships between those parts are fundamental to its performance. Indeed, for a system to exist at all is a consequence of those relationships. We expect the system we call an airplane to fly, but the capability to fly is *not* inherent in the parts that make up the airplane. In fact, "An airplane has been defined as a collection of parts having an inherent tendency to fall to earth, and requiring constant effort and supervision to stave off that outcome. The system called 'airplane' may have been designed to fly, but the parts don't share that tendency. In fact they share the opposite tendency. And the System will fly—if at all—only as a System."[25]

The airplane is a system not because of the structure of its parts (any of which would immediately fall to the ground on its own) but because of its capacity to function as a coherent process. Further, the design of the airplane proceeds as a consequence of the intended process, and the structure is developed only as a consequence of that intention. We see again that process precedes structure.

Filtering data is thus a matter of comparing them to a model and examining the result: Do the data fit the expectation or not? If not, why not? This is the same as steering a car and continuously modifying the direction to remain on the road: Are we heading for the ditch? If so, adjust the course!

Businesses are systems that are regulated by people who use models to assess and regulate performance to make day-to-day decisions about ongoing operations and strategic decisions about the long term. These models include Business Plans, Strategic Plans, Research and Development Plans, Budgets, Sales Plans, and so many others.

Consider two companies that are competitors in a difficult market. Each has a strategy for identifying and selling to potential customers, models called the Marketing Plan. Both plans hypothesize that there are profits to be made. All other things being equal, the company with the superior strategy has the advantage because it has a better model, and thus a better chance of regulating its own performance to actually earn those profits.

The process of building and testing these self-regulatory models is one of the most important activities that managers do, and they do it constantly: analyzing products, employees, competitors, customers, markets, and so on. Actual results are compared with expected results, and the comparison produces information that is very valuable to an organization.

When this information, the results of the comparison, is then used to guide modifications to the behavior of the system, there is a focused and specific basis for action. Is the corporation headed for a ditch? This question is asked continuously, and the answers that are actually used to correct the course constitute 'feedback.' In systems science, "Just calling it 'feedback' doesn't mean that it has actually fed back. To speak precisely: it hasn't fed back until the system changes course. Up to that point, it's merely Sensory Input."[26]

THREE TRAPS OF MODELS

The possibility of developing useful feedback by using a model depends on how good the model is. Many of the models that are actually used to regulate corporations are mental models,[27] approximate ratios, imprecise indicators, undocumented ideas, and vague images. Inherent in mental models are three potentially dangerous traps:

1. Assumptions.

2. Incompleteness.

3. Novelty.

1. Assumptions

The first trap concerns the assumptions that often underlie mental models: unexamined ideas about what is or is not possible; expectations about how competitors will or will not act; beliefs about technology and the marketplace; and dreams about the long- or short-term future. These assumptions usually persevere because people don't realize that their assumptions *are* assumptions. They unconsciously confuse their own models with 'reality,' not realizing that reality is changing, and that yesterday's reality may bear little resemblance to today's. Untested assumptions that were once self-evident and obvious may become significantly, dangerously untrue. This seems to be the trap into which Akers, Robinson, and Lego fell: The 1990s were not like the '60s, '70s, and '80s.

In the 1970s, American auto companies prepared themselves to compete with each other and the European automakers, believing that Japanese cars could not be a factor in the U.S. market. Their assumption was wrong, and they were stunned when Japanese cars redefined quality standards and captured a significant share of the market.[28]

Also in the 1970s, oil experts projected that crude oil prices would climb to $100 per barrel, so oil companies invested in oil-field development projects that were expected to yield oil at a very profitable $35 per barrel. Some years later, prices fell to $20 where they remained, forcing a dramatic retrenchment in the industry. Companies were bought and sold; banks collapsed; projects were abandoned.[29]

Business literature bulges with examples of companies that failed and industries that declined because they were managed according to models that proved to be flawed, models whose assumptions no longer fit a changed marketplace. Believing in untested assumptions is equivalent to seeing things that aren't there. In psychiatry this is called 'hallucination.'

Alternatively, seeing things, but refusing to accept what you see, is called 'denial.'

As markets change, managers are trapped by the hallucinations in their mental models or their denial of reality, and then trapped by the poor decisions that result.

As change accelerates, assumptions and the mental models that are built upon them will be invalidated faster and faster. The rational approach is therefore to bring these assumptions to the surface and test them to expose hallucinations and denial before they lead to expensive, strategic errors in the marketplace.

2. Incompleteness

A second modeling trap is inherent in the necessary incompleteness of models. Models, after all, are simplifications of systems. If the model were a full-scale reproduction of the system, modeled with all of its parts and characteristics, it would *be* the system. Model makers must choose which features and how much detail of a system to include in their models.

There is danger, however, that the actual system will behave in ways that the model cannot predict or replicate. If inappropriate conclusions are drawn from such a model, an organization will not be prepared to deal with actual events.

For example, the Exxon *Valdez* was the 8,859th oil tanker to depart Valdez, Alaska. When it spilled 11 million gallons of oil in Prince William Sound, no one was prepared to respond adequately.[30] In the words of Frank Iarossi, president of the Exxon Shipping Company, "Nobody ever anticipated a spill of this magnitude when the [Alaska] pipeline plan was being assembled."[31]

The complexity of our social and economic systems means that they behave in ways that often frustrate even the best attempts to model them. Since our brains have not been equipped by the evolutionary process to understand the complex and dynamic systems that compose our culture, the incompleteness of our models becomes a fundamental problem that impacts all attempts to improve conditions.

Into this void we leap, pockets bulging with marketing plans and government programs that do not, surprisingly, produce the intended results. In fact, they frequently produce results that are exactly the opposite of our intentions. Jay Forrester calls these outcomes 'counterintuitive,' and notes that the behavior of large and complex social systems is counterintuitive much of the time.[32] The underlying problem is not with the systems themselves, but with our incapacity to understand them. Our thinking, and our expectations about what *ought* to happen in a simple world of cause and effect is mismatched with our increasingly complex culture.

Since our evolutionary 'experience' accumulated in such a cause-and-effect world and our five senses function in the same world, this is our expectation for reality. But cause and effect is but a narrow part of the entire range of phenomena. Scientists have gone beyond the Newtonian models and discovered an underlying universe, one in which models such as Complexity (see Chapter 1) give a much more accurate understanding of the social and economic systems of today.

Society's transition from a time of simple systems that were characterized by cause-and-effect relationships, to complex systems that are characterized by intricate feedback loops, parallels the transition from Newtonian physics to the relativistic universe. It is for this reason that business theorists have begun to explore the new physics for models that might also help explain the new economy.[33]

Science has penetrated to the subatomic realms, and society has encountered the perplexing world of counterintuitive behaviors, but the meaning of this has not yet influenced the broader processes of decision making. For example, the government implemented a 'war on drugs,' the results of which were, disturbingly, increased violence *and* increased drug use.[34] Clearly the model that was used to design the program was simplistic and insufficient.

Another example: Thousands of the former students of public schools are illiterates and dropouts, hardly the intended educational outcome. This school system was designed in the 1850s to prepare a rural population for a lifetime of industrial production, but it is still used today in world whose concerns are far different, far more complex. How surprising can it be that today's public education is a failure? The failure of *education* in a time of rapid change is predictable, inasmuch as education must always be concerned with a past that seems irrelevant so quickly. The discussion above suggests that a *learning* system would be far more useful.

3. Novelty

The third problem with models is that they are inherently weak in dealing with novelty. An old and well-proven model isn't automatically useful for recognizing phenomena that are new. In fact, a model may actually prevent us from even recognizing when we are in the presence of novelty. Unfortunately, new ideas do not generally arrive on the scene complete with a framework for valid comparisons. Because the exponential advancement of technology brings novelty each day, our dependence on models can be a pernicious trap.

This is exactly what happens when a company introduces a product that takes the market by surprise and redefines consumer expectations. To its competitors, such a product is like a threatening virus. When such a virus appears, it is often fatal to the organisms that have not prepared themselves to face this previously unknown threat. For example, television is the virus that forever changed the world of radio, much as cable TV is now changing the world of broadcast. HIV is a frightening example.

Consequently, the ability to respond appropriately to new viruses is among the most important life-preserving qualities that an individual organism can possess.

The first indications of a new virus may be unexpected variations in the behavior of a system, glitches that haven't been seen before. A common reflex is to brush such glitches aside, to explain them away as meaningless anomalies. But actually these may be early warnings, opportunities to grasp the essence of a new situation while there's still time to do something about it. They are also early evidence that mental models may contain untested assumptions, one of which is about to, or has just, bitten us in the rear. Peter Drucker points out that unexpected successes and unexpected failures are the early warnings that define new opportunities for innovation in the marketplace.[35]

Rather than looking at things 'going wrong' as problems, they can also be seen as focused learning opportunities that may hold valuable information about the future. Mistakes can be virtuous in this context and can enable the corporation to avoid bigger mistakes in the future. Thus comes the advice from systems scientists that suggests that you "Cherish your bugs. Study them."[36]

This advice is actually no different from the practice of quality engineers who search persistently to eliminate 'common causes' of trouble and variation that cause systems to perform below expected or desired levels. Upon discovering them, engineers are presented with the opportunity to learn something new about their systems, and thus to improve their performance.[37]

Due to the acceleration of change, there is less time to respond to new conditions in the marketplace. Therefore, the models that are used to regulate the activities of a corporation must be tested and retested continuously. To ensure that it is as comprehensive as possible, this process must involve everyone in the organization, and therefore everyone must learn the language of systems.

PATTERNS AND LANGUAGE

Because of the vital organizing role that language plays in the human intellect, creating models and using them as regulatory tools is largely a consequence of the ability to express them through language. We cannot, in many cases, recognize a pattern that we do not have the words to describe. When a common cause is identified for the first time, it must be named, and that name often becomes a compelling symbol for the problem it represents.

Every organization develops its own code words that express the issues and problems that recur in its environment. In most cases, such language is nearly incomprehensible to outsiders. Even though they may have experienced comparable issues in their own lives, the differences in language become a significant barrier to mutual understanding. There must be an effort made to translate from one to another for communication to take place.

Language is thus the *pattern maker* of the human cognitive process. As society evolves, new words are invented to convey new realities. The dictionary is not a fixed and permanent thing, but an evolving record of our evolving understanding of our evolving universe.

New words and phrases express different ideas differently; this same concept of 'difference' was presented above to define the word 'information.' The evolution of technology, and of the language we use to describe and understand it, is precisely a process of creating differences that did not previously exist. Some of these differences emerge as a consequence of new technology, which enables us to experience the world in new ways. Quasars, quarks, and Q-mesons did not exist in Newton's models, nor did bits, bytes, baud rates, and beta testing exist in his language.

Since models are absolutely necessary for all kinds of regulation and all kinds of management, it is apparent that models are essential in a competitive environment. Continuous improvement of the work and the work process requires continuous improvement of the models used to regulate it, of the flow of information that is fed through the models, and thus of the very language that is used to describe a company and its place in the universe. Stated simply, "They who have the best models will probably win."

MANAGING INFORMATION

The essence of both the global ecosystem and the global economy is not trade, not manufacturing, not services, but that which connects them all together: information. Information connects the parts of the economy into a whole system and provides underlying cohesiveness, just as an engineer's design provides orderliness that transforms the parts of an airplane into a system that flies. Information is the leading economic indicator, the pattern of patterns, and the maker of change.

Information is inherent in the origins and ongoing interactions of cities, inherent in the accumulation of technology that has brought exponential change to the modern world. Change is woven into the very fabric of our culture, and because of the role that information plays in creating change, it is entirely fitting that our era should come to be known as the 'Information Age.' This is indeed an age of constant change!

In this world of tumultuous change, in these times that lack continuity and in which "the center cannot hold,"[38] how can a corporation preserve itself and survive in the changing marketplace? Recognizing the reality of the changing marketplace is the first priority, and that means seeking to identify and understand the patterns that underlie the confusion.

Within the organization, widespread sharing of information is the key to understanding the changing marketplace. Information is the very stuff of decision making, the difference between success and failure when better information means the possibility of better decisions. There is a cost associated with using old, outdated information to make decisions, and, though it is usually an unknown and unallocated cost, the cost of ignorance can be quite high.

The marketplace is focused always on the differences of now and tells us what products and services are in demand only if we *listen*. This is 'news' (never 'olds') and together with prior history, it is the basis for accomplishing work that the market may value. How this information is communicated, digested, stored, and most importantly, used within the organization, is the key issue that confronts all organizations in today's rapidly changing world.

In this context there is one more thing to be said about IBM and its struggles in the changing computer marketplace. Certainly by the mid-1980s, many people at IBM knew that the microcomputer market was growing in importance. IBM salespeople, interacting with customers every day, had to be aware of what customers were buying and what they were considering for their future purchases.

Surrounded by the reality of the marketplace, these people must have seen the implications. The decline of the mainframe must have been as obvious to them as it was to the founders of companies like Sun. Surely many attempted to communicate this information to the leaders of IBM, to John Akers and the other officers of the corporation.

But if this information got to the decision makers, it did not result in corrective feedback, as evidenced by the absence of appropriate action. The corporation failed to manage the internal flow of information, just as NASA failed to heed warnings about O-rings.

This failure cost the company thousands of jobs and billions of dollars, and it cost shareholders many more billions in value as IBM stock plummeted. Although the company's leaders claimed to have been caught by surprise by the rate of change, the real problem had more to do with how they gathered and assimilated information than it did with any great surprises emerging in the marketplace.

The tragedy for IBM, and for every company that gets 'surprised' by this kind of change, is that they had paid for the information that they needed to understand the changing marketplace. They paid the people who sold their products and services day after day. They paid their managers. They paid for thousands of engineers to go to conferences to learn about the industry, and for thousands more to go to graduate schools to learn about the leading edge of advancing technology. They even paid for a great proportion of the R & D that made computer chips more powerful and smaller year after year after year. All the information that they needed to foresee the impending curve in the marketplace road was fully bought and paid for, in advance, many times over.

But because they didn't manage the internal flow of information, they had no way of knowing what information they had. Because managing information is the activity that provides the foundation for knowledge, understanding, and wisdom, *the most important pattern within an organization is the flow of information.*

6

Individuals and Institutions

Corporations exist to own technical information, but only the individuals who represent a corporation can put that information to use. Individuals have become more important than ever, and the balance between individuals and institutions is shifting. In many organizations, however, command and control privileges are used as a weapon by those in power to intimidate those below. These organizations are prone to numerous self-defeating social and information pathologies.

April 1993: The deal for Steve Jobs' Next Computer Inc. to sell its hardware business to Japan's Canon Inc. has collapsed . . . as negotiations dragged on, key engineers in Next's hardware design center left the company, leaving little for Canon to acquire.[1]—Ken Siegmann

The application of unique and specific technical information underlies a company's products and services and differentiates it from its competitors. This information is the difference that makes a difference in the marketplace. As Michael Rothschild writes, "Economic development, and the social change flowing from it, is not shaped by society's genes, but by its accumulated technical knowledge. . . . Throughout human history, profound cultural change has been driven by the evolution of technological information."[2]

Technical information is learned and applied by people, and as Steve Jobs discovered, the key asset of Next's hardware engineering organization was the people who had the technical information in their heads, the engineers themselves. When they left the company, little remained of value to Canon, because the full value of Next's technical knowledge was only partially evident in what had already been accomplished. Canon understood the economic consequences of exponential change. It valued the work that *could be* done in the future far more than that work that *had already been* done.

Technical information is an asset of unique importance in today's economy.[3] The accumulation of this information is a kind of profit, and just as today's financial profits pay for tomorrow's research and development activities,[4] today's technical information is the basis of the innovations that enable a firm to establish, or to preserve, leadership in the marketplace. However, it is an artifact whose value is not easily measured, nor is it recorded on the balance sheet. It is surely one of the paradoxes of modern commerce that although information itself is not quantifiable, its application inevitably leads to higher performance at lower cost. This phenomenon is known as the learning curve, which Rothschild describes this way:

> An organization gains a unit of experience each time it completes one unit of output. . . . a firm's unit of experience is the cycle of producing one unit of product from raw materials. Converting inputs into finished goods and services is the essential function of every economic organization. Each time a company cranks out one more unit of product, it accumulates another unit of experience in solving the problems associated with turning inputs into outputs. . . . over the last two decades, dozens of studies . . . consistently show real cost declines ranging from 10 percent to 30 percent per doubling of experience[5] (Figure 6.1).

Also paradoxical is the realization that technical information is most valuable for what it may allow you to do in the future, in response to prob-

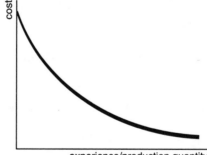

Figure 6.1 **The Learning Curve**
Real productivity improvements of 10 percent to 30 percent are generally experienced in each complete cycle of the production process and the design process. The faster the cycle time, the faster learning can occur.

lems and opportunities that have not yet presented themselves.[6] Existing products and services, and the information upon which they are based, are ephemeral, and their value is likely to steadily and inexorably erode.

The obsolescence of technical information is a critical constraint for the managers of a firm, since specific technical information must be quickly applied to commercial purposes or there may never be a return on the investment that was made in learning.

As we saw in Chapter 5, the act of applying information to create products and services is the act of creating knowledge. Knowledge is created through the process of learning, and learning can *only* be done by individuals.

THE CORPORATION

Since no individual can know everything about the technical disciplines that must be applied to the development and delivery of today's products and services, people join together to share the work, and the hoped-for rewards.

People create new entities to embody their collective actions, and we call these entities 'corporations.' Corporations are separate legal entities, distinct beings with specific rights and responsibilities in society. The root of this word is the Latin *corpus*, 'body.' However, these bodies do not exist physically. They are entirely abstract and exist only because people agree that they do, and because the law (another abstract phenomenon) proclaims that they exist. People and products and services *represent* a corporation, but there is no tangible thing that anyone can touch or interact with that *is* a corporation in and of itself.

The corporate form was established in the laws of American states, beginning with New York in 1811, when the increasing scale of commerce created the possibility of establishing enterprises such as railroads, oil companies, and steel mills that were too large be capitalized by wealthy individuals and their families.[7]

During that era, most individuals were held to be of little importance for the enterprise. When a worker could no longer produce, there was another standing ready to take his or her place without interruption. Industry was gearing up to mass production for a society that embraced mass consumption.

However, for today's and tomorrow's firms such as Next, it is individual people and *only* individual people who know how to use the critical technical information that is translated into useful, marketable products and services. Peter Drucker writes:

> What we now mean by knowledge is information effective in action, information focused on results. . . . in the knowledge society into which we are moving, individuals are central. Knowledge is not impersonal, like money. Knowledge does not reside in a book, a databank, a software program; they contain only information. Knowledge is always embodied in a person; carried by a person; created, augmented, or improved by a person; applied by a person; taught and passed on by a person; used or misused by a person. The shift to the knowledge society therefore puts the person in the center.[8]

We have evolved from a industrial society of mass institutions into an information society of individuals *and* institutions who are now partners in all economic activity. In the framework of this uneasy partnership, human capabilities are organized to serve human and corporate needs, which frequently are not in alignment. The balance between the needs and desires of individuals and those of the larger systems in which they participate fluctuates constantly. It is the subject of continual dialogue and sometimes outright conflict. A labor strike, for example, brings such issues to the forefront, and in its resolution one side, or both, acknowledge more flexibility than they originally admitted.

Reduced to their economic essence, corporations exist to own technical information that is useful in commerce, but which can only be comprehended and applied by individuals. Because corporations are only abstract entities, they cannot learn, any more than they can walk or sing or dance. By imagining that an organization learns, we mistakenly attribute to it capabilities that it does not and cannot possess.

Individuals learn, adapt, choose, apply information, and create knowledge. Organizations are a different logical type, for they are strictly aggregates of individuals, just as societies, economies, governments, and species are also such aggregates. The apparent behaviors of all of these abstract entities are really the sum totals of the behaviors of their individual members. It is a cognitive error to attribute to these abstract creations the qualities which only individuals can express.

While individuals learn, organizations and species *evolve*, for evolution is the expression of the aggregate of all individuals (Figure 6.2).

REPRESENTATION

This important distinction between learning and evolution is the distinction between the individual and the class of which it is a member. The

old way   new way

individuals
learn

organizations
evolve

Figure 6.2 **Learning and Evolution**
Although individuals and organizations are distinct logical types, they are frequently confused with each other. Individuals learn, as represented by the black dot which shifts from an old to a new way of doing things. Organizations are aggregates of individuals that can be represented by a standard bell curve of distribution. While learning is a capacity of individuals, evolution is an expression of the aggregate of an entire population.

individual has the power of choice, while the class is merely a reflection of all individuals. In this regard, we must remember that corporations have no power; individuals exercise power as their *representatives*.

The interactions between corporations occur only through the actions of their human representatives. Nearly all of today's industrialized world exists as a consequence of the behavior of people deploying knowledge on behalf of these abstractions.

Although the actions of corporations are just the actions of people who represent them, the perceived interests of a corporation appear to be different from the interests of people. This difference becomes obvious when a customer is told, "I'm sorry but it's company policy," and "If it was up to me, I wouldn't be doing it this way," and "I wish I could help you, but. . . ."

It is one of the sad truths of our age that no matter what purposes a corporation may have originally been founded to promote or achieve, people representing it will eventually develop an overriding purpose that is distinct from, and often in direct contradiction to, the original purposes that led to its founding.

As individuals become attached to the success of a corporation for their livelihoods, their predominant goal shifts from the corporation's founding purposes to the preservation of the corporation, because the corporation is *perceived* as the source of their present and future earnings. Since corporate longevity is apparently achieved as a consequence of profit,[9] individual perspectives and judgment are subsumed under the overall need to achieve profitability.

Profit is necessary for the perseverance of all systems, not just corporations. Society's profits, collected as taxes, pay for the education of children in schools, for the building of roads and bridges and other infrastructure, and to sustain those who are unable to earn their own way. Profit is the portion of a crop that is not consumed so that it can be used as next year's seed; the reserve of energy stored in the body yesterday that 'pays for' today's work; and the accumulated information that is transformed into products and services.

In response to the increasing cost of energy and materials, research in many industries is focused on using more of this information to replace mass and energy. As technical information advances, still more intelligence is applied to all forms of economic activity. It is precisely this information, which is accumulated on behalf of corporations, and the capacity of corporations to implement commercial action that has made them the drivers of the economy.

Nevertheless, the application of specific knowledge in specific situations is always a result of individual action. Individuals have made each and every innovation in the history of human endeavor, from philosophy to mathematics to science to technology to commerce. Every aspect of every technology that supports the world's 5 + billion living humans has been conceived by people, working individually and working together.

While institutions dominate global commerce and culture, the results that they produce thoroughly depend upon the work of individuals and their ability to apply information to commerce. Similarly, the success of any company in the marketplace depends upon decisions made by individual consumers to purchase, or not to purchase (Figure 6.3).

Since corporations depend on consumers, they attempt at every opportunity to influence the purchasing decisions that consumers make. In doing so they demonstrate the conflict between human values and the corporate drive for profits. A sincere friend, someone who cares about your well-being, would not suggest that you use a product that is likely to kill you. Even a sincere stranger would not try to persuade you to use such a product. Nevertheless, thousands of sincere people who work for tobacco companies and their advertisers do try to persuade you, but only because "their jobs depend on it." Their jobs depend, that is, on convincing you to become an addict and risk killing yourself, to replace the 400,000 customers who will die this year from using their product.

Individual humans are expected to behave one way, but when organized for collective works and acting on behalf of their corporate creations, behaving quite differently may be considered acceptable and rational.

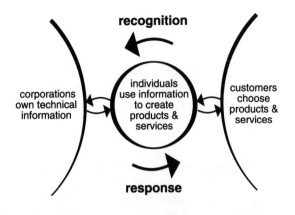

Figure 6.3 **Representation**

How disheartening it is that advertisers are *expected* to lie to promote their products, and that this is considered to be a normal aspect of commercial life. There you are, sitting in front of your television watching a commercial and thinking to yourself, "Now that *just isn't true.*"[10]

It is, at root, the limited purposes of corporations, the limited means that they have of interacting with their environments, and the limited techniques by which they are organized that leads to the exploitative acts that people perform on their behalf. Even their method of making agreements is narrow and limiting, for in the form called the 'contract' only the crudest of issues can be defined. As presently practiced, contracts are not capable of expressing the subtle nuances that differentiate between appropriate use and inappropriate exploitation.

All of these factors contribute to the paucity of information that characterizes the command and control approach. Consequently, the command and control hierarchy has been reduced to a simplistic organizational model in wnich many pathologies are experienced.

PATHOLOGIES OF COMMAND AND CONTROL

These pathologies do not seem to be inherent in the hierarchy, but rather in the way that command and control is exercised in today's organizations. The roots of the problem may be evident in the origins of these two words: The word 'command' comes from the Latin *manus*, hand, from which we get the concept of a 'mandate.' Command has to do with having things 'in hand,' i.e., under control. From the same root we also get the word 'manipulate,' and the idea that, "I've got you in the palm of my hand."

The word 'control' comes from Latin for the process of duplicating a set of records so that the original could later be compared against (*contra*) another copy, or roll (*rotula*), to be sure it had not been altered.[11]

The practice of command and control is focused on maintaining power in the hands of those who already have it, regardless of the conflicts that derive from the very process of exercising that power. As Ricardo Semler comments:

> Outside the factory, workers are men and women who elect governments, serve in the army, lead community projects, raise and educate families, and make decisions every day about the future. Friends solicit their advice. Salespeople court them. Children and grandchildren look up to them for their wisdom and experience. But the moment they walk into the factory, the company transforms them into adolescents. They have to wear badges and name tags, arrive at a certain time, stand in line to punch the clock or eat their lunch, get permission to go to the bathroom, give lengthy explanations every time they're five minutes late, and follow instructions without asking a lot of questions. The organizational pyramid is the cause of much corporate evil.[12]

SOCIAL PATHOLOGIES

It is obvious to even the casual observer that numerous pathologies arise not only in the social relations among the members of the organization, but also in the way that information is managed. Among the many social pathologies are these six:

1. Insecurity.

2. Internal Politics.

3. Making Others Wrong.

4. Conformity.

5. Rules.

6. The Separation of Management and Work.

1. Insecurity

Authority in a command and control organization is derived from one's position in the hierarchy, regardless of one's specific knowledge of a given situation. The persistent and overriding awareness of the very important distinction between 'up' and 'down' leads to interactions between people that almost always begin with a clarification of who's who. Is this person higher than I am in the organization (i.e., can this person hurt me?), or is this person lower (i.e., can I hurt this person?)?

> GE executives who entered [Jim Baumann's] office for the first time would invariably tilt their heads back in an automatic, almost subconscious way. He couldn't figure out why—until someone told him that they were counting the ceiling squares in his office. . . . By counting Jim's ceiling squares, visitors could calculate the square footage of his office, and thus his status in the hierarchy. That told the executives whether to grovel before Jim or to boss him around.[13]

2. Internal Politics

Since those above have the power to command those below, there is a persistent struggle to get into positions of power and get out from under dominating and perhaps arbitrary authority. Such internal competition distracts attention from the marketplace, and focuses it instead on internal politics. Since this rarely adds value to products and services, it provides no benefit to customers. In terms of a company's performance in the marketplace, internal politics is a costly waste of effort: "GEers fawned on their bosses and did what they were told even when their orders made no sense. When criticized by superiors, they turned around and "kicked the dog"— a company argot for passing on the pain to subordinates. Ambitious GE managers kept their ties knotted and their mouths shut."[14]

3. Making Other Wrong

Internal politics and the competition to ascend lead to a persistent pressure to make others wrong, and to avoid being wrong oneself. Thus, although an organization chart is not useful in helping to get meaningful work accomplished, it is quite useful for determining how blame should be apportioned when things go wrong.

4. Conformity

The threat of punishment is a persistent pressure that filters out dissent and diversity and filters in intellectual conformity. Nonconformity is an implicit challenge to authority, and it is reluctantly tolerated only in those individuals whose unique contributions are understood to be indispensable.

5. Rules

Command and control organizations have little tolerance for ambiguity. They come to rely on highly codified rules that specify behavior and punishment in detail. In such an environment, what anyone learns on a given day is irrelevant, because the rules are the rules and they are what matters:

"For executives, mastery of arduous procedures had become an art form, almost a ballet, as well as an unspoken requirement for advancement."[15]

6. The Separation of Management and Work

A corollary of the conformist pathology is that those at the top of the pyramid are individuals who are valued for their individual contributions. Those at the bottom, in contrast, are masses of nameless workers known only for the departments they work in and valued only for the anonymous places they happen to occupy in the production chain. This reflects the belief that management should be separated from work. Managers are in control of the business and of the people below them in the business. Managers think, for which they are better paid. Workers are subordinate to managers. They don't think; they just work, for which they are not as well paid.

In 1984, workers in a GE locomotive factory redesigned the cabs of locomotives they built, reducing the cost by 45 percent. "When a manager inquired why no one had ever mentioned the inefficiencies of the old design, the workers replied, 'You never asked.' "[16]

INFORMATION PATHOLOGIES

The dependence on information filtering in command and control organizations results in one intensely counterproductive result: the sheer annihilation of information. Here are six of the most prevalent information management pathologies:

1. Official Reality.

2. Risk.

3. Information as Power.

4. Information Filtering.

5. Translations and Distortions.

6. Bureaucracy.

1. Official Reality

A company operating in the command and control mode discounts marketplace reality, and its managers come to believe their own assumptions instead. People resist delivering bad news because messengers are routinely shot. Gradually the organization's purposes shift towards doing what it takes to sustain management assumptions, rather than toward the needs of customers. Instead of looking for the important information that challenges management assumptions, people look for information that confirms existing beliefs, while trying to put a positive spin on any information that contradicts the official reality. This pattern has been referred to in systems science as the 'Fundamental Law of Administrative Workings' (F.L.A.W.), which states that, "Things are what they are reported to be."[17]

A strange form of self-referential behavior emerges as the company becomes ever-more self-obsessed. In time, it is widely held that the purpose of the customer is to serve the company.

2. Risk

As regulatory distortion predominates, the threat of punishment inhibits individuals from taking the risks that might lead to innovation because of the possibility that they might fail and be punished. Only when competitors have proven the feasibility of innovations does the risk-averse company take comparable steps. Gradually it becomes incapable of innovation and develops a reputation as a follower rather than as a leader.

3. Information as Power

Since there is an inherent struggle to ascend in the hierarchy, there is inherent incentive to use information as a means of ascent. Information is power. Rather than stimulating an open sharing of information, the very structure of the organization gives incentive to use this value for more limited objectives: "How can I use what I know to help myself to a better position?" In this environment, ideas do not spread freely. They are held captive, to be used as pawns in the unending game: "We learned that information was power in the existing organization, and that if employees wanted to get ahead, they became experts at hoarding information. What they alone knew made them important to the organization."[18]

4. Information Filtering

When information is used as a weapon in this way, the layers of an organization function like clogged drains. Managers must receive all information before it proceeds upward or downward to put the necessary spin on it, and to justify their positions in the hierarchy. Since there's always a pile of paper to be dealt with, all new information has to wait its turn. Whether it is going up or going down the chain, information pauses at each layer. By this process, lag is institutionalized into the very operation of the organization: "It takes hours or days for information to go from an out-box through the mail room to an in-box . . ."[19]

---

5. Translations and Distortions

Frequently, information is translated (and then retranslated) as it is passed from above to below, and from below to above. Such translations are inherently problematic because they present the opportunity for intentional or unintentional misinterpretations. As information gets farther from its source, its meaning can get progressively distorted, and its original value may be lost:

> In The Beginning was The Plan
> And then came The Assumptions
> And the Assumptions were without form
> And The Plan was completely without substance
> And darkness was upon the face of The Workers.
> And they spoke among themselves, saying,
> "It is a Crock, and it stinketh."
> And The Workers went unto their Supervisors and sayeth,
> "It is a pail of dung and no one may abide the odor."
> And the Supervisors went unto their Managers and sayeth,
> "It is a container of excrement, and it is very strong,
> such that none may abide it."
> And The Managers went unto their Directors and sayeth,
> "It is a vessel of fertilizer, and none may abide its strength."
> And The Directors spoke amongst themselves, saying one to another,
> "It contains that which aids plant growth, but it is very strong."
> And The Directors went to the Vice Presidents and sayeth to them,
> "It promotes growth, and it is very powerful."
> And The Vice Presidents went to the President and sayeth to him,
> "This new Plan will actively promote the growth and efficiency of this Company, and these Areas in particular."
> And The President looked upon the Plan,
> And saw that it was good, and The Plan became Policy.[20]

6. Bureaucracy

The source of the pressure that creates middle management can be found precisely in the nature of commanding and controlling. The person whose function is to tell others what to do and to make sure that they do it can only oversee a handful of others, so large organizations require a lot of people in the middle to bridge the control gap between the chair at the top of the hierarchy and the many people working at the bottom. It takes a lot of people to make sure that a lot of people are doing what they're supposed to do: "GE's organizational structure fostered sprawling staffs of supervisors, rule makers, and checkers. Over time the bureaucracy established a life of its own, evolving into a self-sustaining organism with a powerful propensity for growth.''[21]

*   *   *

All of these discordant and counterproductive behaviors express two basic themes. First, because command and control is fundamentally concerned with power, people are constantly dealing with the social pathologies that power evokes: attacking; avoiding being attacked; and defending against attack. Second, all of this adversarial role-playing occurs while there is real work to be done, work that inevitably becomes less important than the life-or-death reality of the power struggle. Personal survival is primary; information is the game piece.

The pathologies that result from these limitations are not secrets. They have been observed, commented upon, and lamented for many decades. That the command and control model has persisted in this form despite these inadequacies is indicative of its enduring strengths in the industrial economy, and perhaps also of the apparent lack of viable alternatives.

RESPONSIBILITY

Since a corporation is not a living entity with its own mind, it does not have consciousness in and of itself, and surely it has no conscience. It is quite incapable of conscious behavior because it has no *inherent* understanding of proper and improper behavior. In fact, it has no inherent *anything*, existing as it does entirely as a matter of social agreement.

Thus, as corporations are presently conceived in practice, in economics, and in law, they are really only able to pursue one purpose, the very limited purpose of commercial success measured as financial profitability.

Any expression of a corporate consciousness is really an action of one of its individual members. This is why corporate officers and board members are required to adhere to external standards when they act on behalf of the corporation. But history has shown, and the example of the tobacco industry makes it quite clear, that the very limited responsibilities of corporate leaders are not anything like the behavior we expect from a stranger who happens to be walking down the street.

A corporation cannot behave responsibly any more than a child can behave responsibly. Children grow to adulthood, and upon attaining the age of majority, are presumed to have learned to be responsible for their actions. As presently conceived, however, corporations cannot grow up, do not grow up, and have no *concept* of responsibility at all, because there is no thinking entity that is a corporation.

Yet corporations have gathered the power to control key resources in every industry throughout the economy: The global economy is the creation of irresponsible, nonresponsible entities.

Having entrusted our fortunes to the power of the corporations, the gigantic, multi-billion dollar children of the modern era, we ought not be surprised at the ambiguous results. The dehumanization of society[22] is inherent in this arrangement and is predictable when the narrow purposes of corporations dominate the economy.

Since corporations are certainly here to stay for as long as our technologically based society persists, the issue is not whether there ought to be corporations, but rather, 'Is it possible for corporations to achieve self-consciousness to the extent that they *can* and *will* act responsibly? And if it is possible, how could it come about?'

EMERGENT PROPERTIES

Organisms that behave responsibly do so because they are conscious of their own behavior and they control it. However, consciousness itself is not present in the physical components of the organism. Neither neurobiologists nor philosophers have found a specific place in the body, a particular neural cluster or a gland where consciousness resides. It emerges, instead, as a consequence of the very functioning of the *whole* organism.

An example from another domain may clarify this distinction: As we discussed in Chapter 5, an airplane flies *only* when its parts are arranged just so, for the property of flight emerges from the coordinated activity of all of the parts when they are functioning together *as a system*. The flight of an airplane and the self-consciousness of an organism emerge from the functioning of the whole. As such they are called *emergent* properties.

Emergent properties are characteristic of systems. In fact, you can detect the presence of a system when you recognize behaviors that are not inherent in parts, but can *only* occur when parts are joined into wholes. Life itself is an emergent property, for it is clear that 'livingness,' like consciousness, is not resident in any single part of our bodies. The process of evolution seems to be an emergent property of genetics and natural selection; exponential change is an emergent property of economic competition.

Human consciousness seems to have emerged as a consequence of the number of neurons in the body, the way they are organized, and the quantity of messages that they transmit to one another. The nervous system is "the most complex organ produced by biological evolution on earth."[23]

The human brain alone consists of approximately 10 billion neurons, but it is not just the number of neurons that matters. The size of the human cortex, as compared with early humans, allows more space for *connections* between neurons: "from the Australopithecines on, the major changes in the brain would have involved increasing degrees of complexity . . . through increase in connectivity."[24]

COMMUNICATIONS

In comparison to the subtlety of human consciousness, corporations ignorantly and clumsily pursue their existence through the aggregate and relatively uncoordinated behaviors of their members. In the information economy, the renewed importance of individuals creates conditions in which there is progressively more coordination occurring among the individuals within all corporations.

With increased emphasis on the 'intelligence' of products and services, the process of designing products is more comprehensive than ever before and generally involves the coparticipation of more people. Improvements are discovered and applied before a product is ever made, and design decisions are based on information about customer wants and needs, on competitor capabilities, and on technological trends. To accomplish the increased design activity, more people are necessarily involved in compiling information that pertains to the design process itself. This drives corporations toward greater volume and complexity of communications.

Since, as we will see in Chapter 7, the design process includes not only the traditional research and development activities, and also the activities of users, design is never ending.

Consequently, many new communications channels and systems are being implemented. Some of them utilize the capabilities of computers and computer chips, which is discussed in Chapter 8. In addition, organizations are implementing new methods to support enhanced face-to-face communications through the design of the work place itself, by which people can work together more effectively, the subject of Chapter 10.

Another driver of increased communications is the concentrated collaborative processes through which individuals work together to solve quickly complex problems, the subject of Chapter 9.

Although the communications needs of large organizations are expanding exponentially, even individuals and small business are taking great advantage of the new technologies. Because personal computers enable individuals to use computing and communications power that was not long ago beyond the capabilities of even governments and large corporations, individuals and small businesses can today provide innovative products and services to consumers that are much more precisely custom-designed than those provided by large corporations. In this regard, the emergence of small business during the last decade is another dimension of the widespread substitution of intelligence for mass and energy, a side effect of which is that many large corporations find themselves surprised to be in competition with former employees whose capital is knowledge that was accumulated at the corporation's expense.

Individual consumers, entrepreneurs, small businesses, large corporations, and government agencies are all participating in the increased communications activity in the marketplace. Perhaps as communication increases, it will one day yield the rich connectivity that differentiates the human brain from that of our evolutionary ancestors. Maybe this trend has already begun, for as global dialogue about issues such as the use of earth's resources and the social responsibilities of nations and corporations broadens each year, agreements such as the treaties negotiated in Rio de Janeiro in 1992 will lead to new standards for the performance of all human institutions.

INTERLUDE

7

The Design Process

The design process is a universal approach to defining and solving problems. It provides a framework that can be used by individuals and teams to handle all kinds of complex issues. At root, the process of design is also the process of learning.

Trying to define what will happen three to five years out, in specific quantitative terms, is a futile exercise. The world is moving too fast for that. What should a company do instead? First of all, define its vision and its destiny in broad but clear terms. Second, maximize its own productivity. Finally, be organizationally and culturally flexible enough to meet massive change.[1]—Jack Welch

Among the eight practices of the recognition and response organization, two are fundamental to the process of defining goals for the future and achieving them: *learning* and *design*.

As we saw in Chapter 5, *learning* is the process of developing knowledge through the integration of theory, information, and experience (Figure 7.1). Perhaps this is a key to the failure of the command and control organizational model, for in command and control it is assumed that those in command already know what is important. Because of their superior knowledge, their role is to give direction, while the unique knowledge of all others is discounted, as are their experiences. Two of the outcomes of command and control are the suppression of learning and the suppression of its application.

In contrast, high performance organizations support learning in all of its various forms. Individuals in these organizations learn, and they learn voraciously.

Design is the process of systematically responding to needs by 'marking out' the future, defining how things ought to be different, predicting,[2] and

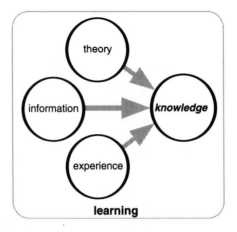

Figure 7.1 **Knowledge**

planning how to realize *vision*. It is a process of creating and selecting, of determining the characteristics of a thing or of an idea. Ultimately, it is a uniquely human undertaking: Architects design buildings; engineers design products; generals design military strategies; entrepreneurs design companies and industries; teachers design curricula; scientists design investigations and experiments; legislators design policy.

In one form or another, design is practiced by people of all backgrounds and in all cultural contexts, and in a broad sense, *design is the application of learning to human life.*

As such, it is fundamental to the economy that is based on technical information, for design is the method by which information is translated into useful products and services. Design is simply a systematic approach to learning, to discovering whatever it is that you must come to comprehend to accomplish whatever it is that you are inspired to do.

In this context, the distinction between design and engineering is sometimes unclear. If you already know what the specific desired outcomes are and how they can be achieved technically, then what you are doing is probably engineering. Design, in contrast, is a venture into the unknown that is rich with discovery, risk, uncertainty, and the possibility of failure. It is trying new things, testing to find out what works and what doesn't work, and why.

As described here, engineering is a subset of the broader process of design. While design explores the possibility of something entirely new done in a new way, engineering will provide certainty, based on past knowledge, that it will work properly. Both have important roles in the creation of value for society (Figure 7.2).

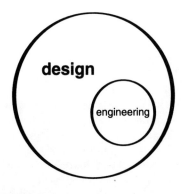

Figure 7.2 **Design and Engineering**
Engineering is a subset of the broader process of design.

THE DESIGN PROCESS

Although each individual may approach design differently, there is an archetypal *process* of design beneath these differences, a disciplined series of steps that constitutes a generalized model.

This proposition that design is a discipline suggests something far different from the common stereotype of the wild-eyed, creative (mad?) genius working in a cluttered laboratory on dark and stormy nights.

Einstein with a tidy haircut just doesn't inspire the same awe. But with his hair exploding in all directions, surrounded by the apparent chaos of papers piled high, standing in his frumpish sweater beside rows of unintelligible blackboard scribblings—*this* is the creative genius.

Design, interestingly, is both discipline and wild-eyed creativity. It brings out this creative genius hidden in everyone, and at the same time it is a process consisting of steps that can be managed with great clarity and considerable precision:

1. Create the problem.

2. Create the solution context.

3. Create solutions.

4. Define the details.

5. Implement.

6. Use and give feedback.[3]

As a discipline, design provides an approach to the complex problems that society and its organizations are facing more and more frequently. As Peter Drucker points out:

> the ability to connect and thus to raise the yield of existing knowledge (whether for an individual, for a team, or for the entire organization) is learnable.... It requires a methodology for *problem definition*—even more urgently perhaps than it requires the currently fashionable methodology for 'problem solving.' It requires systematic analysis of the kind of knowledge and information a given problem requires, and a methodology for organizing the stages in which a given problem can be tackled—the methodology which underlies what we now call 'systems research.'[4]

What Drucker refers to as 'system research' is what is meant here by 'design,' and this process can be applied in all kinds of situations, including the transformation of the organization itself.

1. Create the Problem

Design begins with vision. When Martin Luther King Jr. proclaimed, "I have a dream!" he condemned the reality of his day and simultaneously expressed determination to fulfill his vision. His powerful voice still echoes, transcending time and distance.

President Kennedy expressed the vision of humans walking on the moon, and eight years later astronauts Neil Armstrong and Buzz Aldrin stepped from the Eagle and extended the reach of humanity farther into the universe.

The protesters of Tian'anmen Square shared a vision of society that compelled them to risk their lives. Today, individuals throughout the world persist in the quest to fulfill the visions of Dr. King, NASA, and Tian'anmen Square.

A compelling vision, well expressed, is one of the most powerful of forces in human society. It sets up the contrast between what is and what could be, and in this contrast emerges a driving force, a compelling motive. This contrast is the source of *creative tension*, the energy that drives visionaries, whether they are artists or scientists or entrepreneurs or educators; missionaries or presidents or revolutionaries or parents (Figure 7.3).

Great leaders define visions that express the spirit and the potential of their times, infecting others with a compelling anxiety, a creative tension that suffuses the atmosphere and begs for action. Such visions contrast so strongly with current conditions that the ideas of *what could be* are overwhelmingly powerful. They are motivating and magnificent, so much so that personal sacrifices are made willingly in the quest for their fulfillment.

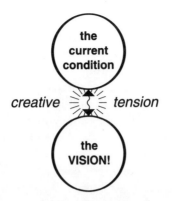

Figure 7.3 The Design Process: Create the Problem
The problem comes into being as the difference between the current condition, with all of its flaws, and the vision. Until there is such a difference, there is no problem. Once it is defined, no matter how vaguely, this very difference is the source of *creative tension* that motivates the process of fulfilling the vision.

A vision becomes the defining element of a professional life or perhaps a personal life, and gives meaning to an otherwise mundane existence.

But what do you do with vision? How do you translate its breadth and scope into specific and coherent actions that constitute progress? Somehow you must *bring the future into the present,* transcending time to transform that which *could be* into that which *is.*

If you do not somehow take action to fulfill the vision, it will remain in the vague and distant future, inconsequential. But once the quest for fulfillment is begun, this vague future is given distinct shape and form in the present and offers possibilities that once were only dreamed of. In this regard the fulfillment of a vision also transcends time.

The vision and its contrast with the current condition has, in effect, *created a problem.* The current condition is undesirable or even unacceptable, and the vision offers a solution. But caution is needed here, for although the act of defining a vision has led directly to the creation of a problem, it is important to discern if it is an appropriate vision, and therefore a problem worth solving.

The recent struggles of General Motors illustrate this point. During the 1970s and 1980s, GM wanted to bring efficiency to its auto manufacturing efforts by standardizing the look of its cars. An entire generation of Chevrolets, Buicks, Oldsmobiles, Pontiacs, and Cadillacs looked so similar to one another that customers couldn't tell them apart. Sales declined, and GM's market share plummeted.

However, the cars that looked similar on the outside were very different on the inside. Because of this there were no significant economies of scale in their manufacture. What GM should have done, of course, was to make the cars look different on the outside but be the same, or similar, on the inside. This would have enabled the company to offer more variety to the marketplace while still achieving significant economies of scale in design and manufacturing. How could they have gotten it so wrong? What strange vision must have inspired GM's leadership to formulate the problem precisely backwards?

While GM was losing customers, companies like Toyota, Honda, and Nissan were achieving success, motivated by visions of steadily increasing quality, marketplace variety, and manufacturing cost control. They gained market share by introducing new cars that were assembled around a few basic chassis and engine configurations.

A misdirected vision creates the wrong problem and is the beginning of an organizational wild goose chase.

Vision is also fundamental in the creation of customers for a company's products and services, for marketplace competition is just an expression of differing visions. Advertising is designed to influence the process by which customers choose by influencing the customer's vision: Drink this beer and you'll be attractive; drive this car and you'll be successful; wear this clothing; smoke this cigarette; eat this food; use this product. Products often fail because they do not inspire the customers' vision: If the difference between the way things are now and how they would be different after the purchase is not sufficiently compelling, there are few customers.

2. Create the Solution Context

Solving the problems that a vision creates by transforming vision into reality requires resources. What resources are available? Must the entire corporation be risked, or just one product line?

The scope of ambition must be tuned to fit the resources that are available (Figure 7.4), and eventually a fit is established between the scope of the vision and the resources available for its implementation. This fit *defines the context* in which solutions (there may be more than one) can be created.

History offers countless examples of underfunded visions, projects abandoned before they were completed because the money ran out or the magic of the vision was lost, or both. In our times, the Superconducting Supercollider began with promise of advancing fundamental science and ended billions of dollars later as a hole in the ground that one entrepreneur suggested may be a good place to grow mushrooms.

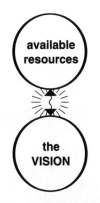

Figure 7.4   **The Design Process: Create the Solution Context**
The quest to fulfill the vision must be tempered by a realistic assessment of available resources. This creates the solution context.

3.   Create Solutions

Solutions can be derived from either questions or assumptions about the status quo and how it came to be. Solutions derived from questions bring with them the possibility of innovation, while those that derive from assumptions are likely only to recreate the past from existing knowledge. The rate of change throughout the economy means that everything you know today must be thoroughly reexamined tomorrow, for it may no longer be valid.

Thus, the process of creating solutions must begin with vigorous questioning and analysis to provide a firm foundation. Why are things the way they are? What decisions from the past have influenced the way things are now? What were the assumptions that led to the existing situation?

The *analysis* that results in a thorough understanding leads to *insight*, from which *new options* can be developed: We could do it this way, or this, or this!

The best solutions are *selected* from such options, and they themselves are then analyzed. The learning curve model shows that in each cycle through the production process, improvements of 10 to 30 percent are achieved, and such improvements are also achievable in the iterative design process. Thus, multiple iterations of the design process are likely to yield results that cannot be achieved in a linear process (Figure 7.5).

The cycle of *analyze/insight/create options/select* is followed repeatedly until it is clear that the best possible solutions have emerged. This does not need to be at all tedious, and it can be very inspiring, as is described in more detail in the section on Collaborative Design in Chapter 9.

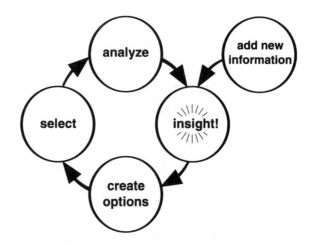

Figure 7.5 **The Design Process: Create Solutions**
This cycle develops new solutions that are beyond recreations of the past. By cycling through more than one iteration, the productivity improvements that characterize the learning curve are applied to the problem-solving process as well.

It is the leap from analysis to insight that constitutes the essential power of the design process, for at this vital moment, clarity and synthesis provide the capability to make the future different than the past.

The capacity to achieve such insight requires the preparation of the earlier stages of the design process itself, and also perhaps a lifetime of preparation. It is here that the deeper benefits of the proclivity to learn are realized as the three components of learning come together in the creative act of insight: Theory, information, and experience must be well integrated to result in solutions that are truly comprehensive.

The power of such an insight must match the power of the initial vision. If the insight falls short, it will never inspire the level of commitment that is needed to achieve fundamental change.

Creativity is essential to this stage of the design process, but why do some people seem to be so creative while others are not? One reason is that they *want* to be creative, and another is a basic quality that distinguishes creative people from all others: They ask questions. In fact, they ask questions incessantly, and they also persistently attempt to answer them.

Most people are born with tremendous curiosity and quickly acquire the habit of asking questions. Why is the sky blue? Why does it rain? Where are you going? What's that? How does it work? What is it good for? All of this leads, of course, to "Can *I* try?"

As they grow up, some sustain this questioning habit while others do not. Those who continue to ask questions learn to see the world in unique ways, to explore the ideas that hide behind commonplace explanations.

The very act of asking "Why it is so?" soon leads to a subsequent question, "Why can't it be better?" Those who ask questions do not necessarily accept the status quo. Instead, they use their imaginations to create entire worlds, entire universes, better mousetraps, and new industries (possibly all at the same time).

Although not everyone continues the childhood habit of asking questions, this spirit can be reawakened. Most command and control organizations, however, take the opposite tack. Social pressures tend to filter out questioning and, in the process, suppress the very creativity upon which a company depends. This tendency is expressed from the top of the organization in the desire for control, and from the bottom in the desire for predictable and steady employment. Both are debilitating.

The eighth practice of recognition and response organizations, *Organized Abandonment,* could also be described as systematic questioning: It is a technique for ensuring that habits do not mesmerize everyone into losing sight of the marketplace. It can lead to systematic innovation in an organization's products and services as well as in the design of the organization itself.

Even the solutions that emerge from the design process must be methodically questioned, for just as there is danger in adopting the wrong vision, so there is also danger in selecting the very first solution that emerges before it is fully understood. Designers who seize on the first answer may simply be reviving old solutions, disguised in new wardrobe, perhaps, but old nonetheless. This often occurs when design is based on information that is already well-known, for reworking old information is unlikely to yield truly innovative solutions. In this context we encounter the pervasive phenomenon of reorganization:

> Apple Computer Inc. reported its biggest ever quarterly loss yesterday after taking a huge charge [of $320.9 million] to pay for layoffs, restructuring and excess inventory. Joe Graziano, Apple's Chief Financial Officer admitted that the computer maker got caught with its pants down by the free-fall in PC prices. Apple thought its superior technology could command premium prices, but consumers balked.[5] The very next day came the announcement of yet another reorganization Apple: "This week's restructuring is Apple's third shakeup since 1990. Hoping to right itself, Apple unveiled a new structure. . . ."[6]

How many reorganizations does a company go through before its leaders realize that they are caught in a trap? Where is the vision that might motivate such a reorganization? Far better solutions may await discovery, never to be found because the design effort has stopped prematurely.

Without new information, a team of designers has little choice but to repeat the past, and so the habit of asking questions is a necessary technique for bringing new information into the design process. You might ask, 'How are these problems handled in other industries?' or 'How are these problems likely to be handled fifty years from now?'

Thus, *creating solutions* is most effective when it is integrated with new information and when it is done iteratively. The selected solutions are analyzed, leading to new options, among which the best are selected and analyzed yet again. This is a cycle of progressive refinement that leads to clarity and carefully crafted solutions.

4. Define the Details

Eventually, after many questions and iterations, solutions that reflect the best ideas emerge (Figure 7.6). Now there must be a shift in the thinking process, for the concern is transferred from understanding the problem and solving it to understanding how to implement the solution that finally has been selected.

We ask, '*Precisely* how much will it cost? How long will it take? How much will it weigh? What color will it be? How will it be assembled and delivered?' These are the questions of *defining the details*, the fourth step in the design process (Figure 7.7).

Much of this work is the process of engineering, and is certainly a strength of the Western mentality. Engineering has provided two thousand

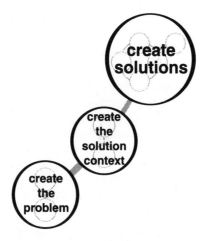

Figure 7.6 The Design Process: Steps 1, 2, and 3

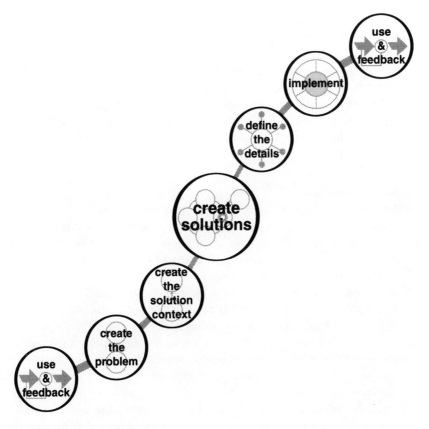

Figure 7.7 The Design Process

years of technology that has been applied in the creation of infrastructure which now unifies the globe into a single economy, and although our absorption with engineering has its drawbacks, it is fundamental to the marketplace economy.

So, we develop detailed specifications and blueprints; we prepare extensive management models, budgets, and project teams—this provides the capability to implement solutions.

5. Implement

Implementation is the next step in the design process, for now the vision will be translated into reality (Figure 7.7). Materials are obtained and fashioned to match the engineered design, or in any case to match as closely as possible. Tests are run. Drawings are consulted; progress is assessed; money is spent. And then, *voila!* Something new emerges.

Although some would suppose that the design process is completed once the implementation phase begins, new information is still waiting to be discovered during this process, information that may have a substantial impact on the final solution. New materials with new performance characteristics become available, offering the possibility of unforeseen cost savings or performance enhancements. Sudden shifts in marketplace demand emerge, making features that were once considered options suddenly mandatory. Parts don't fit together correctly, forcing design teams 'back to the drawing boards.'

6. Use and Feedback

All through the design process, learning is occurring that is directly and indirectly related to the project at hand. The assessment of this learning, and the application of its consequences, means that even a finished, built solution is *still* in the design process (Figure 7.7).

In addition, users will express their own creativity by finding new ways to use a product that its designers may never have imagined.

From an inspiring vision and its implicit condemnation of conditions at the time has come an end product that has brought the future into the present. Does this new reality measure up to the expectations that drove the process? Do customers appreciate the benefits that they were imagined to favor so strongly? Is the creative tension resolved?

Use is the ultimate assessment of the vision and its implementation, and from this a new condition emerges. Life is different. But is it as it should be? Or is there a gap between the new reality and a new vision that is dawning, against which today's condition is suddenly inadequate? If a new vision comes into focus, creative tension grows, and there is a problem, a new problem. The design process begins again. How can it be done better? What resources are available . . . (Figure 7.8)?

*   *   *

This sequential presentation of the design process helps one to understand its scope, but in practice most designers do not necessarily follow the steps in any particular order. A vision may arrive accompanied by detailed engineering ideas, images of the new design in use, and a sense of what it will cost. The designing mind jumps forward and backward from step to step, answering the call of the vision and following wherever inspiration leads, regardless of the sequence on the diagram.

Likewise, each step may require differing degrees of precision and completeness in different situations. What makes the design process model so useful is its generality, the guidance it provides to individuals and teams of designers who are faced with complex challenges. No matter how much

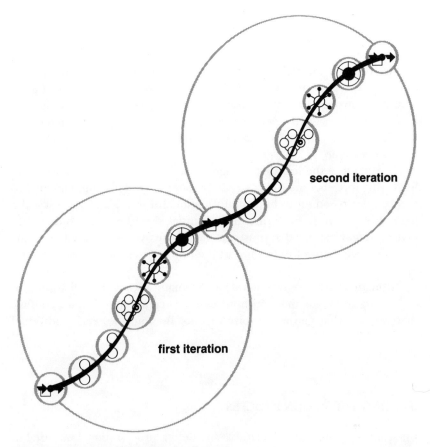

Figure 7.8 **Iterations of the Design Process**
Solving problems through the design process results in . . . new problems. Thus, the last step of the process is also the first step.

detail is eventually accomplished at each step, and no matter in what sequence the steps are accomplished, each step is part of an overall process and must be addressed to some extent, however much or little.

DESIGN AND LEARNING

Design and learning are reciprocal processes, and they occur simultaneously. Questions drive the process of design, just as they drive learning. Learning does not occur when an institution puts students, teachers, and textbooks into a classroom together; it occurs only when the learner is motivated to learn, motivated by curiosity or desire, motivated, ultimately, by questions that beg to be answered.

Learning is the inward process of creating knowledge by assimilating new information through listening, imagining, watching, touching, reading, and experimenting, while design is the outward expression of such knowledge through the acts of drawing, building, writing, dialoguing, and many others. Design is *always* learning, for it is testing, experimenting; learning is *always* design, for it is the reformulation of knowledge, and thus the *recreation of self.*

The result of the learning/designing activity is, inevitably, innovation, the driving force behind today's global economy. Design is fundamental to the economy based on technical information, for the design process is the method by which that information is translated into useful products and services. Organizations that must innovate to survive (which is all of them) must organize themselves to support the processes of learning and designing.

In many ways, design is simply a systematic approach to learning, to discovering what it is that you must come to comprehend to accomplish whatever it is that you are inspired to do. By doing so, each individual changes the world.

APPLYING THE DESIGN PROCESS

It may not surprise you to learn that the design process model was used to organize this book (Figure 7.9).

The Introduction and Chapter 1 describe the current condition of the changing economy and its impact on management, and it frames the creative tension as the difference between structure thinking and process thinking. The rest of Part One describes the vision of process thinking and the recognition and response model.

Part Two analyzes the current condition and key ongoing trends, from which comes the depth of understanding that leads to insight.

This chapter points out that organizations fail to innovate when they use old information to solve their problems. Without going outside to actively, persistently look for new information, they are doomed to recreate the old, failed ways.

Together, the description of the current condition, the vision, and the design process constitute a model of the discipline of design and its application to organizations, which together *create the problem,* the *solution context,* and *solutions.*

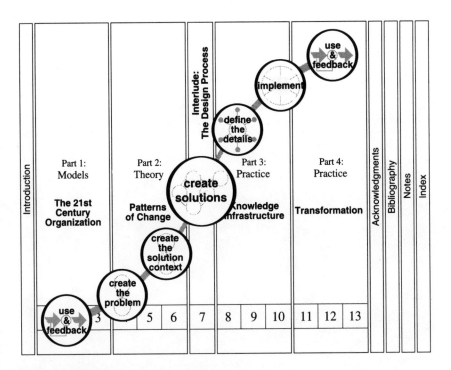

Figure 7.9   **The Design of This Book**

In Part Three, practical issues concerning the *details* of an organization's infrastructure are described. Part Four is also focused on practice, for it is concerned with *implementation, using,* and *feedback,* the final stages of the design process.

PART THREE

PRACTICE
Knowledge Infrastructure

The application of knowledge to work created developed economies by setting off the productivity explosion of the last hundred years. . . . Increasing the productivity of manual workers in manufacturing, in farming, in mining, in transportation, can no longer create wealth by itself. The Productivity Revolution has become a victim of its own success. From now on, what matters is the productivity of non-manual workers. And that requires applying knowledge to knowledge.[1]—Peter Drucker

One of the key elements of the industrial economy is its infrastructure of roads, bridges, rail lines, communications systems, airports, canals, ports, et al. Without this infrastructure, the process of transforming resources into products and delivering them to market cannot occur on a large scale.

In addition to these basic capacities required for industrialism, the information economy also requires specific infrastructure to support the creation of knowledge.

Such knowledge enables individual companies to differentiate their products and services from those of competitors. It is a never-ending process, always accomplished in the framework of a marketplace in which competitors constantly seek to better position themselves based on their own accumulated knowledge. Which corporations have better knowledge? It probably doesn't matter. What does matter is which corporations can best *utilize* their knowledge to improve their market position. This depends, to a great extent, on the knowledge infrastructure, for this infrastructure provides essential tools that enable individuals to transform information into knowledge.

Widespread awareness of the importance of the knowledge infrastructure has only recently emerged in conjunction with the renewed emphasis on learning. A few pioneers have been working in this field for decades,[2] and now there are many experimenting in this field as its economic importance becomes clear. In fact, there is now a discipline that addresses these issues: Knowledge Infrastructure Engineering.[3]

In Part Three, we examine three components of this infrastructure. In Chapter 8, key aspects of information and communications systems are described. In Chapter 9, the practice of collaborative work processes by which individuals integrate their separate perspectives and thereby create new knowledge is presented. In Chapter 10, the design of the work place itself is discussed.

8

Information and Communication

Real time information systems that handle both quantitative and qualitative information provide vital support to recognition and response organizations. These information systems, together with extensive communications systems, are key elements of the infrastructure of evolving corporations.

Jay Forrester once remarked that the hallmark of a great organization is "how quickly bad news travels upward."[1]—*Peter Senge*

March 25, 1989: David Parish, a spokesman for Exxon, said the company did not expect major environmental damage as a result of the [Exxon Valdez*] spill.*[2]—*Philip Shabecoff*

Six days after the Exxon *Valdez* ran miles off course, ran aground, and spilled millions of gallons of oil into Prince William Sound, company officials acknowledged that they would not be able to contain the oil that was spreading throughout one of North America's richest marine ecosystems. The damage eventually cost Exxon $3.4 billion in clean-up costs and $1.325 billion in reparations, and because of its awkward handling of the situation, a substantial amount of corporate good will.[3] Plaintiffs in a court case that Exxon has already lost have asked for an additional $15 billion in punitive damages.

In situations as dramatic as the Exxon *Valdez* oil spill, and perhaps even more importantly in situations of far greater subtlety that occur regularly throughout the corporation, information is the key to recognition and response in the short term, and to adaptation and evolution over the long term. The design and functioning of the knowledge infrastructure that is used to gather, integrate, and transmit information is therefore critical to success; the systems that perform these vital tasks are the subject of this chapter.

The people in an organization are likely to be disbursed over space and time, and so the systems that handle information and communications among them are important tools for supporting unity of purpose and co-ordination of action. This capacity is now substantially dependent on computers, which can handle a tremendous variety of message types and messages: "Updated daily on handheld terminals by 10,000 Frito-Lay salespeople, information on 100 Frito product lines in 400,000 stores appears on company computer screens in easy-to-read charts."[4]

The level of detail handled by Frito-Lay's computer system shows the enormous variety that computers are adept at managing: 10,000 sales people delivering 100 products to 400,000 stores generates a variety that is the multiplicative combination of each of the three variables, a total variety of *at least 400 billion*. Of course, the point of tracking such data is to know if things are going well or badly, which is a variety of 2 times the 400 billion, so we're really talking about a variety of 800 billion. And then we wonder, did it rain today? Or did the delivery truck get a flat tire? Or was it a holiday? Or is there a strong competitor? Very rapidly the pertinent variety escalates toward infinity, precisely as the variety of the marketplace also does.

At Chase Manhattan Bank, 2 million checks are processed each *day*. Chase also performs trend analysis on sets of 50 million credit card transactions, which requires a computer that can accommodate a terabyte of data, more than most computers can manage but nevertheless a realistic possibility with today's technology.[5]

These numbers are staggering, yet computers accommodate such problems routinely. No human analyst, or even an army of analysts could make much sense of a single day's activities in a large organization as it happens.

This massive number crunching is what computers were invented to accomplish during the 1930s and 1940s, when the army needed to calculate ballistics tables for artillery but could not manage the job quickly enough, even with rooms full of mathematicians. The development of mathematical calculating machines (computers) was initiated, and a mere 50 years later, Frito-Lay and Chase Manhattan are the beneficiaries of decades of research, along with every other company in the industrialized world.

But influenced by their fantasies and advertising campaigns, people believed for decades that computers would *replace* humans in managerial and decision-making roles. The myth of an all-knowing, all-seeing computer distracted attention away from a more pertinent issue, which was to understand what computers can do that humans cannot do, and vice versa.

Clearly, gathering and filtering data is something at which computers excel, and at these tasks they outperform people by a wide margin, as we see with Frito-Lay. But here is the rest of the story:

Early this year, Frito-Lay Inc. had a problem in San Antonio and Houston. Sales were slumping in that area's supermarkets. So CEO Robert H. Beeby turned to his computer, called up the data for South Texas, and quickly isolated the cause. A regional competitor had just introduced El Galindo, a white-corn tortilla chip. The chip, it turned out, was getting good word of mouth—and as a result, more supermarket shelf space than Frito's traditional Tostitos tortilla chips. Within three months, Beeby had Frito-Lay producing a white-corn version of Tostitos that matched the competition and won back lost market share."[6]

It is also apparent to those who have worked extensively with computers that they are generally unable to do what Beeby did, which was to understand the *meaning* of the pattern embedded in the numbers, a meaning that was only suggested by the sales reports but which the reports were not competent to describe.

It is for this reason that computers must be seen primarily as tools that *augment* human effort, rather than ones that replace human effort. There are roles for which computers are uniquely suited just as there are roles for which human intelligence is indispensable.

As universal information-encoding tools, computers augment the human capacity to create, store, analyze, and transmit information. These are uniquely human activities that are undertaken for uniquely human purposes, and each can be augmented through the application of computer technology. Not coincidentally, these are the critical capacities for all management in the information economy and the exponentially changing marketplace. Hence, our reliance on computers becomes steadily more pervasive.

The awareness that computers must augment human intelligence is not widely understood. One of the originators of this concept is computer scientist Douglas Engelbart, whose approach to augmentation has focused for three decades on both the philosophy and its practice. Engelbart originated many of the capabilities that are now widely taken for granted, such as the mouse, display windows, display editing, and outline processing. He comments,

Over the centuries our cultures have evolved rich systems of things that, when humans are conditioned and trained to employ them, will augment their basic, genetically endowed capabilities so that they, and their organizations, can exercise capabilities of a much higher nature than would otherwise be possible. . . . I have become ever more convinced that human organizations can be transformed into much higher levels of capability. Digital technologies [computers], which we have barely learned to harness, represent a totally new type of nervous system around which there can evolve new, higher forms of social organisms.[7]

Clearly, then, the intent of the knowledge infrastructure isn't merely to implement the mother of all databases, which as NASA has discovered is certainly a double-edged sword (see Chapter 5). Rather, the computer's role in the knowledge infrastructure is to make it easier for people to create ideas, to understand them, and to share them. It is thus most of all a tool for the most fundamental of processes, learning.

It is interesting to note in this context that the increasing importance of computers in human society has become a self-generating phenomenon. We use computers to help us make sense of the world's increasing complexity. At the same time, we observe that a great deal of this very complexity exists as a consequence of the widespread usage of computers. There is surely a trap contained in this situation, one that we have not yet devised a way out of, and meanwhile the evolution of the computer industry consumes ever more resources as individual companies are compelled to continue this information version of the arms race in their continuing struggle for survival.

Yet we remain optimistic, for there is a glimmer of hope that computers may still fulfill their promise. The focus on augmentation and its application as infrastructure are key, for this plays to the strengths of technology and to the complement between human capacity and technology.

We know now what the computer must do in addition to the voluminous number crunching that it and it alone is competent for: It must augment human thinking *and* the processes of communication. Although there is considerable overlap between these two, they are surely as distinct as the vehicle is distinct from the roadway, even as both are components of a transportation system. We also know why the computer is necessary: The variety of the marketplace has simply surpassed our capabilities.

REAL TIME

Historically, computers have processed information in but one time frame—later. It seems that people have always been waiting around for one computer or another to finish processing their jobs.

This is a consequence of what computer designers refer to as the overall 'architecture' of their computers, the designed relationships between hardware and software. The prevalent approach to computer architecture is the concept of 'batch processing' that was established 40 years ago to fit the capabilities of the hardware of that time.

The batch architecture organizes the computer's processes into steps that are executed sequentially. In batch accounting systems for example, sales, cash receipts, inventory changes, purchases, payables, and all other financial transactions are entered into a computer where they are stored *en masse* until later, when at daily, weekly, or monthly intervals they are finally processed. Only then are the accounts of a company updated and reports produced, and only then it is revealed what has happened.

Most companies are operated in this way, and they therefore receive financial statements in the month following the occurrence of the events. Managers have become accustomed to this kind of lag, and have come to regard it as a fact of nature, along with spring rains and gravity. It is, however, but one approach, and there are other possibilities today.

The problem with batch processing is that lag is literally built in, so reports describe events that are at least 10 days old and commonly as many as 40 days old. By then, it may be too late to take subtle corrective action; what remains is to clean up a mess, whether it is lost market share, or an oil spill. Managers constantly look towards the past, and wonder what happened.

This lag may have been acceptable in the slower-changing economy of 1955, but in the very fast-changing economy of today the lag built into batch architectures is a serious problem. Everyone needs information, and the answer to the question, 'when' is simply, *'now.'*

In response, there has been a gradual shift from batch architectures to *real time* architectures, which has been made possible by faster and more powerful computer chips that have made the batch processing model obsolete.

'Real time' means that there is no lag between an event and an organization's knowledge of the event. At all times, the organization knows all that it needs to know about what is happening in its environment and what is happening with itself. If this definition seems familiar, that's because it is. This wording expresses the same intent as the definition of 'recognition' in the recognition and response organizational model: "Individuals recognize important information in the marketplace, and communicate it to others who need to know" (see Chapter 3).

The role of the computer is to *augment in real time* the processes by which people seek to recognize the overall character and underlying patterns of the marketplace. We see a complement between the design of the organization and the knowledge infrastructure that enables it to operate effectively: Real time information processing and recognition and response organization design are two aspects of a single phenomenon.

Real time systems are now widely used in manufacturing, inventory management, and distribution. Entire factories are run on real time or near–real time computer systems that reduce costs while improving coordination. Curiously, however, many companies that operate in real time in their factories still endure considerable lag in their accounting functions. Having factories and distribution systems operating at one rhythm and offices operating at a slower one prevents the full power of real time from being realized. It is as though a driver would accelerate the car with the right foot while the left remained on the brake pedal.

Nevertheless, the shift to real time is under way, and it is inexorable. Although the costs of such a shift can be significant for an individual company, the benefits make it worthwhile. In any case, the pressure from competitors who are already in real time will force any company that wants to remain in business to make the shift.

FORECASTING AND PATTERN RECOGNITION

An important difference between real time companies and their batch rivals is that while batch companies look backwards to figure out what happened, real time companies manage in the present with events as they happen.

Companies that operate in real time know exactly where they are now, and they can accurately forecast as far as 90 days into the future with astonishing reliability, enabling them to learn about the future, manage the future, and *create* the future.

Such a forecasting capability might result in a four-month lead on competitors who remain in batch mode, which in some consumer products markets could be an entire product generation. Imagine the market leadership that a company could achieve if they could consistently stay four months ahead (Figure 8.1).

Operating in real time also means that problems are more likely to be exposed as they occur, rather than weeks or months later, as the Frito-Lay story demonstrates. The pattern recognizing capacity of real time systems can identify emerging conditions, calling attention to situations that are *about* to occur, enabling their users to *manage the future* (Figure 8.2).

Pattern recognition systems operating in real time use models that are already defined, a reminder that all regulation requires a model, as discussed in Chapter 5. For example, while few would care if a particular product were sold for a particular price at a particular store, many would care to know if thousands of them were sold at thousands of stores in two days (it may be a great product; should we get more?); or if none of them were sold in thousands of stores in an entire season (get them to an outlet

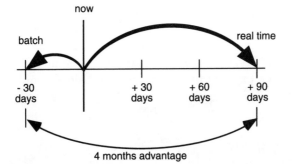

Figure 8.1 Four Months Advantage
Real time systems that accurately forecast 90 days in the future provide an advantage of 4 months over batch systems operating 30 days in the past. In some industries, this can be an entire product generation, which is a significant difference.

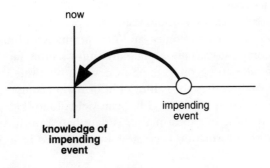

Figure 8.2 Managing the Future
Pattern recognition in real time systems provides knowledge of impending events far in advance, enabling you to *manage the future*.

store at any price, don't order more, and why did we expect them to sell?); or if hundreds were sold at the wrong price, in thousands of stores (is there a problem with our systems? is our pricing wrong?); or if 10 were sold for the wrong price at one store (is someone stealing?). With this technology and the information that it yields, merchandise buyers, store managers, and clerks can do a much better job of selecting and selling their products to meet their customers' needs.

Overall, such patterns constitute powerful and important feedback. Whereas it used to take weeks, months, or longer to determine how the market responded to a particular product, it can now be known almost immediately. Today it is possible to conduct live market tests and to learn the results on a daily basis. Actions and their results are much more closely linked, so product management takes on a whole new meaning: It is explicitly a learning process, and one that occurs in real time.

Because computers can simultaneously monitor millions, and as we have seen even billions of variables, many subtle variations in the patterns of events can be exposed by computers long before people perceive the same patterns.

QUALITATIVE INFORMATION

Real time systems function where the information is based on transactions, in manufacturing control, inventory control, distribution, and sales. This is quantitative information, which can by itself be quite deceptive. Another kind of information is also vital to the future of the corporation. This is information that describes the character of the marketplace through stories, experiences, and images that make it dynamic, real, and, most of all, intelligible. It is information about vision and purpose and strategy, about the discovery of new technologies, and new products and marketing campaigns from competitors. This is qualitative information, far different than the aggregate sales and profit numbers on accounting reports, but equally important. Together, these two kinds of information compose a whole picture that is more complete than either can yield alone (Figure 8.3).

Whereas quantitative information is data based on financial transactions, qualitative information is created and collected by individuals. It is

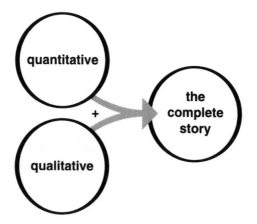

Figure 8.3 Quantitative + Qualitative Information
By themselves, neither quantitative nor qualitative information provides a complete picture, but together they can provide a distinct competitive advantage.

rumors and desires and opinions that individuals hear while interacting with customers; it is observations and conversations at trade shows and in stores; it is comparisons between their own products and those of competitors; it is what they learn at universities and conferences, from books and journals and E-mail.

Nearly all qualitative information deals with the results of experiences that are far too complex to be conveyed in financial statements. In a narrow sense, the limitations of the numbers alone make it necessary for an auditor's financial reports to be accompanied by notes that explain occurrences that the numbers do not convey. In a broader sense, the important qualitative ingredients are nuances, feelings, intuitions, and opinions, which rarely can be quantified. These are the differences that make a difference.

Correctly interpreting such information and applying it to new action yields knowledge, which is just what each and every manager desperately needs and wants. To make such interpretations correctly requires well-developed models.

Thus, managing qualitative information has two components: There are libraries of models, and there is an ongoing flow of new information that is filtered through them. Through this process these models are continually challenged, validated, revised, or discarded.

We see an example of this dimension in the Frito-Lay story. While it is impressive that Beeby and his staff were able to discern an important pattern from their own computers, it shows that the existing communications channels may have been quite limited. There ought to have been another way for the message about new competition to reach headquarters, especially with so many Frito-Lay salespeople in the grocery stores each day. Was there no way that they could convey this important message? Was there no way for a local Exxon manager in Alaska to convey the seriousness of the situation to New York? And was there no way for the knowledgeable NASA engineer to convey the message that it was unsafe to launch the *Challenger*? Apparently not.

In the command and control environment, the vertical linkages between layers of hierarchy represent communications channels. Organizations attempt to stuff a tremendous variety of messages through these very limited channels, but they simply cannot accommodate it all. Consequently, a tremendous amount of information is permanently lost.

Therefore, another purpose of qualitative information systems is to provide communications channels that operate in parallel with the quantitative ones, giving everyone more access to useful information and to the possibility of engaging dialogue directly with each other.

An example of the increase in qualitative information is the explosive growth of Internet, the global network of networks that is used primarily as a medium through which millions of people participate in numerous dialogues on topics which they themselves have chosen. Interactions on Internet are entirely self-organizing, consisting of individuals who exchange information that is predominantly qualitative.

Through such dialogue there emerges a critical element in the confusion of exponential change: context. Qualitative information is the *source* of context, the essence of discerned and shared meaning that is the expression of philosophy, of belief, and of commitment. In contrast, a financial statement of numbers is quite lacking in context, which is its strength but also its danger.

For example, in comparing the financial performance of two companies, the fact that one is a maker of weapons and the other a maker of food may not be evident from their financial reports, although it might be decisively important in the broader philosophical context, which can only be conveyed qualitatively.

Until quite recently, computers have not been adept at handling qualitative information, due to the enormous amount of data contained in a document such as a photograph. Now, the steady advance of computer technology has made it possible for computers to store photos, films, and recorded sounds, and these capabilities are the basis of the new industry called 'multimedia.'

Another qualitative application of computers concerns 'hyperdocuments' that enable people to organize and present information in nonlinear formats. This is the work of Douglas Engelbart.

Printed books are linear, and we have become accustomed to information presented in this format: First you read Chapter 1, then you read Chapter 2, and on you go until the end. Computers are not limited to linear formats, but most software encodes information that way simply because this has been our habit.

In contrast, hyperdocuments are like interactive, computer-based games in which players make decisions that determine the subsequent course of the game. There is no single path; there are many paths. Users of hyperdocuments have tremendous control over the information they access, and thus over the experiences that they have. It is because of this that hyperdocuments will become increasingly important, for the trend toward more power in the hands of the individual is inexorable.

A third approach to providing qualitative information on computers is 'groupware.' Groupware will also play an increasingly important role by enabling computer users to share ideas with each other through electronic networks. Groupware programs support varying degrees of structured collaboration to bridge between the complementary worlds of information and communications. Some are very open ended, while others lead groups of users through specific sequences in the process of decision making.

Together, multimedia, hyperdocuments, and groupware systems will be used to develop and present the entire knowledge base of an organization, enabling anyone, anywhere in the world to access and share a specific idea or sets of ideas using a personal computer. Such a knowledge base is both a record of the current state of an organization's understanding about itself and its marketplace, as well as the medium for ongoing dialogue about the further refinement of the knowledge base itself, providing the capacity to deal with philosophical issues in parallel with financial performance.

COMMUNICATION

The utilization of new communications technologies has increased exponentially because they enable people to communicate with each other through media that precisely suit the nature of the information, and they do it fast. Fax machines instantly transmit paper-based information. Computer modems and networks transmit electronic files. Pagers transmit short, character-based messages. Cellular phones transmit voice messages anywhere.

The demands of competition have compelled producers and distributors to create closer relationships with each other, and as a consequence they have more to communicate about. One technology, Electronic Data Interchange (EDI) is part of this trend. Already in use throughout the retailing industry, EDI links the computers of different companies to each other, enhancing the interdependence between customers and suppliers and reflecting the trend in the marketplace toward increasing customization of products and services.

As producers and distributors learn more about each others' needs, they organize themselves to respond more precisely, as this story about Wal-Mart and its relationship with Proctor and Gamble shows:

Pampers is a bulky item that requires a lot of storage space relative to its dollar value. Wal-Mart maintained Pampers inventory at its distribution centers, from which it filled orders coming from the stores. When the distribution center inventory began to run low, Wal-Mart would reorder more diapers from P&G. With the idea of improving this aspect of its business, Wal-Mart approached P&G with the observation that P&G probably knew more about diaper movement through warehouses than Wal-Mart, as it had information about usage patterns and reorders from retailers from all over the country. Wal-Mart suggested, therefore, that P&G should assume responsibility of telling Wal-Mart when to reorder Pampers for its distribution center and in what quantity. The new arrangement worked so well that over time Wal-Mart suggested that P&G henceforth skip the purchase recommendations and just ship the diapers it thought Wal-Mart would need.[8]

COMMUNICATION AS SELF-REGULATION: BALANCING FREEDOM AND CONTROL

Since recognition and response corporations will be organized around the work that needs to be done, rather than around arbitrary concepts of structure, there is no predicting who will need to dialogue with whom, and there is no point in attempting to predict. Self-organization will emerge as a consequence of the flow of information, and since computer-based communications technologies enable each person to be linked to everyone for an astonishingly low cost, the question is not *whether* it ought to be done, but *how*.

Linking everyone to everyone else eliminates the hierarchy's role as an information filter, opening the organization to broader autonomy for which shared commercial and social purposes create context and cohesiveness. Individuals need autonomy to respond appropriately to the unique situations they face amid the complexity of the marketplace, but if they are not sufficiently coordinated, the actions of many individuals may nullify each other.

To achieve balance between the extremes of rigidity and anarchist disintegration, Stafford Beer suggests that self-organizing systems require ongoing dialogue on specific topics that pertain to self-regulation. To help sort out exactly where that knowledge is, Beer's viable system model defines different types of messages, which are delivered through different communications channels. This approach greatly increases the capacity of an organization to handle information, as the very choice of channel creates context that makes the messages it carries easier to understand. Critical nuances are enhanced in this way, rather than being obliterated: Communication is also self-regulation.[9]

Separating these distinct conversations into separate channels enables ongoing, focused, and action-oriented dialogue to be sustained while avoiding confusion over what is an instruction as distinct from what is a question, or an observation.

The context for each of these conversations is a set of base models about which assumptions are documented and expectations are defined. As events unfold, expectations are either fulfilled, or surprises emerge.

Surprises indicate aspects of the models that now need adjustment, or perhaps the models are entirely inadequate and new models are needed.

Ongoing refinement of such models is achieved by addition of new information that is constantly gathered from the environment by everyone in the organization. Models are thus the explicit regulatory framework of an organization, and by incorporating new information they evolve as reflections of the market that they describe ever more precisely.

Meetings, conferences, phone calls, voice mail, electronic mail, computer conferences, research and development work, and even casual musings on napkins are all methods through which the dialogue is carried on. Documented bodies of knowledge are built, refined, and applied to the tasks of operations, management, and survival.

THE MANAGEMENT CENTER

An abundance of information is swirling through the organization, carried by multiple communications channels. Somehow, an organization's leaders must maintain an overview of the whole system. But how can they possibly comprehend all of the information and ideas in this knowledge system in which so many people are participating?

One way to do so is to create a special place where individuals and teams can collect, analyze, and share information. This is a center for information and design, like the control room of an electrical power company, where generators, transmission lines, and substations are monitored and controlled to optimize the distribution of electricity. It may also be like the bridge of an aircraft carrier (or of a starship) where the captain gathers information and consults with senior officers to make decisions amid battle.

The organization's version of this facility is a place where ongoing financial activity is monitored on real time computer displays, and simultaneously where the ongoing refinement of the information base and the library of models is focused. Surrounded by parallel streams of quantitative and qualitative information, this is the ideal place for teams of strategists to explore and define long-term business strategy while designing immediate action in anticipation of and in response to ongoing events.

In 1973, Stafford Beer established such a facility for the government of Chile, but the experiment was abruptly ended when president Salvador Allende was assassinated.[10] Using the much more powerful PCs of today, this management center can be achieved much more easily than in 1973.

It can also be achieved in virtual form on desktop computers, accessible to anyone, anywhere, who can connect a PC to a telephone line. Soon, with advancing cellular communications, even the phone line will be unnecessary. Such a management center is an important part of the new work place, and it is described more thoroughly in Chapter 10.

Picture, then, individuals who work in the evolving corporation. They gather in a management center, monitoring their organization as it operates in real time and thus fully aware of the flow of financial transactions as they occur. Simultaneously, they monitor the entire organization, which is involved in conversations about the business of today and of the future. Their corporation is a leader, anticipating the trends in the marketplace. When unexpected conditions do emerge, they are able to quickly coordinate the dialogue among the key people in the organization to understand the significance of what's happening and to develop and implement the appropriate responses.

FUTURE COMPUTING

To complete this description of computers in the knowledge infrastructure, something must be said about the computers of the near future. Soon you will have supercomputer power on your desk, the size, perhaps, of a medium-sized book. This will be your personal assistant, augmenting your creativity by filtering ongoing streams of information to provide you with only that which is likely to interest you. And how will your computer find out what interests you? It will ask, of course!

While it's doing all this filtering, it will also help you do your work using sophisticated modeling programs that run day and night, testing concepts and designs that may play a part in the future of your organization.

The widely used applications of today's computers, the word processors, spreadsheets, and databases, are bringing us to the end of an era. The PCs of the late 1990s will change work and the work place abruptly and definitively, making obsolete billions of dollars worth of existing computer systems.

Researcher Hans Moravec forecasts the future of computer technology, giving perspective to its rapid development:

> The amount of computational power that a dollar can purchase has increased a thousandfold every two decades since the beginning of the century. In eighty years, there has been a trillionfold decline in the cost of calculation. If this rate of improvement were to continue into the next century, a humanlike computer would be available in a $10 million supercomputer before 2010 and in a $1000 personal computer by 2030. But can this mad dash be sustained for another forty years? Easily! The curve . . . is not leveling off, and the technological pipe-

line contains laboratory developments that are already close to my requirements. The industry's success is one reason the success can continue—its enormous, and rapidly increasing, wealth supports more and better research and development of further advances. Also the very computers that the industry makes are employed in the design of future circuits and computers. As they become better and cheaper, so does the design process, and vice versa. Electronics is riding these vicious cycles so quickly that it is likely to be the main occupation of the human race by the end of the century[11] (Figure 8.4).

Reports of the progress along this trend line can be found nearly every day in newspapers. Here is one: "In recent Department of Defense tests, the Wavetracer Model 8 costing $150,000 processed a complex image in little more than twice the time a $10 million Cray X-MP required for the task."[12]

Profiled in the *New Yorker* magazine, computer scientist Gregory Chudnovsky offered this perspective on advancing technology:

The gigaflop supercomputers of today are almost useless. What is needed is a teraflop machine. . . . Now a better machine is a petaflop machine. . . . The petaflop machine will exist by the year 2000, or soon afterward. It will fit into a sphere less than a hundred feet in diameter. It will use light and mirrors— the machine's network will consist of optical cables rather than copper wires. By that time, a gigaflop 'supercomputer' will be a single chip. I think that the petaflop machine will be used mainly to simulate machines like itself, so that we can begin to design some *real* machines.[13]

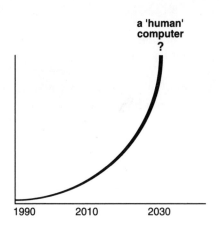

Figure 8.4   **Future Computing**
Hans Moravec forecasts that by 2010, computers will be capable of emulating human thought.

A few years from now, desktop computers costing perhaps less than $10,000 will do what no person (and no mainframe computer) has yet done. They will:

- Evaluate millions (or billions) of options and make operational decisions about the course of action of large-scale systems of public works, in real time.

- Monitor transactions in a global business and reliably alert management to changes in the overall health of the business as they happen, or before.

- Simulate the performance of systems that only a few years ago could not be reliably modeled on even the largest supercomputer.

- Produce for hundreds of dollars images, graphics, animation, and movies that look as good as the best Hollywood movies.

In short, computers will not only create ever-proliferating data, but they will finally manage honest-to-goodness information. The processing power of computers will augment the human thinking process, and thereby change the way we think and the way we work.

Because the way we work is intimately linked with the way we organize ourselves in the work place itself, organizations will change significantly. For example, people won't do clerical work; computers will. There will be few, if any clerks; people will imagine, think, design, and create, while computers do the drudgery. Such will be the knowledge infrastructure of the 21st century.

Because even today the possibility exists to implement true real time systems and advanced modeling capabilities are already arriving, all investments in computer technology must be scrutinized carefully to ensure that today's choices leave open the pathway to tomorrow's capabilities. There is the danger that you may go shopping for a new buggy only to discover soon thereafter that you could have gotten a car instead. *Caveat computor.*

9

Collaboration

Due to the complexity of the business environment and its increasing technical specialization, the collaboration of many people with diverse backgrounds and expertise is frequently necessary in dealing with today's issues and problems. Collaborative techniques that enable these people to work together quickly and effectively to solve problems can be far more productive than traditional meetings. Work can be done in days that might otherwise have taken weeks or months.

How can a team of committed managers with individual IQs above 120 have a collective IQ of 63?[1]—*Peter Senge*

A firm's efficiency is constrained only by its technology, and its technology is limited only by its members' ability to work together as an intelligent, creative organization.[2]—*Michael Rothschild*

we need also a methodology, a discipline, a process to turn this potential into performance. Otherwise, most of the available knowledge will not become productive; it will remain mere information.[3]—*Peter Drucker*

As a corporation evolves away from organizational patterns of command and control, another pattern emerges that is based on individuals cooperating by choice. Their affiliation is likely to have both commercial and social purposes, and it inevitably exists in the context of a market, which itself is likely to be in constant flux.

As the recognition and response model becomes its way of organizing, responsibility for decision making in this milieu of complexity spreads to more and more people in the corporation. Each individual will sooner or later make and implement decisions that impact the future of the entire corporation, and therefore the future of everyone else.

At Semco, the organizing assumption is that each individual can responsibly represent both his or her personal interests as well as those of the organization as a whole:

> We insist on making important decisions collegially, and certain decisions are made by a company-wide vote. Several years ago, for example, we needed a bigger plant for our marine division. Real estate agents looked for months and found nothing. So we asked the employees themselves to help, and over the first weekend they found three factories for sale, all of them nearby. We closed up shop for a day, piled everyone into buses, and drove out to inspect the three buildings. Then the workers voted—and they chose a plant the counselors didn't really want. It was an interesting situation—one that tested our commitment to participatory management. . . . We accepted the employees' decision, because we believe that in the long run, letting people participate in the decisions that affect their lives will have a positive effect on employee motivation and morale.[4]

Another advantage of broad participation is realized through the very process of recognizing and responding to change. To become aware that something notable is happening in the marketplace, and to comprehend precisely what is different about it, often requires the combined knowledge of many individuals. Their varied perspectives must be integrated to compose a model of the totality that is clear enough to be useful. From such a model appropriate strategies and actions can be developed.

In the process of comprehending such conditions and designing responses to them, each individual creates the new knowledge that literally becomes the future of the corporation. This is possibly the most important process that the corporation can nurture and manage. Peter Drucker states:

> The productivity of knowledge is going to be the determining factor in the competitive position of a company, an industry, an entire country. No country, industry, or company has any 'natural' advantage or disadvantage. The only advantage it can possess is the ability to exploit universally available knowledge. The only thing that increasingly will matter in national as in international economics is management's performance in making knowledge productive.[5]

Collaborative processes which facilitate the creation of new knowledge by teams of people working together are vital to the knowledge infrastructure and to recognition and response organizations. By combining the diverse perspectives of many individuals into coherent wholes, they help the company to regulate itself and to maintain its balance amid the changes of the marketplace.

When there is a hint of important change on the way, perhaps a team of people is assembled and goes to work gathering information, filtering it, analyzing it, and devising preliminary models of its meaning. Such a collaboration is simultaneously a process of learning and design, but the structure through which the team works is often adopted spontaneously and with little design.

Experience shows, however, that there is no reason to expect that people will create an effective working structure just because they happen to be together in a room. In fact, a group is as likely to have trouble accomplishing their goals as they are to have an easy time of it.

This is precisely what the designed collaborative process seeks to improve, and it is the subject of this chapter.

THE INTERACTION METHOD

The practice of meeting design was brought into focus in 1976 by architects Michael Doyle and David Straus, who developed a technique that they called the 'Interaction Method.' Recognizing the waste caused by the poor productivity of typical meetings, they published *How To Make Meetings Work*, in which they presented their model.

They observed, "In almost every field remarkable advances have come in the last decade, but there has been no major improvement in the way meetings have been run in the last twenty years—in fact, not even in the last century."[6] They went on to point out that, like any complex activity, successful meetings happen because of good preparation and design:

> Productivity, creativity, efficiency, participation, and commitment are results. If you want these results from your meetings, you have to understand the process that produces them. . . . A football team may practice forty hours for every one that counts. After every game the players analyze the films to figure out what worked and what didn't. That's how they develop teamwork. They break down the complex activity of football into fundamentals and plays, practice them, and then put them all together in a game. Meetings are one of the most complex activities you do.[7]

The interaction method is still being used successfully all over the world, and you will find that even after all these years their book is probably still available at your local bookstore. The firm that they established, Interaction Associates, is still quite active, teaching and facilitating their techniques.

FOUR COLLABORATIVE MODELS

Numerous other models of the collaborative process have also been created in recent years. Some have been developed within corporations, while others have been developed by consultants and academics. Some are narrowly focused on specific kinds of problems, while others are applicable to a wide variety of problems and issues.

Here are descriptions of four diverse approaches to collaborative process that demonstrate a wide range of possibilities:

1. General Electric's Work-Out.

2. Collaborative Design.

3. Reengineering.

4. Open Space Technology.

1. General Electric's Work-Out

At General Electric, a three-day collaborative technique called Work-Out was developed by internal staff members working with outside consultants in 1988. Its purpose was to enable thousands of GE employees to participate in the transformation of the corporation by working together to identify and solve problems.

For decades, GE employees had been constrained by the company's rigid hierarchy. CEO Jack Welch saw, however, that the future success of the corporation depended on developing a much more participatory work environment, one in which each individual could contribute their best ideas to improving productivity. Thus, Work-Out was designed to help overcome GE's pervasive command and control culture by engaging everyone in the process of improving the company, while simultaneously exposing managers who would not adapt to the participatory culture that Welch was committed to.

In Welch's words, ''The point of Work-Out is to give people better jobs. When people see that their ideas count, their dignity is raised. Instead of feeling numb, like robots, they feel important. They *are* important. . . . we're trying to differentiate GE competitively by raising as much intellectual and creative capital from our work force as we possibly can.''[8]

Under the guidance of a trained facilitator, Work-Out was

> patterned after New England town meetings. In groups of 30 to 100, the hourly and salaried employees of a particular business would spend three days at an off-site conference center discussing their common problems. No coats. No ties. To ensure that people could speak candidly without fearing retribution,

bosses were locked out during discussion times. Meeting in small groups, the employees would define problems and develop concrete proposals. On the final day, the bosses would return. According to Work-Out's rules, they had to make instant, on-the-spot decisions about each proposal, right in front of everyone. As Welch had hoped, the process quickly exposed those GE managers who didn't 'walk the talk'.[9]

By mid-1992, more than 200,000 GE employees had participated in Work-Out sessions, and the results were helping GE achieve the higher levels of performance that Welch was after. GE's Appliance business unit, for example, reduced its inventory by $200 million and thereby increased its return on investment by 8.5 percent due to improvements that were developed during Work-Out sessions. Other GE business units reported similar success stories.

2. Collaborative Design

Collaborative Design is a process that enables groups to solve complex problems such as developing business strategies, planning organizational transformations, and designing complex products. It has been developed and applied by a network of consultants in projects with corporations, schools, and government agencies around the world, for groups ranging in size from 10 to 20, to even 200 people. Events last from one-half day to five days, and frequently accomplish work that would have taken weeks or months to complete using traditional meetings.

The theory of knowledge that was presented in Chapter 5 is the conceptual basis upon which the process is designed (Figure 9.1). The objective of a collaborative design event is to create a work process in which the exact new information will emerge to enable the participants to create new knowledge, and thus to solve the problems at hand. The focused dialogue that inevitably occurs in Collaborative Design frequently leads the participants to a much deeper understanding of the issues they face, and of each

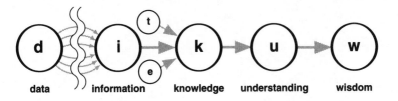

Figure 9.1 **Collaborative Design**
The Collaborative Design process integrates theory, information, and experience into learning events for groups of 2 to 200 people, or more. Through condensed interactions among the participants, understanding emerges, as well as wisdom.

other. Wisdom also emerges, for as people work through complex issues, they engage with each other in identifying visions of what ought to be done, as well as how it could be accomplished.

The model shows that to create new knowledge, three distinct elements must be integrated into a single process: *theory, information,* and *experience.* Here we see the simultaneous expression of learning, design, and the creation of knowledge, for these are all words that ultimately describe the very same thing.

Theory In the Collaborative Design process, three underlying *theories* are applied, one of which is of course the theory of knowledge itself. Another is the design process that was presented in Chapter 7 (Figure 9.2), and the third is derived from the disciplines of systems science.

In most cases, a group arrives with a compelling vision or an unacceptable condition at the start of the process, for this is what has led people to commit time to solving this particular problem in the first place. When vision is already present, much of the initial work is spent in defining the condition; when the condition is dominant, work is done to define the vision. In both cases, the intent is to *create the problem* in very clear terms, and to catalyze the creative tension that will energize the process toward creating solutions.

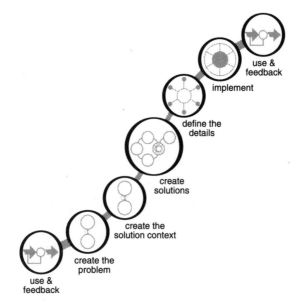

Figure 9.2 **The Design Process**

The use of the design process in collaborative problem solving was pioneered by consultant Matt Taylor. Like Doyle and Straus, Taylor is an architect, and his experience of the design process in that field led him to apply it to helping corporations solve complex management problems.

The disciplines of systems science provide operational theories that have proven very useful to groups dealing with complex and systemic issues. Understanding the character and operation of systems seems to be fundamentally important for participants in all organizations. These disciplines, developed by innovators such as Stafford Beer and W. Edwards Deming, provide tools by which people can explore the hidden theoretical roots of the issues at hand, enabling them to reframe their experiences and see the world in new ways, thereby designing new approaches.

Information The *information* component of collaborative design depends upon the issues that a group has decided to address. In general, the process is most effective when there is a wide diversity of information and opinion so that new information will be available throughout, and this occurs when a diverse group of participants take part. In addition to employees from throughout an organization, outside experts, vendors, customers, and community members may add depth to the perspectives that are represented.

The issues will be explored in great detail from many different vantage points, enabling each participant to understand how others view the situation. By clearly framing these differences, new insights often emerge that become new knowledge, solutions that no individual participant could have developed on his or her own.

Experience *Experience* is the third element in the theory of knowledge, for it has been shown that people learn best when they actually experience the issues that they're exploring. Whereas seeing and hearing are limited learning methods, *doing* provides the totality of involvement that enables people to fully grasp the meaning of new information. The technique of creating such learning experiences is the subject of an emerging discipline called 'accelerated learning,' which synthesizes recent discoveries about how people learn most effectively.[10]

About this issue Peter Senge writes, "Human beings learn best through firsthand experience. We learn to walk, ride a bicycle, drive an automobile, and play the piano by trial and error; we act, observe the consequence of our action and adjust."[11] The Collaborative Design process includes experiences that help to contextualize the issues that a group is dealing with. These may be simulations, model building projects, and games that transcend the purely intellectual by engaging the whole person.

A Typical Event When a large group gathers to participate in a three-day Collaborative Design event, they are first introduced to the process by a facilitator or a team of facilitators, and within an hour they are working in teams of three to five people each, exploring various aspects of the issues they face. After an hour or so all the teams may report what they have learned to each other, and then they will work in teams again. Later, they may all work together to develop models that require everyone's participation.

This rhythm of small and large team work will continue until the issues have been explored in considerable detail. Participants will examine the issues from many different vantage points, and over a time span of 100 or even 200 years. They will examine history, and they will project themselves forward into the future and look back at the present.

They may build conceptual models of their problems using toys or wooden blocks. They may play learning games that enable them to experience their issues in new ways, and to help them to communicate and design together effectively. Through all of this, each participant gradually builds understanding and develops a large context in which the specific issues at hand reside.

This is the process of creating solutions, and there will be many iterations of analysis and insight and creating options and selecting (Figure 9.3). New information will be introduced showing how similar issues are handled in other disciplines, or in other industries. Experts from outside will be brought in to share their experiences in other companies.

Through this process issues that seem intractable and massively complex become clearer and sort themselves naturally by the second or third

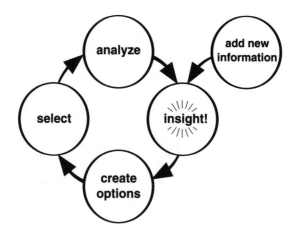

Figure 9.3 **Creating Solutions**

day. Solutions begin to flow from the diversity and depth of knowledge of all of the participants, and the broad range of vantage points ensures that all vital perspectives are represented.

To make the process of creating new knowledge easier, a support staff documents the ongoing dialogues that occur throughout the event. This document is done in real time and is used by the participants as a form of feedback about the content and the process that they are engaged in.

Soon the group reaches the critical point, and like a heated popcorn kernel, suddenly it pops. Insight! Understanding emerges that is deep and complete: There are elegant solutions, and they can be implemented (Figure 9.4)!

This has happened again and again, with all kinds of problems and all kinds of organizations. Collaborative Design creates a cognitive process in which participants become experts with a thorough understanding of the problems and opportunities they face, as well as the understanding and commitment to implement the solutions that they devise. Because the work is likely to be comprehensive, it will include detailed action plans that can be used on Monday morning to begin the work of implementation.

Figure 9.4 **Insight!**
After three or four days of design, the moment of insight arrives. Photo by the author.

Complete documentation will be available almost immediately to be shared with those who did not participate in order to give them a detailed understanding of what happened. It is also useful as a reference document. Frequently, a summary document captures the highlights and the key conclusions, as well as the complete action plan.

Collaborative Design is thus a systematic approach by which groups can solve complex problems, and it has been used to support systemic change in numerous organizations. Recently, for example, a five-day Collaborative Design event helped the Department of Education of Guam to initiate the transformation from a bureaucratic, centralized organizational structure to an organizational model in which individual schools respond specifically to local needs and opportunities.

Collaborative Design has also been used in an oil company to initiate a broad-ranging process of reengineering; in an insurance company to design and implement a new organizational model; on a military base to design responses to changing conditions due to the end of the Cold War; in a high school district to design programs to deal with issues of drug abuse and drop-outs; with a nonprofit organization to design new educational curricula; and in an auto rental company to develop key strategic initiatives. In dozens of events in large corporations, government agencies, and community organizations, the Collaborative Design process has enabled groups to solve complex problems, to achieve unexpected breakthroughs, to develop deeper understanding, and to experience those potent moments of insight when things fall into place and it becomes clear that visions can be achieved.

3. Reengineering

Michael Hammer and James Champy point out that,

> American companies perform so badly precisely because they used to perform so well. . . . Advanced technologies, the disappearance of boundaries between national markets, and the altered expectations of customers who now have more choices then ever before have combined to make the goals, methods, and basic organizing principles of the classical American corporation sadly obsolete. Renewing their competitive capabilities isn't an issue of getting the people in these companies to work harder, but of learning to work differently. This means that companies and their employees must unlearn many of the principles and techniques that brought them success for so long.[12]

They observe that companies have grown around tasks organized into the simplest and most basic of steps, leading to fragmentation, poor performance, and now excessive cost. In response, they propose that companies should 'reengineer' themselves by remaking their operational processes to serve their customers' needs as directly as possible. They define this as "the fundamental rethinking and radical redesign of business processes to achieve dramatic improvement in critical, contemporary measures of performance, such as cost, quality, service, and speed."[13]

The key to this approach is the concept of a 'business process,' which is, "a set of activities that, taken together, produce a result of value to the customer."[14] The purpose of reengineering is to eliminate the boundaries between functional departments and the limitations of structure-oriented thinking by organizing work around such processes.

Hammer and Champy describe a series of steps in the reengineering process that is much like the design process described in Chapter 7. First, existing processes are broadly mapped, and those processes best suited for reengineering are selected. A reengineering team is assembled, which consists of:

- A team leader.
- The 'process owner' who represents the process that is being reengineered.
- A group of people who do the reengineering work.
- A steering committee who oversee the work from the perspective of senior management.

A reengineering team's first task is to understand the existing process from the customer's perspective. They may also explore how other companies handle similar issues, an investigation that is called 'benchmarking.'

Once they fully understand what is now being done and how others do it better, the process is redesigned to take eliminate all unnecessary steps and to take advantage of new technology that will enable the necessary work to be done most effectively. A design prototype is tested on a small scale so that it can be refined under real circumstances, and finally it is ready to be implemented throughout an organization.

Throughout this process, people with different roles in the organization from various departments participate in the analysis of the existing condition and the development of new possibilities, and it is primarily through these interactions that reengineering takes place.

4. Open Space Technology

Open Space Technology was developed by consultant Harrison Owen, who has used it successfully all over the world with all kinds of organizations since 1985.

Owen designed Open Space Technology after a meeting with a group of organizational experts in Monterey, California. At the end, everyone confessed that they got more out of the coffee breaks than the meeting itself. 'So my question was, Is there a way of producing the kind of good, intense interaction you get in a coffee break while achieving the output and performance you get in a meeting?'[15]

In response to his own question, Owen devised a few simple principles through which he believed that a group could organize itself, just as the coffee-break discussions were also *self-organizing*. Owen found that they worked quite well, even when the issues at hand were tremendously complex.

At root there is the simple idea that what is required is "a profound commitment to the notion that given the appropriate space and time, people will utilize their freedom and exercise their responsibility for their own personal empowerment and the achievement of the task at hand, whatever that task might be."[16] Success comes when the individuals in a group bring two key elements, passion and responsibility. "Without passion, nobody is interested. Without responsibility, nothing will get done."[17]

As to who should participate, there is but one criterion: voluntary self-selection. Thus the four principles are, "First, whoever comes is the right people; second, whatever happens is the only thing that could have; third, whenever it starts is the right time; and fourth, when it is over it is over."[18]

Journalist Don Oldenburg described a one-day Open Space event that Owen facilitated for senior managers of the U.S. Forest Service:

His instructions to the forestry managers are brief: Each is to think of an area or issue he or she is passionate about that relates to the conference's theme ('Enhancing Relationships With Our Customers'); then title it, be prepared to take responsibility for it, step forward and write the title on a piece of poster paper, and tack it to the wall. The room buzzes with doubt and excitement. . . . One man rises reluctantly, states his name and issues and starts marking it on poster paper. Two more stand up, followed by a flurry of others. As suddenly as it started, it stops. The posted topics are arranged in immediate, late morning, and afternoon time slots and are designated locations. Anyone interested in an issue signs up and shows up. Thirty-two minutes into the conference, the forestry managers have created and scheduled 13 workshops.[19]

Open Space has been used on five continents with corporations, government agencies, and community groups in sessions of one to three days:

The purposes have ranged from corporate redesign in the face of intense competition, to national redesign in the face of massive transformational forces such as South Africa. The technology is not magic, nor does it solve all problems. However, in those situations where highly complex and conflicted issues must be dealt with, and solved, by very diverse groups of people, Open Space Technology can make a major contribution.[20]

In his book on Open Space, Owen presents examples of the technique used in Venezuela to help the fastest growing cellular phone company in the world come to grips with the issues of its own phenomenal growth, a one-day event for the National Education Association among 420 people, and numerous other events in gatherings of 5 to 500 people.

He comments, "Over the years of development, Open Space has moved from its genesis in frustration as a joke, to become a very effective means for empowerment."[21] He also discovered that before starting, every group was sure that, in spite of what others had done, the process would *not* work with them. So far, he reports, they have been consistently incorrect about that.

* * *

Each of these models provides a structure through which collaboration leverages the knowledge 'assets' of individuals and groups who are dealing with complex issues. They demonstrate varying degrees of openness, for a reengineering project may be tightly structured, while Collaborative Design is less so; Work-Out is still less structured, since many of the issues that are dealt with arise spontaneously from the participants. At the nonstructured end of the spectrum is Open Space Technology, which surely demonstrates that the concepts developed by complexity scientists are as applicable to groups of people working together as they are to economic systems. Given an appropriate set of rules, preferably simple rules, very complex systems can indeed be self-organizing (Figure 9.5).

As they differ in their degree of openness, they also provide different approaches to the creation and management of knowledge. Work-Out enables teams of workers to air their complaints and apply their knowledge to their own work. Collaborative Design enables groups to understand the

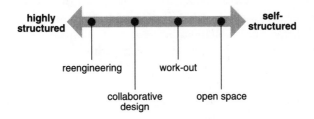

Figure 9.5 **A Spectrum of Structures for Collaboration**

issues they face and achieve key insights that lead to solutions, accomplishing weeks or months of complex design work in a matter of days. Reengineering a company's work processes brings the customer's perspective to the forefront, while Open Space enables hundreds of people to organize themselves within an hour to deal with complex issues.

These processes were all developed for groups that work together face to face, but recently another aspect of collaboration has emerged using computers to support work that may occur in many places simultaneously. These are computer-enhanced meetings which use 'groupware' to enable people to work together on line, as mentioned in Chapter 8. Computers are being used by groups in many ways to support open dialogue, to provide structured approaches to investigation and decision making, and to present and document work as it being done. More of these applications will be developed in the future simply because they overcome barriers of time and space, enabling people to collaborate from a distance.

FACILITATION

An element that these models share is the participation of someone whose responsibility is to facilitate the process itself. To facilitate, after all, means 'to make easy,' and thus it is the facilitator's role to enable the processes of collaboration to be as easy as possible to create the needed knowledge. This fits the perspective of systems science, which emphasizes that the regulation of a system must occur from outside of it. By focusing on the processes of the system called a meeting rather than on its content, a facilitator functions as regulator, applying an understanding of factors such as problem-solving, psychology, creativity, learning, and design.

One aspect of this regulation is simply removing obstacles that make it difficult for groups to achieve their goals, and in this regard the new work place can play an important role. The formal conference room may be too small or too large, too cold or too hot, too dark or too bright, and its furniture may be uncomfortable or too rigid, while necessary equipment may be lacking. Thus, collaborative processes often work best in project rooms or management centers, whose large writing walls also make it easy for many individuals to work together to map out complex topics. This is discussed in detail in Chapter 10.

Even more important is ensuring that the those involved understand that their role is to participate as members of a design team, rather than as defenders of the established order, their department or their boss. If individuals come into a process to deflect change away from themselves and on to others, the process will never achieve success.

Facilitators also seek to eliminate other, more mundane obstacles, such as:

- Missing information.

- Personality conflicts.

- Unclear instructions.

- Time constraints.

- Schedule conflicts.

These obstacles recur in most organizations every working day, causing productivity to suffer unnecessarily. Facilitators of the collaborative process consider these issues and work to overcome them even before groups meet.

At their best, the results of collaboration are increased productivity through faster decision making, more clarity about the real issues that organizations face, and the discovery and implementation of better solutions. Because of the increasing pressures of competition and the need to develop and implement new designs and solutions more quickly than ever, collaborative design processes are becoming ever more vital elements of the knowledge infrastructure.

10

Places for Learning

The work place itself is a key element of the new organization. Carefully conceived and designed work environments can help individuals, teams, and entire companies to achieve much higher levels of performance than might otherwise have been possible. These environments include the work spaces for individuals, project rooms for teams, and management centers for the entire enterprise.

CTC [Chrysler Technology Center] is going to be the finest automotive technical center in the world. Nobody will have the kind of tools we'll have to design and develop products for the next decade and the next century. But it will be just a tool—just bricks and mortar and sophisticated technology. What will really breathe life into CTC is our people. It's designed to help people work together better than ever before.[1]—Lee Iacocca

Chrysler Corporation created its billion-dollar Technology Center to accommodate the 7,000 Chrysler employees engaged in the design and development of new cars. Constructed between 1986 and 1993, the 3.5 million square foot facility supports a new approach to organizing the automobile design process, platform teams. Working in these teams and in the CTC has enabled Chrysler to reduce its automotive development time from 5 years to 3.25 years, a critical competitive advantage in the demanding auto market.

Chrysler's platform teams have been very successful, developing new products for the company that have propelled it to record profits. Consequently, other auto companies such as Ford are now copying the platform team concept.

The shift from the departmental organization to platform teams is a significant departure that exemplifies the shift from structure-oriented thinking to process thinking, but Chrysler seems to be one of the few companies to recognize that such new organizational models can be significantly enhanced through the design of the work place itself.

* * *

In the factories of the early and mid-20th century, work was divided into small tasks, fragmented and performed on production lines by tens, hundreds, or thousands of workers. Frederick Taylor initiated a productivity revolution by defining each worker's job in precise, invariant steps, bringing new levels of order to manufacturing. Each worker did only one task to ensure that it would be done consistently and correctly.

This same approach, based on fragmentation and specialization, was also applied to work in offices, where legions of specialists examined the contents of only their particular box on only their particular forms and shifted papers from the pile marked 'in' to the pile marked 'out':

> from start to finish there were at least thirteen handoffs among different work groups and some twenty-seven different information systems were involved. . . . while the interval between receiving an order and turning the service over to the customer was fifteen days, our actual work time was only about ten hours.[2]

Michael Rothschild has observed that the ubiquitous, multistory office tower filled with clerical workers is a response to the problem of organizing work space to efficiently move paper from person to person.[3] With row after row of desks and small cubicles, surrounded by row upon row of small offices, all driven by logistics of paper, these are places where individuals work in separate little cells like so many penitent monks.

Most people are not conscious of the impact that the work place has on how work is done, but it does have an impact, and in many cases it is an enormous impact. As with the organization itself, this work place was once *designed* to be the way it is, but people have lost sight of this fact, and they simply assume that offices have to be the same as they have been for decades.

As it is a specific intent of the process orientation to re-integrate work into coherent wholes, the work place designed for fragmentation and specialization does not provide adequate support for organizations that adopt process-oriented organizational models such as recognition and response. In the new organization, the work place is not a place for segmentation, but a place for learning.

This chapter presents approaches to the new work place. The ideas that are presented here are based on projects that have been completed by a team of designers, including the author and others, that have resulted in high performance work places which support new organizational models.

ELIMINATING EXCESS TIME AND COST

Overall, two factors have converged in the knowledge economy to bring an end to the pattern of fragmented work. Both are consequences of the dynamics of the competitive marketplace, and the astonishing inefficiency of clerical work as it was performed during the industrial era.

First, increasing competition is squeezing excess *time* out of all work processes. Sequential work is slow, but the marketplace is moving faster and faster all the time.

The learning curve model shows that those who achieve faster cycle times in the production and marketing of products and services will have more opportunities to learn and will gain a distinct competitive advantage.[4] Since clerical work is very time-consuming, but is among the least value-added activities in any organization, it is being eliminated through the implementation of new organizational models and through work process redesign (reengineering).

Secondly, increasing competition drives prices down and squeezes *cost* out of the work process, and there is simply no money available to pay people who do not contribute discernible value. If a company is paying workers who are engaged in nonproductive tasks, competitors can probably do the same work at a lower cost.

Consequently, clerical work is being designed out of existence, and much that cannot be entirely eliminated is being handled by computers.

In addition to the decline of clerical work, the work of middle management is also being eliminated. People at all levels are working with greater autonomy, and through the application of computer networks that enable people to exchange information with each other directly, hierarchical layers of middle managers have become unnecessary.

As a result of these trends, organizations are doing more work with fewer people, and the consequences are unmistakably clear: Jobs must be *made* unnecessary.

At GE, for example, between 1981 and 1991, total employment declined from about 400,000 to 300,000 people even as total revenues increased from $28 to $60 billion; revenue per employee increased from $70,000 to $200,000.[5]

This creates a dilemma for government officials responsible for the economy as a whole, for even as many companies increase their revenues and profits, they do so with fewer employees. There is a disturbing possibility of increasing, systemic unemployment, and no one can be sure if this is a temporary phenomenon related to the transition from an industrial economy to an information economy, or if it will be permanent.

KNOWLEDGE WORK

As a result of the economic changes and the changes in the nature of the work itself, a new kind of worker has come to the forefront. Twenty-five years ago, Peter Drucker identified this growing segment of the work force as 'knowledge workers,'[6] and he accurately predicted that their importance to the economy would steadily increase. Knowledge workers add value, in his words, by applying *knowledge to knowledge.*[7]

Robert Reich calls them 'symbolic analysts,' and he identifies them as people who "solve, identify, and broker problems by manipulating symbols. They simplify reality into abstract images."[8] These symbols are drawings, diagrams, and of course, the written alphabet. As most professional work is dependent on information and is recorded in symbols, symbolic analysts are at the heart of the information economy.

In the language of the design process, these people are engaged in continual learning and in applying their learning through the process of design (Figure 10.1). Whether you call them knowledge workers, symbolic analysts, or designers, they are professionals of all disciplines, including writers, programmers, nurses, engineers, lawyers, producers, accountants, marketers, architects. . . .

Knowledge work, like the process of learning to which it is so closely related, begins with the individual. Knowledge workers engage in the design and creation of informed *distinctions* that differentiate an organization's products and services in the marketplace.

Frequently, this work is dynamic, engaging, and often fast-moving. It can also be painfully slow and exactingly detailed, but whether it is fast or slow, it nearly always involves complexity. It may be the complexity of a medical diagnosis; a computer chip design; a class action law suit; the engineering of a high-rise building; or any of thousands of activities undertaken throughout an organization that require years of education, subsequent years of concentrated practice, and an abundance of creativity.

Such complexity can only rarely be well represented on a pad of legal paper or well described in a four-page memo, or even four hundred pages

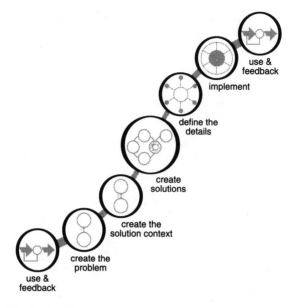

Figure 10.1 **The Design Process**

of text. It takes *images and objects* to model complexity, diagrams, photographs, calendars, flow charts, blueprints, mock-ups, prototypes, samples, schematics, and illustrations.

Frequently, these complex problems and design challenges involve the knowledge of many different specialties and can rarely be fully modeled and understood by individuals working alone. Thus, many people must work together to comprehend them, specialists from different disciplines who combine their diverse knowledge into a complete picture. Dr. William Miller, Director of Research and Business Development for Steelcase notes, "Most innovation today occurs through combining skills from different disciplines. It's very hard to push the state of the art in one discipline."[9]

Working amid such complexity, the activities of knowledge workers are almost always *projects;* they are almost never 'jobs.'[10] A project may last for a day, a week, or a year, and an individual may participate on only one, or simultaneously on five project teams.

It is clear that knowledge work is fundamentally different from the fragmented, repetitive clerical and middle management work that most office buildings were originally designed to accommodate. With its rows of desks, cubicles, and small offices, the old work place is simply not competent to support the kinds of collaborative dialogue, creativity, and exploration that individuals and teams of knowledge workers regularly undertake. Nor does it readily accommodate rolls of large drawings, scale models, test parts and samples, large calendars and flow charts that are the common artifacts of such projects.

As the work place itself is a vital part of the knowledge infrastructure, the expanding importance of knowledge work calls for a new kind of work place, one that is designed to fulfill the specific and unique needs of knowledge workers.

THREE SETTINGS FOR KNOWLEDGE WORK

In most organizations, knowledge workers need three different settings to accommodate the different aspects of their work:

1. Individual work spaces.

2. Project rooms.

3. Management centers.

1. Individual Work Spaces

The individual's work space must be a place for learning and for designing, the two things that knowledge workers spend most of their time doing. This takes many forms, such as reading, writing, drawing, inventing, studying, exploring, and thinking. About such work Ricardo Semler comments that, "Thinking is difficult. It requires concentration and discipline. Give it the time it deserves."[11] To this we would add, in the theme of this chapter, "Give it the space it deserves." This work space must be large enough to spread out the documentation that complex projects generate, for it takes space to be able to use these documents effectively.

Perhaps most important is that the individual be in control of this space, for no one knows more than the individual about how to support his or her own learning process. Some need a large space piled with accumulated documents; some need orderly shelves; some want a compact space, and others a large one.

As learning is deeply personal, the place for learning must be personal as well. Thus, individuals should arrange their own furniture, and set the sound, light, air temperature, and decor to suit their own needs. This may be considered revolutionary in view of the limited and standardized approach that is taken with most offices, but it fits well the individualistic character of knowledge work and the organization's dependence on the productivity of these workers.

2. Project Rooms

Many knowledge workers spend as much time working in teams as they do working alone. In most office buildings, teams are forced to meet wherever they can find enough space, whether it happens to be in large offices, not-so-large offices, meeting rooms, training rooms, cafeterias, classrooms, hallways, or empty offices (there will be more of these due to continued downsizing). But none of these rooms is designed to support the kind of open-ended learning that knowledge work projects involve.

What project teams really need are project rooms that they can call their own. These must be large enough so that each individual has room for a desk for their own work, without having to go four floors away to do it, and with enough additional space so that an entire team can easily work together at once.

Michael Hammer and James Champy describe the importance of the project room this way:

> To function as a team, members need to work together in one place, which is not as easy as it sounds. Most companies don't design their facilities with collaborative work in mind. They maintain lots of private or semiprivate rooms designed for solo work and conference rooms for meetings, but they don't have many large spaces suitable for a team to work together over an extended period of time. This isn't a minor issue; it can prove a serious impediment to a reengineering team's progress.[12]

The work habits and thinking habits derived from standardized and fragmented offices reinforce the pattern of command and control management. As colleague Bryan Coffman recently observed, "the 'old philosophy' space design inhibits reengineering and transformation more than any other single factor, although it will not of itself prove a sufficient tool to complete the transformation."[13]

Project rooms designed specifically for collaborative knowledge work are therefore crucial to the infrastructure of organizations committed to working in new ways. Since these rooms do not already exist in most offices, they will have to be created.

Like individual work spaces, one of the most important qualities of project rooms is that the people who are doing the work must be in control of the places in which they work. Their needs may change from hour to hour, and it simply won't do to have someone from the building department come in every time something needs to be moved.

There is a constant reconfiguration of the team that occurs in response to the rhythm of the work itself, and to accommodate this flow of work and the continual regroupings, the space itself and the furniture within it will be moved many times. When it is needed, a conference table can be composed from four smaller work tables, and it can also be used in smaller pieces for small team work. Computers, file cabinets, desks, and chairs are rolled in and out as they are needed. Flexibility is the key.

The flow of a typical day in a project room illustrates this: At the start of the day, a team of 10 people may be working separately at their own desks, making phone calls, writing, and reading. The full team gathers at 10:00 A.M. for a brief update, and then breaks into three separate work sessions at 10:30. After working in these teams before and during lunch, the whole team flows through an uninterrupted afternoon in which they work intermittently as a full team, individually, and in small groups. To accommodate this flow, people and furniture are continually moving, for it is the work itself that determines how the space is used, and this cannot be predicted in advance.

As simple as this sounds, the fact is that most work spaces and most furniture are designed with assumption that people are incompetent to make such choices, and their placement is fixed by an architect or a facility manager. The space is expected to remain unchanged for years, regardless of the composition of the team or the nature of the work that they do.

Most conference rooms are dominated by large, fixed tables that are attached to the floor so that they cannot be moved, even when a large, open space is what is really needed. This is the facility's corollary of the rigid hierarchy that impedes organizational flexibility.

A project room can be more than just a big, square room. To support a variety of work styles and needs, it may be a group of connected subspaces of different sizes and shapes. Figure 10.2 shows a project room consisting of a large round space which is well suited for large conferences and design sessions, with a series of adjacent smaller spaces for individual and small group work (Figure 10.2).

Once the flexibility of recognition and response is understood, its expression has an infinite variety of forms in the work place. Anyone should be able to set up or remove any element of a work space quickly and easily. The work drives the individuals and the teams, and they must configure their work environments to accomplish the best possible work.

3.   Management Centers

In Chapter 8 it was mentioned that Stafford Beer installed a management center (or as he refers to it, a control centre) in Santiago, Chile in 1971 in conjunction with his work for the government of president Salvador Allende. Photos and a discussion of this facility were published in Beer's *Platform for Change*,[14] and a description of its genesis and function was published in *Brain of the Firm*.[15]

Figure 10.2 **A Project Room**
A project room provides its users with a place to focus their efforts as a team. This project room was developed in 1992 for the Capital Holding Corporation, Louisville, Kentucky, based on concepts developed by Matt and Gail Taylor. The design team consisted of Matt Taylor and William Blackburn of Athenaeum International, Inc., Langdon Morris of Strategic Planning Guild, and Donnie Weber of WBW Group, Inc. Photo by the author.

In *Brain of the Firm*, Beer wrote, "I propose a control centre for the corporation which is in continuous activity. . . . All senior formal meetings would be held there; and the rest of the time, all senior executives would treat it as a kind of a club room. . . . It is what the Greeks called a *phrontisterion*—a thinking shop."[16]

The intent of developing such a facility must be, ultimately, to provide a place where learning takes place in the most effective ways possible to support individuals and teams in the design of ever-more effective actions. Thus, an organization's management center is a central learning hub, a place where people come together to learn and to design, to synthesize a broad range of information, people, and ideas, to create the knowledge that makes it possible to understand the present and to create the future.

The use of this facility, however, need not be limited just to senior managers. Everyone in the organization will need this facility at one time or another. For some this will occur infrequently, while others will be there nearly every day. Thus, by 'management center' we must expand our thinking beyond 'bosses only' to the idea of management as an activity that includes those who participate in managing the organization, which is of course absolutely everyone.

Designing a Management Center There are probably hundreds of ways to configure a management center. After observing many and helping to design some, the general layout presented here seems quite effective, and will provide a good starting point for thinking about the design issues that must be considered.

Figure 10.3 shows how a management center might be arranged for a typical corporation. It is a gathering place, a place where information is collected and people work together to solve problems. It must, therefore,

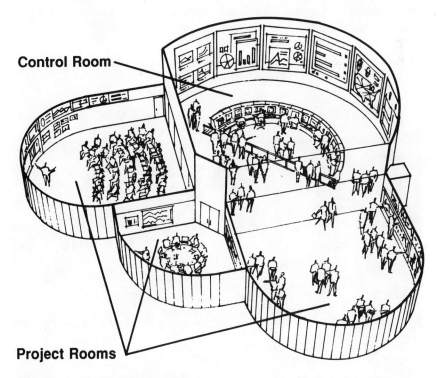

Control Room

Project Rooms

Figure 10.3 **The Management Center**
This drawing of a management center shows a central Control Room and three adjacent Project Rooms. The control room is used for the analysis and display of quantitative, real time information, as well as qualitative information. Working in the project rooms, teams develop strategies, products, business plans, and quick responses to emerging conditions with full access to the rich information stream. This is the facility for managing the process-oriented organization in real time. Drawing courtesy of Patri.Burlage.Merker based on a design by Langdon Morris.

be a place where people want to be, a place with a feeling of welcoming and openness, and as Beer suggests, a club room that is rich in information and interactions.

Overall, this is a large space of approximately 5000 square feet. Within it there are two different kinds of spaces, a control room located at the apex of the primary sight lines, and three project rooms. The project rooms are divided from one another by movable partitions that can be opened to create one very large space, or closed to provide privacy.

The Control Room The control room is an information hub that is linked to the organization's electronic network of communications channels and can access the organization's real time financial information and its qualitative databases. Large projection screens display real time financial activities in flow charts and diagrams, as well as images and models that enable people to grasp the significance of the broadest concepts as well as the specific details. They can also display broadcast TV and cable TV, whether local news or CNN (or the Super Bowl). These display screens can also be used for video conferencing (Figure 10.4).

Figure 10.4 **Large Screen Displays**
Large projection screens are used in the management center to display all kinds of information. Photo of the EDS Information Management Center courtesy of EDS.

The control room is staffed by a team of knowledge workers, shown at workstations facing the large screens, who provide information, facilitation, documentation, and logistics support to the people who are working in the center. They also select the information that is shown on the large-screen displays to provide the most relevant and interesting information that is pertinent to the work that is being done.

At any given time, knowledge workers may be analyzing reports, preparing documents, or gathering data for projects that are under way or are about to start. Tapping into the ongoing data stream, they also design and run business simulations that model alternative future possibilities for the organization.

The center is linked with all of the organization's offices, so participation in the center's work is not limited to those who happen to be there on any particular day. Through two-way video conferencing, the center can be expanded to include any number of people, from tens to hundreds to thousands who are elsewhere in the building or an ocean away.

In addition, the 'virtual management center' will be accessible on line through computer networks, enabling individuals working remotely to see on their own computers the same information that is being displayed in the center. Groupware will support interactive dialogue between those in the management center and others who are elsewhere, so even those who happen to be traveling can directly participate in making critical decisions, or casually check in just to see what's happening.

Project Rooms The two large project rooms and the smaller one can be used for collaborative design events, formal meetings, or for informal brainstorming. They are adjacent to the control room and positioned to have a good views of the large screen displays, making it easy to link the ongoing flow of information with the design activities of project teams.

On any given day, there may be a team working on developing strategic initiatives in one project room, while another team uses the collaborative design process to solve a complex tactical problem in the adjacent room. Still others may come by for half an hour simply to take the pulse of the ongoing activities of the business.

This mingling of project teams in a single large space creates opportunities for people to interact spontaneously and to draw from each others' experience as they solve specific problems.

A curved wall is the focal point of each project room. Seven feet tall and 30 or 40 feet long, these walls are enormous white boards that are big enough to develop and present models as complex as the entire corporate strategic plan, detailed briefings on critical issues, or even elaborate marketing campaigns (Figure 10.5). The curve enables one to stand in the

Figure 10.5 **A Curved Writing Wall**
Photo by the author.

center of the space and clearly see a display of 300 square feet of information. There is simply no better way to see the overview *and* the details of complexity at the same time.

Depending on their size and their style of working, some organizations will need to have only one project room. Others may wish to have 10, making for a full-fledged conference center.

*   *   *

Management centers are lively places where people come to test out new ideas with their colleagues; to solve complex problems; to participate in large-scale business simulations and educational events; to catch up on the latest events. They will be centers for active learning, for dialogue and speculation and argument, and most of all for creating the future.

Management centers are also, of course, the ideal facilities for managing during crisis. Here, many people can work side by side with immediate access to complete information, developing and testing alternative responses, while others working remotely participate electronically. As information comes in, strategy can be mapped out in detail, and as it becomes clear what actions need to be taken, an entire organization can be communicated with and immediately mobilized for action.

Management centers are also ideal places for boards of directors to learn about what's really happening in their businesses. Whereas the former board room emphasized the importance of the hierarchy and expressed the stability of the enterprise with expensive wood paneling and an enormous table surrounded by stern, high-backed chairs, the new board room represents the need for continuous learning amid the rapidly changing marketplace. Whereas the members of the former board studied financial reports and one-page memos in quiet isolation, the members of the new board interact with everyone, from the CEO to the shipping dock workers, gathering information and giving it out at every opportunity.

Management centers are a long way from the four walls, desk, and chair occupied by the clerical workers of 1950; they are key components of the high performance knowledge infrastructure of the 21st century. By enabling so much information to be integrated in one place, management centers will have tremendous influence on the thinking of everyone who uses them, and on the effectiveness of organizational self-regulatory processes. They will, therefore, contribute enormously to the adaptiveness of the organizations that implement them.

COMPONENTS OF THE NEW WORK PLACE

Individual work spaces, project rooms, and management centers utilize four major design elements that provide the functionality that is essential for managing complexity:

1. Writing walls.

2. Furniture on wheels.

3. Aesthetics.

4. Technical systems.

1. Writing Walls

Many of the walls in these spaces are covered from top to bottom with white boards, so that an entire surface, seven feet tall by twenty, thirty, or even forty feet long is a single, continuous *tabula rasa* for drawing and writing. This work surface is hundreds of times larger than a pad of paper, and large enough to enable everyone on a team to work together on a single diagram, mapping out and understanding a complex problem. Tools such as magnetic symbols, rulers and compasses make it easy to design and display complex information (Figure 10.6).

Figure 10.6 **A Writing Wall**
This large writing wall enables individuals and groups of people to understand the detailed ramifications of complex ideas far more easily than they could using a smaller work surface. Photo by the author.

There is an ambiguity to spoken and written language because words mean different things to different people. Pictures eliminate much of this confusion, for pictures show relationships clearly and directly, helping people to share their ideas with the confidence that they are communicating effectively. Large working surfaces enable people to create images, flow charts, Venn diagrams, and illustrations that represent complexity in ways that words simply cannot convey. Thus, the irresistible axiom: "One picture is worth a thousand words."

Using partitions that are mounted on overhead tracks, on hinges, and on wheels, large spaces can be subdivided into smaller ones, so any room can be easily rearranged into two, three, or even four smaller rooms. These moveable dividing walls are also writing surfaces.

2. Furniture on Wheels

Nearly all of the furniture in the space is on wheels. Desks, tables, equipment stands, and chairs can be moved by any individual. For example, 10 individual desks could be instantly rolled aside, and replaced by four tables that join together to compose a large conference table. Later, they can be separated back into four components for four smaller team meetings. Later still, they can be moved aside and ten desks are brought back.

3. Aesthetics

The best of these facilities have yet another important attribute, a quality of aesthetics that both soothes and entertains the mind. When someone leans back to reflect on a new idea, or to formulate an intricate concept, the room itself offers something beautiful to engage the eye, while the mind pursues it own journey. Just as a walk in the park helps one to focus and relax, a mental stroll in a project room is aided by an aesthetically rich environment with engaging colors, forms, plants, and interesting things to look at and touch. There may be paintings, maps, sculptures, and even toys, rich and stimulating things that help to evoke those very qualities in the ideas that are generated there.

4. Technical Systems

The users of a work space, a project room, and a management center are able to adjust all of the environmental factors, including air temperature, music, natural lighting, and artificial lighting, to suit their needs and their moods.

In addition, there are power, phone, and computer network access jacks wired throughout the floor and walls that are immediately accessible: Pop open the lid, plug in a computer, a phone, or a modem, and immediately anyone can go to work. Centralized audio and video recording and playback systems can be remotely controlled from throughout the space.

Dedicated equipment, including, for example, laser printers and a fax machines, is available so that teams can work without interruption.

*   *   *

Project rooms and management centers with the qualities described here are not speculative, for many companies are already using these facilities, and more will do so in the coming years.

For example, Labor Secretary Robert Reich recognized the need for such a space in his organization, and after a year-long struggle with an entrenched bureaucracy, a 5,000 square foot project room was created by removing walls to make a large and open space. Teams from throughout Washington now come together to work on complex projects in the Labor Department 'skunkworks.'

Furniture manufacturers such as Steelcase now recognize that there are enough knowledge workers to constitute a market that worth serving. The company recently introduced a product called 'Personal Harbor and Commons' that elegantly provides both work spaces for individuals and project rooms for teams of knowledge workers. One user commented, "Decision-making time has been drastically reduced. . . . We're talking constantly and resolving issues on the spot. . . . We even developed a diagnostic test in five months that normally would have taken 14."[17]

Meanwhile, in the Steelcase R&D labs they are working on even more advanced tools for knowledge workers, including products which fully integrate computers and the workstations that they occupy.[18]

All of this makes it clear that offices that are designed and built in the future will probably not look or feel at all like the ones of the recent past. They have, after all, a much different purpose, that of leveraging every individual's capacity to learn and to take action. To do so, they will incorporate new tools and components that are just now merging into the mainstream. The prospects are excellent that these new tools will support new levels of productivity, enabling many organizations to experience the kind of productivity transformation that Chrysler demonstrated in the early 1990s.

PART FOUR

PRACTICE
Transformation

Change has no constituency. People like the status quo. They like the way it was. When you start changing things, the good old days look better and better. You've got to be prepared for massive resistance.[1]*—Jack Welch*

The practices by which corporations organize themselves are developed over time through processes of trial and error. Ultimately, a corporation succeeds in organizing itself, in regulating itself, when its leaders devise models and practices that enable it to adapt to its environment.

When the environment is changing rapidly, as it is today, these models must be frequently reexamined, and it is likely that they will also need to be frequently changed. When the necessary changes are fundamental and concern the basics of what the organization does, and how and why, then self-regulation must give way to something deeper. The shift from command and control to recognition and response is one such shift, a process of transformation by which a corporation's entire approach to organization is redesigned. Corporate transformation is thus a special case of self-regulation.

11

Transformation by Design

Organizational transformation is a complex and sometimes overwhelming process, but the design process can be used as a guide, making the shift from the old organization to a new one coherent and efficient. From the creation of the problem through the implementation and use of a new organizational model, teams with specific assignments search for and find the new information that make possible for lasting and appropriate change to occur.

e have we had so little time in which to do so much.[1] *—Franklin D. 942*

The work of transforming an organization can be overwhelming. There will be a flood of ideas, dreams, possibilities, and constraints confronting those who come face to face with the need for fundamental change, and somehow it must all be organized. The design process provides such a method. Just as it pertains to developing products and services, to authoring books, to developing corporate strategy, and to creating works of art, the design process can also be applied to the process of corporate transformation (Figure 11.1). It can provide coherence and sense of order, while enabling the broadest possible participation throughout the corporation. When it is combined with the practice of Collaborative Design described in Chapter 9, the transformation process can be accomplished even more quickly.

Fundamental change such as this begins with an organization's leaders, who must define both the condition and the vision in clear, explicit terms that no one can pretend to ignore. It will take more than a commitment from senior management, though, for ultimately people throughout an organization must participate in the change process:

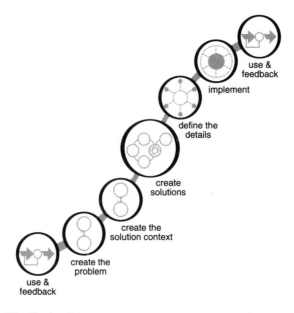

Figure 11.1 **The Design Process**

The Delta Consulting Group and Columbia University studied some two hundred and eighty-five companies during a fifteen-year period and found that forceful, larger-than-life leadership is critical to successful change. But they also found that the story is a little more complicated than the mythmakers would have us believe.... The companies most successful at change have nurtured skilled leaders at all levels.[2]

STEP ONE: CREATE THE PROBLEM

When marketplace reality does not match a corporation's expectations, and its vision of success remains unfulfilled, the problem is precisely that there *is* a gap between reality and the vision. The creative tension that results from this excruciating difference *compels* an organization to move forward, to throw off the past, and to create itself anew.

When the issues have been sufficiently well framed and a clear commitment has been made to transformation, a rigorous process of organizational redesign can begin. Instead of imposing change from the top of the hierarchy, however, the design process can be used to guide a process through which the whole organization can participate in creating comprehensive change. Because of the broad participation, this is likely to be faster and more effective than any decisions imposed by fiat.

This approach to corporate transformation relies on teams of people drawn from the entire organization working together in a coherent sequence to carefully frame the important issues and then solve them. In the process, they will create a new organization almost as a by-product of their focused efforts on improving the products and services that they produce, market, and sell.

In this process, senior management must define the overall context in which these changes will be implemented, and then create the teams that will do the work. Three different kinds of teams will participate (Figure 11.2):

a. The *avant garde*.

b. The facilitation team.

c. Analysis and solution design teams.

a. The Avant Garde

The team that initiates the transformation is the *avant garde*, a group of six to eight leaders from all levels and departments of the organization. At least one of the *avant garde* must be a senior manager, while others can be

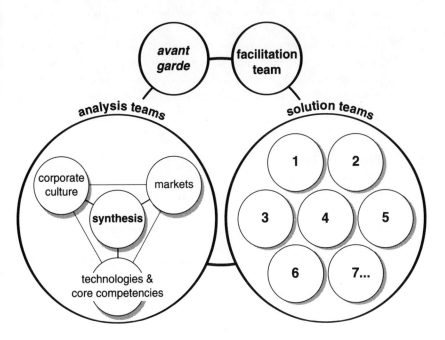

Figure 11.2 **Transformation Teams**

drawn from the leaders among the middle managers and line workers. Some of these people may also be from outside of the organization, for they bring a different perspective that will help the *avant garde* to avoid the tunnel vision that can develop when people have worked together in an organization for a long time.

This team will explore new models of organization and develop the language and concepts of transformation that will be used to create a new context for the entire organization. They will define the key terms and issues concerning the current condition and the vision, and they will design and guide the overall process through which the corporation will transform itself. Thus, the primary role of the *avant garde* is to establish the appropriate overall context in which transformation will take place.

The development of new language will be tremendously important in this process, for the ideas and concepts that people able to comprehend are closely linked with the language that they use to express them. While the language of command and control organizations includes phrases such as 'the chain of command,' 'climbing the corporate ladder,' 'the power struggle,' and 'decision-making authority,' the language of the transformed corporation is likely to include concepts such as 'the design process,' 'self-organizing systems,' 'knowledge workers,' and 'recognition and response.' These concepts were irrelevant, or perhaps nonexistent in the command and control environment, but now they will become central, organizing themes.

The *avant garde* must understand these new models and the language that describes them, and exemplify these concepts as well as the discovery process that others will experience as transformation proceeds. As the design process expands to include more people, the *avant garde* will stay in front, mapping the new territory in advance to help others find the best paths.

b. The Facilitation Team

The facilitation team is a group of five to ten people who support the *avant garde*. They are facilitators, researchers, writers, consultants, advisors, and artists who make the transformation process as easy for everyone as possible by designing and facilitating collaborative events. While the *avant garde* must focus on the key organizational issues of transformation, the content, the facilitation team focuses on the process itself, enabling individuals and teams to work as effectively as possible.

They also help the *avant garde* to define and communicate the specific issues of transformation. They may prepare reports, presentations, brochures, and videos that deliver the transformation message. Overall, their efforts complement and provide leverage to the work of the *avant garde*.

The facilitation team cannot be made up of senior management's already busy assistants, for their jobs must continue to focus on managing the daily flow of work. This team must be free to focus exclusively on the transformation process, to do whatever is necessary to support the individuals and teams that will be working throughout the organization. This is likely to be more than a full-time job.

In many organizations, these will be the only people working full-time on transformation, as everyone else will participate in conjunction with their ongoing responsibilities.

c. Analysis and Solution Design Teams

Together, the *avant garde* and the facilitation team work to support design teams that are drawn from the entire organization. Some teams, described in detail below, will be formed to analyze existing problems and practices and the world outside the corporation. Other teams will design and implement solutions that fit the changed conditions.

To ensure that every meaningful perspective is represented in the design process, the participants on these teams will include people from every department, every office, every hierarchical level throughout the organization, and the entire range of social and cultural perspectives.

Through participation in this process, everyone in the organization will have the opportunity to learn and to design, to question and experience for themselves. Transformation by design is a large-scale learning process, one involving everyone in the organization in *dialogue* about the organization, its present, and its future.

Peter Senge draws upon the work of physicist David Bohm to describe the specific character of dialogue and its importance in developing a clear understanding of complex issues:

> The purpose of dialogue is to go beyond any one individual's understanding. "We are not trying to win in a dialogue. We all win if we are doing it right." In dialogue, individuals gain insights that simply could not be achieved individually. "A new kind of mind begins to come into being which is based on the development of a common meaning . . . . People are no longer primarily in opposition, nor can they be said to be interacting, rather they are participating in this pool of common meaning, which is capable of constant development and change." In dialogue, a group explores complex difficult issues from many points of view. . . . *people become observers of their own thinking.*[3]

STEP TWO: CREATE THE SOLUTION CONTEXT

To create the solution context, analysis design teams consisting of four to ten people each will develop models of the present reality and the future requirements in three key areas:

a. Corporate culture.

b. Markets.

c. Technologies and core competencies.

a. Corporate Culture

A corporate culture naturally emerges when people interact with each other over a long period of time. Such a culture becomes a set of overriding models that define an organization's identity. If you talk to a Wal-Mart employee about his company, you're likely to learn something about Sam Walton's philosophy. In a five-minute conversation, one Wal-Mart employee suggested that I ought to read Sam Walton's biography. "It's all there," he said.[4] Then he said it again.

When I talked to a Nordstrom employee, I learned about the founding grandfathers, their small shoe store, and their determination to be the best. "They were very competitive," she said, and so is the entire organization today, 90 years and three generations of the Nordstrom family later.[5]

Similarly, Senior Vice President Pamela Godwin comments about the corporate culture of Direct Response Group: "We had been told—and now we know it's true—that before you can effect any significant change, you've first got to understand your company's culture. People behave logically in the context of their environment, so if you want employees to change their behavior you've got to create an environment that's aligned with your business strategy."[6]

One of the results of culture is to preserve a pattern of relationships that has become successful. Another is to distinguish between insiders and outsiders, between 'us' and 'them,' and so to help identify and resist outside influences. 'The way we do things around here' and 'the way we've always done it' are not just instructions, they are deeply held beliefs that provide cohesion. Consequently, outside influences that challenge these beliefs are suspect: *Corporate cultures resist change because that is what cultures do.*

All transformation efforts inevitably come face to face with adherents to an existing culture and their inherent resistance to change. From their perspective, transformation appears as a threatening outside influence, one that probably brings discomfort.

> The work of change agents is made enormously more delicate and uncertain by the fact that the mere presence of a change agent (recognizable as such) has about the same effect on an organization as an efficiency expert seen strolling across the factory floor with stopwatch in hand: it promptly induces bizarre and unpredictable alterations in the behavior of the System as the System begins to Kick Back against real or imagined intrusions upon its current equilib-

rium. Because of this effect, anyone who identifies him/herself as a 'change agent' is self-convicted of incompetence.[7]

The corporate culture design team develops a model of the current organization and its culture, describing its overall character and its strengths and weaknesses. They explore how the culture responds to change, which will assist the *avant garde* in selecting key leverage points that will help them overcome the inevitable resistance to change that develops (or may already have).

Overcoming this resistance is one of the most important challenges that the *avant garde* team must accomplish. Ultimately, significant change will occur as people come to understand its necessity, and this understanding will come about when people have had the opportunity to learn about the key issues.

b. Markets

There must be a very clear model of the needs of customers and of their capacity to pay for the products and services that enable those needs to be fulfilled. This design team has the task of understanding the corporation's overall market and its specific niche markets by defining the needs, expectations, and capabilities of today's and tomorrow's customers.

Organizations that produce disparate products and services for many kinds of customers may have subteams exploring them individually, in order to understand issues such as the following in detail:

- How do our products and services compare with those of competitors?

- How does the competition view the market?

- How do they plan to meet the customers' needs?

- What is most important to customers today?

- What will be most important in five years?

- How does technology impact the needs of customers?

- What are the long-term trends that will influence customer behavior?

- What could cause unexpected change in this industry?

Some of this information may already have been gathered, for this is what many research and development and marketing specialists spend a lot of time doing, and they may wonder why so much effort is now being put into work that has already been done. However, if the organization really needs to transform itself, if its products and services really do not fit the current needs and desires of customers, then it is likely that the existing models are inadequate in fundamental ways, and therefore the work that has been done may be correct in the specific but wrong in context, or vice versa. It's necessary to find out.

c. Technologies and Core Competencies

Rapid change in the marketplace means that the technologies that compose a corporation's products and services may soon be out of date. This design team develops a model of the current technologies and core competencies that the corporation depends on, as well as the short-term and the long-term technologies that the corporation will depend on in the future.

They seek to understand, most importantly, the life cycle of each technology on its own overall S-curve, how the organization's application of these technologies compares with its competitors, and what investments will be required to stay current with the overall marketplace.

- How do the technologies in use today compare with the technologies used by others?

- What are the advantages and disadvantages of each?

- Which technologies will become obsolete?

- How will future demand impact the development of replacements for existing technologies?

- What new technologies will become part of the products and services that our customers will expect?

- What will it cost to develop competence in these technologies?

- What will it cost to maintain competence in the existing technologies?

These questions lead to an evaluation of the core competencies that will be required for the short- and long-term futures of the organization. Honda is an example: "It is Honda's core competence in engines and power trains that gives it a distinctive advantage in car, motorcycle, and generator businesses."[8] Honda's engine development team consists of about 700 engineers who are working on gasoline engines, electric vehicles, and hydrogen and methanol engines:

Honda's Formula One engines have powered the Honda McLaren Marlboro team to seasonal championships for six years running, sealing Honda's reputation in Japan as an innovator and recharging company morale. More important, Honda's foray into racing has proven a fertile training ground for brainy engineers and spawned such technologies as the more efficient variable valve-timing system, which now shows up under ordinary Honda hoods.[9]

Another example is Hewlett-Packard, which has recently been organized around three core competencies that will enable the company to develop successful products in its critical markets. Says CEO Lewis Platt, "There are only a couple of other companies in the world that have the measurement, computation, and communications capabilities that we have."[10]

Determining a set of core competencies also determines which will *not* be core. Access to those competencies must be obtained though vendor relationships, alliances, and joint ventures.

Interactions Between Teams

As with reengineering projects, the modeling work of these teams will involve the development of 'process maps' that show in detail how the organization relates to the marketplace, for they will reveal the underlying character and leverage points for new opportunities.

As each of these teams develops their models, they will work to understand and contextualize the well-known and dominant trends of the marketplace. In addition, they will seek to identify the 'weak signals' that portend important events that are just now emerging and are not yet widely recognized or understood.

The assessments of corporate culture, markets, and technologies and core competencies cannot be done independently of one another, for each influences the others. To explore the many relationships between these areas, the three design teams work simultaneously, and interact with each other frequently. While each team has its own project room, the work will be most effective if all of the project rooms are part of a single, larger space that will enable people to have the spontaneous conversations that add so much value to the exploration process.

It is likely that some of the assessments will contradict one another. Members of one team may disagree significantly with the conclusions that another team reaches, and there may even be significant disagreement among the members of one team. These disagreements are valuable and important, for they expose differences in underlying assumptions or methods of analysis. When these assumptions are exposed, *they* enable fundamental issues to be resolved. *However, it may not be possible, at this time, to determine which assumptions are correct.* Many disagreements will concern expectations for the future, about which no one can be sure despite their strong opinions.

Since decisions will have to be made before it is clear which assumptions will prove to be true, understanding the differing viewpoints and their underlying assumptions creates the conditions for learning. This will lead to better choices in the future, as unfolding events reveal which assumptions were valid and which were not.

To support this learning, a key role for the facilitation team is to document these important dialogues so that there is a clear record of the differing viewpoints. This will enable future results to be compared with today's expectations. The record of this dialogue is a key element in the organization's library of models and supports the process by which these models can be tested and revised as conditions change.

As most organizations do not have sufficient resources to enable the participants on these design teams to leave their existing jobs, much of this work will have to be done in conjunction with ongoing responsibilities. This has the benefit of keeping the work focused in real-world concerns, but there is also a down side, for if the design work is not pursued diligently, it may not get done quickly enough and the whole process may get bogged down. Thus, the work can be compressed and done quickly by using the Collaborative Design process. Working without interruption for a week at the beginning and for another at the end of the project, with only a few weeks in between, prevents the process from dragging on indefinitely, and it limits the extra workload for the participants to a manageable period of time.

Synthesis

After each team has completed the work in its own domain, a fourth design team is constituted from the three to synthesize the separate assessments into an overall model of the corporation-in-its-markets for the present and the future. This is a model of the corporation on the S-curve of its own development and in the context of the industries in which it competes.

- What is our current position?

- What are the consequences of our position?

- Where are our competitors in relation to us?

- How long is it likely to be before we reach the crest of the S-curve?

- What alternatives are we likely to have then?

- What actions should be taken now?

The combined results of all the design teams reveals where the largest gaps between current reality and the vision really are. It is the basis from which a realistic assessment can be made of the resources that will be required to undertake the transformation process, and this is the *solution context*.

STEP THREE: CREATE SOLUTIONS

When the gap between current reality and the vision is clear, it will also be clear that the biggest obstacle to achieving success is the lack of specific knowledge in specific areas. Thus, the next step of the design process is to establish solution design teams to gather the new information that enables them to create the new knowledge that is needed. This is a very focused process of learning about what is necessary to achieve success in the marketplace.

By combining analysis of existing conditions with relevant new information, people will discover new ways of doing things that had not been apparent before. The lightbulbs of insight will flash on as people see how the future can be different (Figure 11.3).

These teams will seek new information from many sources. Some of the new information may be technical, and it will come from experts and

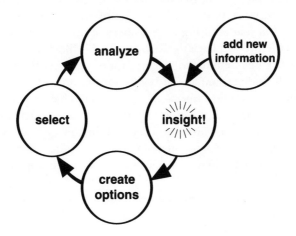

Figure 11.3 **Creating Solutions**

from other companies. Some of it will certainly be cultural, and it will come from careful study. Some of it will be market-oriented, and some of it will be strategic.

In the search for this information, solution teams will experiment with new ways of working, perhaps testing new ways of organizing a manufacturing process. Perhaps they will use reengineering to change the approach to administration, or accounting, or product development.

At Bell Atlantic, a reengineering team was established to redesign a vital element of the company's telephone service, one that accounted for 20 percent of its revenues and 50 percent of its profits. The company was losing customers to competitors who provided better service, and had to act quickly:

> The team took over operational responsibility for servicing customers in a part of central Pennsylvania ... empowered to make whatever changes in work methods and procedures that were necessary to cut the process time, reduce expenses, and produce a defect-free output. They were to discard all of the functional and departmental measurements and management objectives under which they used to work in their separate departments. Their only concern was figuring out how they could reduce cycle time, and improve the quality of the output concurrently. Within several months, the team was working with cycle times measured in days instead of weeks. In some cases they had reduced them to hours. The quality of the service began to improve dramatically, too.[11]

Some teams will visit other companies to explore how they handle specific issues. Others will literally move in with customers, working side by side to understand their needs and desires and the opportunities for new products and services. In the midst of GE's process of transformation, one team spent a full year studying the practices of nine leading global corporations, and their report became the basis of GE's 'Best Practices' program, which has since been emulated by corporations all over the world.

Some will study mountains of books and reports, seeking specific answers to detailed technical questions, or they will challenge themselves to develop better teamwork through experiential learning activities, such as ropes courses. Some individuals will reenroll in college courses; some will enroll for the first time. Some will negotiate new relationships with vendors and customers, while others will work with vendors to improve their own practices.

During the process of designing solutions, no existing practice will be left unexamined. In the process, new language will emerge to describe phenomena that are newly discovered, and a new corporate culture will emerge.

STEPS FOUR AND FIVE: DEFINE THE DETAILS AND IMPLEMENT

In the midst of the widespread design activity, it will become evident that transformation proceeds simultaneously from two different vantage points.

At the level of specific action, solution teams will discover and invent answers to their questions, define the details of their solutions, and implement the solutions. In so doing, they will change the way work is done in the organization. At the same time, the *avant garde* team continues to refine and spread the language of transformation from the vantage point of philosophy, leading the way with the definition of the vision and the strategies that will enable it to be achieved. The integration of the specific solutions and the philosophical perspective creates a completely new framework, a new context through which a new understanding of organization emerges through the acts of implementation (Figure 11.4).

As successful natural systems organize themselves spontaneously and specifically in response to environmental conditions *at the time,* so can the corporation. The design process is a method of systematically exploring the environmental situation and understanding it. By responding to this understanding, the character of the organization will then exist as a *consequence* of the environmental situation.

It is clear, then, that the primary objective of the design process is to create a dialogue that is comprehensive. This will yield the competence that will result in the appropriate design of the organization itself.

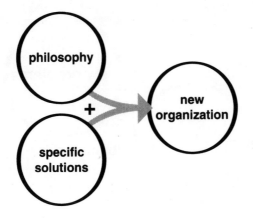

Figure 11.4 **New Organization**
A new organization emerges from the synthesis of an *overriding philosophy* and *specific solutions* that are developed by design teams working to solve specific issues and problems throughout the organization.

Implicit in this process is the awareness that conditions will definitely change, perhaps as soon as this afternoon, perhaps tomorrow. Perhaps they have already changed, and we just haven't become aware of it yet. Because the dialogue is now ongoing, when change is recognized, the dialogue itself will lead the members of the organization to take the actions that constitute adaptive responses.

STEP SIX: USE AND FEEDBACK

Once the specific implementation projects are under way, there is a broader issue which can then be dealt with, the design of the knowledge infrastructure. Through the transformation process, the learning modality and the habit of dialogue have been established through which a new organization has emerged. Together, these create the context in which it then becomes possible to engineer the organization's knowledge infrastructure to fit the new organization.

This infrastructure, consisting of elements including communications and information systems, the work place, and collaborative processes (which presumably the organization has become proficient at in the course of the transformation process itself) will support the now-ongoing dialogue through which the organization will continue to evolve. It will also, of course, support the work of producing the company's products and services

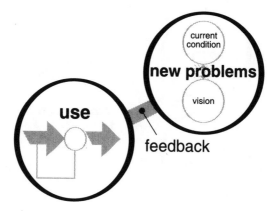

Figure 11.5 **New Problems**
Solving problems enables us to look at the universe in new ways and to discover thereby new problems that did not exist in the old universe. The design process starts again (see Figure 7.8, page 115).

that go out into the marketplace, which constitutes the use of the designed organization to fulfill the purposes for which it was designed.

From this use, feedback will arise as individuals discover what is now working, what is not, and what new problems have arisen.

As Buckminster Fuller pointed out, when you solve problems you do not just get solutions; perhaps more importantly you also get new problems to solve, problems that simply didn't exist in the old universe.[12]

The last step of the design process may also be the first step of another iteration. For the act of using creates anew the distinction between whatever the current condition is and the vision, from which comes the creative tension that again compels the design process forward (Figure 11.5). Evolution is never finished.

12

Transformation Strategies

There are four key strategies that can be used as levers to initiate transformation, and there is also a fifth that is often attempted but rarely succeeds. Each of the four strategies, or combinations of them, can be used to bring fundamental change to an organization.

Everybody wants to go to heaven but nobody wants to die.[1]—*Don Nix*

I want a revolution![2]—*Jack Welch*

The transformation of a large organization can take a long time, and the design process may involve many people, which may be feasible for organizations with plenty of cash and lots of time. For example, the transformation of Xerox took seven years, and former CEO David Kearns writes that one shouldn't expect it to go much faster in a large organization:

> It is foolish to think that it will happen overnight. In fact, it will not happen anywhere near as swiftly as most managers would like. Most of the time, it seems to move through a company at geological speed. It's a safe bet that the change in most organizations will take five to seven years. Not surprisingly, that five-to-seven-year time frame is offputting to a lot of chief executives. They would like to see change tomorrow, and if they have to they'll settle for it taking a year. But the thought of waiting more than five years is disconcerting. Yet if you don't accept this timetable going in, you will never accomplish your goals.[3]

The process of transformation by design described in Chapter 11 simultaneously addresses the entire scope of a corporation, but many organizations do not have the resources to engage in so broad-ranging a process. Cash is limited, and the precious time of talented people is even more so.

This chapter describes transformation strategies that are based on the process described in Chapter 11, but adapted to diverse perspectives and focused more specifically on key leverage points.

After surveying numerous approaches that have been implemented, they seem to group themselves into five basic themes:

1. Pretending.

2. A new organizing principle.

3. Learning.

4. Technology.

5. Procreation.

It may also be appropriate to combine these strategies.

1. Pretending

Although the strategy of pretending has never been known to be successful, that doesn't stop CEOs from attempting it. Companies pretend to be leaders, or they pretend to undergo transformation, but when prevailing managerial assumptions remain unquestioned, the voice of marketplace reality is too strongly suppressed to penetrate to the isolated inner core of corporate culture.

Reflecting this tendency to resist real change, Hammer and Champy report that:

> many companies that begin reengineering don't succeed at it. They end their efforts precisely where they began, making no significant changes, achieving no major performance improvement, and fueling employee cynicism with yet another ineffective business improvement program. Our unscientific estimate is that as many as 50 percent to 70 percent of the organizations that undertake a reengineering effort do not achieve the dramatic results they intended."[4]

Another way to pretend to transform is to apply business strategies that create the illusion of leadership without the insight that makes it substantial. In his distinctive *Innovation and Entrepreneurship* (1985), Peter Drucker analyzed IBM's strategy and pointed out the likelihood of the company's demise because of its strategic approach to product development. Drucker's prediction was published, it must be emphasized, a full *seven* years before IBM's weaknesses were acknowledged by company's directors by their firing of John Akers. Not only did IBM's leaders miss subtle warning signs, they also missed this very direct one: Prevailing assumptions can indeed be strong filters.

Drucker predicted that the company would falter because its product development strategy was based on a practice he identifies as 'creative imitation'. Creative imitators seize on innovations developed by others, but they do a better job of commercializing than the originator:

> IBM, the world's foremost creative imitator . . . has successfully imitated every major development in the office-automation field. As a result, it has the leading product in every single area. But because they originated in imitation, the products are so diverse and so little compatible with one another that it is all but impossible to build an integrated, automated office out of IBM building blocks. It is thus doubtful that IBM can maintain leadership in the automated office and provide the integrated system for it. Yet this is where the main market of the future is going to be in all probability. And this risk, the risk of being too clever, is inherent in the creative imitation strategy.[5]

This incremental and opportunistic strategy ignored the broader patterns of technological evolution that were driving the marketplace, and the company realized the truth too late to prevent more than 100,000 people from losing their jobs. A year after Akers was fired, IBM's new CEO, Louis Gerstner, presented a predictable strategy, one intended to reduce the company's reliance on mainframe computers.[6]

Pretending to be a leader or pretending to undergo transformation may be attractive options because they avoid the very difficult work of rethinking an organization, but such strategies cannot be successful over the long term.

2. A New Organizing Principle

When leaders realize that there is a need for transformation, they may also realize that it is the central, organizing idea of a corporation that must be reconsidered. Facing a deeply held assumption and admitting that it no longer fits reality creates the space for new ideas, new visions, and new principles to emerge. Perhaps eventually one emerges that is inherently compelling, one that creates an entirely new context that enables everyone in the organization *to see themselves differently than before.*

By seeing themselves differently, individuals can then accept new organizational images that support new ways of working, new policies, and new strategies that bring a company into alignment with the reality of the marketplace.

This is the most powerful of the transformation strategies—and the simplest. It is also perhaps the most difficult to accomplish, for issues are rarely so clear.

The transformation of Semco is an example of the power of a new organizing principle:

> When I took over Semco from my father twelve years ago, it was a traditional company in every respect, with a pyramidal structure and a rule for every contingency. . . . One of my first acts . . . was to throw out the rules. Semco's standard policy is no policy. . . . Today, our factory workers sometimes set their own production quotas and even come in on their own time to meet them, without prodding from management or overtime pay. They help redesign the products they make and formulate the marketing plans. Their bosses, for their part, can run our business units with extraordinary freedom, determining business strategy without interference from the brass. They even set their own salaries, with no strings. Then again, everyone will know what they are, since all financial information at Semco is openly discussed. We simply do not believe our employees have an interest in coming in late, leaving early, and doing as little as possible for as much money as their union can wheedle out of us. After all, these same people raise children, join the PTA, elect mayors, governors, senators, and presidents. They are adults. At Semco, we treat them like adults. We trust them. Semco has grown six-fold despite withering recessions, staggering inflation, and chaotic national economic policy. Productivity has increased nearly sevenfold. Profits have risen fivefold. And we have had periods of up to fourteen months in which not one worker has left us. We have a backlog of 2,000 job applications. . . .[7]

The practice of business process reengineering also utilizes the power of new organizing principles (if the company undertaking reengineering happens to be one of the 30 to 50 percent that follow it through to completion). Most companies are segmented into departments, and work is passed from department to department in a linear fashion. Communications are obstructed by departmental barriers. Reengineering eliminates this segmentation of work by identifying the underlying processes that add value to the company's products and services. The barriers to cooperation between departments are eliminated as people focus on understanding the real work required to fulfill the needs of customers. The distinctions between departments then appear arbitrary, which, of course, they are. This very shift from 'departmental thinking' to 'process thinking' is the equivalent of a new organizing principle around which a business can then be operated.

3. Learning

In its fullest expression, process thinking leads to an understanding that supports organizational flexibility. Individuals respond immediately to new information that comes their way, even when it calls for new processes that contradict established practices. This, of course, is the learning process.

Since learning occurs when an individual wants to learn, it is beyond the control of any organization. Nevertheless, many corporations offer education programs in the hopes that they will stimulate learning to occur, and many of them have been very successful. Hammer and Champy present it this way:

> If jobs in reengineered processes require that people not follow rules, but rather that they exercise judgment in order to do the right thing, then employees need sufficient education so that they can discern for themselves what the right thing is. Traditional companies stress employee *training*—teaching workers how to perform a particular job or how to handle one specific situation or another. In companies that have reengineered, the emphasis shifts from training to education—or to hiring the educated. Training increases skills and competence and teaches employees the 'how' of a job. Education increases their insight and understanding and teaches the 'why.'[8]

During the 1980s, both Xerox and General Electric underwent corporate transformations that were driven by educational processes. Former CEO David Kearns presented the story of the Xerox transformation in *Prophets in the Dark* (co-authored with consultant David Nadler):

> One of the fundamental things organizations instinctively do is institutionalize the things they did that made themselves fat and sassy. They sort of hardwire these behavior traits into the way they work. In reasonably stable environments, that's a perfectly good procedure to follow. What has worked well for me ought to continue to work well for me. But environments rarely remain stable, and so what happens is that the sources of success in the past become the seeds of failure in the future. Over and over again, we've seen this pattern. That's exactly what happened at Xerox. We had lots of people at Xerox who were proficient at selling copiers into an expanding marketplace in which there was virtually no competition. Once the environment changed, the old mind-set worked against the organization in a deadly way.[9]

By 1982, Xerox's share of the American copier market had dropped from an estimated 80 percent to only 13 percent in a span of just six years, and Kearns saw that the company might be out of business entirely by 1990 unless it dramatically improved the quality of its products and services. To do so, Kearns initiated a program called 'Leadership Through Quality' through which *all* 100,000 Xerox employees were educated in the concepts and methods of continuous quality improvement. The education process alone took four years. The time spent educating Xerox's 100,000 workers, "totaled one thousand six hundred and forty-four man-years. That was a big investment, but it was one of the best we ever made."[10]

By applying the total quality approach to Xerox products and services, Kearns hoped that the company could be saved. It took a full seven years to turn the company around, but by 1989 Xerox's share of the American copier market had increased to 19 percent, and its revenues, income, and return on assets had all increased significantly. At the end of 1989 Xerox received the Malcolm Baldridge National Quality Award, marking the company's ascent to the pinnacle of the quality movement.[11]

At General Electric, CEO Jack Welch faced a situation similar to the one that Kearns faced at Xerox. When he took over the company in 1981, Welch saw that GE would soon begin to decline unless fundamental organizational issues were addressed. This story is presented in Noel Tichy and Stratford Sherman's *Control Your Destiny Or Someone Else Will:*

> Where others saw strength, Welch saw weakness. GE's executives, disciplined but submissive, knew how to follow the company's rigid rules. But when the outside world started to change, many of GE's procedures and systems became irrelevant. The self-confidence that had characterized the company's managers began to erode. Left to pursue its course for another decade or so, this apparently healthy company might have become another Chrysler. Instead of waiting for trouble, the CEO pushed for radical change long before most people recognized it as necessary.[12]

Even before he had become CEO, Welch knew that he would implement major changes, and he had told the head of GE's corporate education center, "I want a revolution!"[13] Doing as he proclaimed, Welch changed the composition, structure, and the practices of GE in many ways during the 1980s.

Most of all, Welch wanted to change GE's culture, to make people in the giant corporation more responsive to the market, and to do so he eliminated three to five layers of management throughout the GE hierarchy. Still, by 1988 he felt that there were too many GE managers who had not accepted the open management approach that he believed was necessary. To take his revolution to everyone in the corporation, Welch's ideas for a wide-open educational process to transform GE became the Work-Out program described in Chapter 9:

Work-Out began with four major goals:

1. Building trust: GEers at all levels had to discover that they could speak out candidly without jeopardizing their careers. Only then would GE get the benefit of its employees' best ideas.

2. Empowering employees.

3. Elimination of unnecessary work.

4. A new paradigm for GE: In effect, Welch wanted the whole organization to participate in defining itself.[14]

*   *   *

The Xerox and GE examples show that learning and education are powerful methods through which transformation can be implemented. Today, countless companies are implementing quality improvement programs through which learning is changing all aspects of their operations.

4. Technology

Sometimes it is not possible to articulate a new organizing principle, perhaps because no one has actually thought of one that makes sense. In the absence of such a principle, it is still possible to initiate transformation by implementing technology that changes an organization's knowledge infrastructure and thereby increases the level of interaction within the company and between a company and its environment. For organizations whose leaders are able to express new organizing principles, the implementation of communications and information technologies can expedite the transformation process.

For example, technologies that augment communication pervasively influence relations between individuals by making it easier for people to interact, thereby influencing all aspects of an organization's culture.

Real time technologies that eliminate information-processing lag change the way people think about business information by speeding the time index of thinking and action to match the pace of activities in the marketplace. Suddenly it becomes possible to anticipate the market in new ways, which is why real time is being applied throughout the retail industry.

Military organizations worldwide are specifically organized around technology because technology is fundamental to military strategy at all levels, whatever current the technologies happen to be. Reflecting this close linkage, when a new generation of technology comes into usage, the organization of the military changes almost immediately as a consequence.

Real time systems have had a tremendous impact in the military. They have shifted many of the command functions of battle away from the battlefield itself and into remote command posts from which senior officers can issue commands directly to individuals in the fighting force that is hundreds or thousands of miles away. Similarly, ordinary citizens observe the battle from its midst while sitting in their living rooms, and then impact the conduct of battles and wars through the political process.[15]

Neither politics nor war will ever be the same now that control of television broadcasts can be the decisive difference in military and civil conflict, as exemplified by recent events in the Philippines and Russia.

The Philippine revolution against Ferdinand Marcos was carried live on local TV. When Marcos showed his weakness during a live broadcast, popular opposition ignited immediately, and it was only a matter of days before he was forced to leave the country.

In a short article on the failed Soviet coup of August, 1991, technology observers Don Clark and Ken Siegmann point out that:

> Western news broadcasts, telephone calls, fax and electronic messages played pivotal roles in coordinating popular opposition. Amazingly, Cable News Network actually used a Soviet satellite to beam its reports back to the United States. ... Whatever the reasons for the free flow of information, the events of the week show that technology doesn't simply concentrate power in the hands of central authority. It also shares that power with people—and can bring them together for a higher purpose.[16]

Elsewhere, the Palestinian Intifada was coordinated by fax machines, which Israeli soldiers destroyed at every opportunity, while in China, four years after Tian'anmen Square, high technology communications are opening a country that has kept itself closed for centuries. Fax machines are being used widely, as are computers. Many people are using electronic bulletin boards and electronic mail to communicate within and outside of the country. Even satellite dishes are becoming common, and although government leaders would like to restrict their use, the Army earns profits by selling equipment to the public, and a government factory planned to build 60,000 to 70,000 satellite dishes in 1993 alone.[17]

Applying technology to achieve organizational transformation inevitably brings existing organizational structures into question, for a free flow of information transcends old ideas and old boundaries. It doesn't necessarily have to lead to a *coup d'état*, but there is likely to be a revolution of some sort, and there will certainly be a great opportunity to introduce transformational change into the corporate culture.

5. Procreation

Another approach to transformation is procreation, which occurs when a company creates a new offspring with the autonomy to create its own identity. For example, GM established its Saturn division with a clean slate, with no history or bad habits to inhibit its full development in the marketplace. In that choice was a tacit acknowledgment that *fundamental* change would not be successful within the existing divisions of the company under the current corporate leadership.

The subsequent success of Saturn has been reassuring to GM stockholders, but the growing adolescent absorbed billions of dollars of GM's capital, forcing the company's other divisions to slow the development of new cars. The very existence of Saturn may have indirectly increased the pressure on the others GM divisions while simultaneously making it more difficult for them address the causes of their decline. As Saturn edged toward and finally achieved profitability, some GM divisions slipped further and further into demise.

Oldsmobile slipped furthest. In 1986, Olds sold about one million cars, but by 1992 the company sold only 389,000 cars, while 16 of its 3000 dealers *did not sell a single Olds* in 1992.[18] It gets worse. The Olds image is considered by GM management to be so badly tarnished that the new, 1994 Oldsmobile Aurora will carry the Olds name only inside, *under* the glove compartment door.

Meanwhile, due to the shortage of capital at GM, new Oldsmobiles now on the drawing boards won't be introduced until as late as 1998, and one has to wonder if the division will even exist then.

Saturn, on the other hand, will still be going strong if current trends continue, and therein lies the essence of the procreation strategy. Saturn is a new entity, conceived and raised to live in an environment in which the old entity no longer fits, and in the case of many of GM's divisions, may never fit again.

It should be noted, however, that the parent doesn't necessarily have to die in the process of giving birth. For example, during the 1980s, Japanese auto companies Honda, Toyota, and Nissan all established new divisions to market cars in the U.S. Honda was immediately successful with its Acura, Toyota with its Lexus, and Nissan somewhat less so with Infiniti. While investing in these new divisions, market shares of the Japanese parent companies remained steady, showing that the parent need not sacrifice all for the child.

United Airlines is another example of procreation. United has lost business to competitors such as Southwest, which has much lower costs and can therefore charge lower fares. In response, United sold itself to its own employees in exchange for $5 billion of reductions to its payroll cost structure, thereby recreating itself with a lower cost structure that it hopes will be competitive. In addition, the new United spawned a separate airline offspring that will compete directly with Southwest by copying Southwest's cost and pricing structures and operating methods.

A third example of procreation is the laser printer division of Hewlett-Packard, which was established in 1981. Rather than opening the new division at its Palo Alto headquarters, HP established the division a safe distance away in Boise, Idaho, to give it freedom to develop a culture suited to its market. Today the division accounts for 40 percent of HP's income.[19]

VISUALIZING TRANSFORMATION

Once a corporation has embarked on the transformation journey, it is likely to encounter landmarks that vary surprisingly little from one organization to the next: There is a pattern to transformation.

To visualize this pattern, we return to the S-curve model. By definition, an organization that must undergo transformation is one that has reached or will soon reach the crest of its S-curve, a peak beyond which decline of some sort is inevitable.

Recognizing that this is happening, perhaps because of faltering business in the marketplace, it becomes undeniably clear to an organization's leaders that transformation is required.

In Figure 12.1 we see an organization approaching the crest of its S-curve. As it passes the crest, the pattern of declining marginal returns sets in to its operations (see the Introduction). The cost of being in business gradually increases, while the profits do not. Performance, productivity, and morale falter.

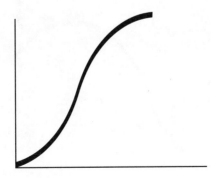

Figure 12.1   **The Crest of the 'S'**
Once an organization reaches the crest of its S-curve, its past successes may be gone forever.

Perhaps the market has shifted to new technologies that the firm does not have access to; or to a new price structure that cannot be matched. Perhaps new competitors are capturing market share through intensive marketing and promotion.

Some will interpret the situation as a temporary blip, beyond which there is yet promise (Figure 12.2). Perhaps they are right; perhaps not. A design team will have to gather all of the available information and make a decision.

The ultimate cause, or causes, may presently be well concealed, but persistent inquiry eventually turns up root causes. If the decline is, upon examination, inexorable, then one of the strategies described above, or some combination of them, must be brought into play. In this action, the seed of a new entity comes into existence (Figure 12.3).

The seed can take many forms, depending on the selected strategies. It may be a figurative entity, a new principle that gloriously lights up the night sky. It may be an education program that leads to changes in how everyone thinks and works. It may be new infrastructure that subtly changes communications within the corporation, enabling new, adaptive behaviors to emerge. Or it may literally be a new division or a new company.

Whether it is a literal offspring or only a figurative one, it is a separate entity, existing outside of the parent.

If there has been sufficient lead time or a visionary in the organization who foresaw this situation in advance, the development of the seed may be a gradual process. If, however, this development takes place during a crisis, then the seedling may be hurriedly incubated and rushed into the market, incomplete but better than nothing. Either way, those involved in creating

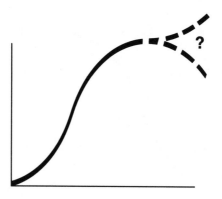

Figure 12.2 **A Temporary Plateau?**
It may be possible that this is a temporary plateau, or it may be the beginning of the ultimate demise. Which will it be?

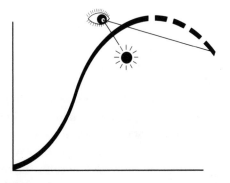

Figure 12.3 **The New Entity**
In response to imminent decline, a new entity is established with an identity that is separate from the existing organization. This entity embodies the qualities that are needed in the new marketplace, qualities that the old organization is unable to develop for itself because of its inability to change.

the fledgling work day and night to clarify its identity, and to understand and implement the intricate details of its design and operations. This can be a feverish, exhausting, and exhilarating process, filled with hope and expectation.

When the time has come, ready or not, the new entity is pushed out into the marketplace, and begins its development at the base of its own S-curve. Almost immediately it is likely to encounter the old organization, and there is a collision as the older, and probably much larger organization becomes aware of the infant's existence (Figure 12.4).

Figure 12.4 **Collision**
Almost immediately, the new entity encounters the old organization and a conflict ensues. The old organization attempts to control the new entity, to overpower it and neutralize its innovations because they pose a threat to the old ways.

There is likely to be resistance, for the established order will resist change, as culture does, and it will attempt to use its larger size and momentum to envelop and overwhelm the new order to overcome the threat of change that the new one represents. Despite their success, innovations developed by Saturn were adopted by other GM divisions only slowly, reluctantly: "One company that could pay more attention to Saturn's innovation is GM. Some outsiders are pushing it to implement Saturn-style training programs. Others want to see GM divisions adopt rewards for high customer-satisfaction ratings. But so far, with the exception of anti-lock brakes developed for Saturn and now used in some other makes, there has been little cross-pollination."[20]

There is a difficult interaction between the two vectors, as old and new coexist in a power struggle which may be subtle, or it may be out in the open.

Some will see the new entity as a welcome opportunity. "At last," they will say, "something is really going to happen around here!" Others will doubt, sincerely wondering if this is really necessary. There is risk inherent in the emergent entity, and it is probably frightening.

Others will suggest that the new entity is just a fad, and they will attempt to wait it out as many managers at GE did. Perhaps they will point to the disturbing failure rate of reengineering projects. Still others will see that they stand to lose protected positions in the bureaucracy, and they will resist, perhaps fiercely.

Many will have never experienced anything like this kind of change in their entire professional lives, and they will not be prepared for it now. Imagine the feelings of an Oldsmobile employee who, despite a dedicated career of good work and the sincere good work of thousands of his colleagues, sees his company in fatal decline. Assembly plants close, and people who have only worked in one place, at one job, for 20 or even 30 years find themselves unemployed and without recourse.

However, it is not just businesses that experience such transformations, for they occur throughout human culture and the natural world. The same pattern exists in the age-old conflicts between parents and energetic teenagers, and in conflicts between established rulers and the leaders of revolutions.

It even occurs in the shift from one conceptual framework to another throughout the sciences. In his study of the process of scientific discovery, historian Thomas S. Kuhn points out that established scientific theory provides a framework in which researchers explore and interpret the universe. Inevitably, they discover discrepancies in established models, and as they probe more deeply they find more cause to doubt those models. Eventually enough evidence accumulates to enable someone to formulate a new and different theory, which then stands in contrast to established theory.

In physics, Newton's model defined the scope of research for hundreds of years. As technology advanced, new techniques enabled researchers to identify a world in which Newton's models did not seem to work. At this stage, some saw only a Newtonian universe, while others saw only the universe where Newton's models did not apply.

Kuhn identifies these contrasting viewpoints as 'paradigms,' and he describes the difficult tumult that occurs as scientists grapple to understand strange new worlds:

> The proponents of competing paradigms are always at least slightly at cross-purposes. Neither side will grant all the non-empirical assumptions that the other needs in order to make its case. . . . Though each may hope to convert the other to his way of seeing his science and its problems, neither may hope to prove his case. . . . Just because it is a transition between incommensurables, the transition between competing paradigms cannot be made a step at a time, forced by logic and neutral experience. Like the gestalt switch, it must occur all at once (though not necessarily in an instant) or not at all.[21]

Just as Einstein captured the essence of a new perspective of the physical world with the theory of relativity, the emergent business entity must likewise break through the resistance to preserve its identity and its opportunity. Leadership plays a predominant role in this process, for no organization can make this transition without leadership that protects the new venture in its inevitable conflict with the old culture.

As we have seen, CEOs who do not grasp the essence of this situation lack the means to transform their corporations. Since today it is an accepted practice to fire CEOs whose corporations do not perform up to expectations, mastering the strategies of transformation is surely fundamental to success as a corporate leader.

While the conflict between two organizational paradigms is at its peak, an abundance of information throughout the organization contributes to a rational and coherent dialogue, while secrecy and the withholding of information creates an environment of fear. The knowledge infrastructure can thus play an important role at this stage, for if everyone has the means to communicate openly with everyone else, the likelihood of sincere dialogue increases. Many of these issues can also be resolved through the processes of collaboration, as GE's Work-Out demonstrates.

If the new entity prevails in its struggle for existence, it consolidates its start-up and seeks to establish itself as a mature and profitable entity, advancing up the S-curve. Only then it is possible to transfer its innovations

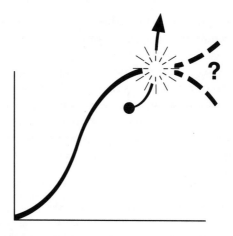

Figure 12.5 Innovation Transfer
If the new entity is well designed and receives strong support, it can prevail and continue to develop its own identity. Only then can its innovations be transferred to the old organization. These innovations may stimulate the renewal of the old organization, in which case it begins the ascent again.

to those who were steeped in the old culture in a systematic way (Figure 12.5). The old vector may then begin to be transformed following the example set by its offspring.

Over the course of decades, it is likely that an organization will repeatedly be faced with such transformative challenges. Each crisis presents the opportunity for transformation into a new entity, and to thereby achieve new standards of organizational performance. This process of leaping from

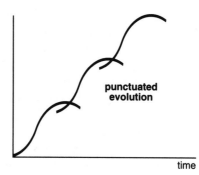

Figure 12.6 Punctuated Evolution
The model of punctuated evolution describes the development of new adaptive qualities and new species and is similar to the development of organizations and their products.

200

S-curve to S-curve is called punctuated evolution,[22] and it is the same process that characterizes the evolution of products and services. They are progressively refined over time, in response to marketplace demands and expectations, and in response to innovations by competitors (Figure 12.6). Each generation restates that which is still viable from the previous generation and adds new capabilities that contribute to the overall acceleration of change throughout society.

As the process of product development leads to the evolution of the marketplace as a whole, the same process must be applied to the evolution of the corporations that participate in the marketplace. If corporations do not evolve with the market, they will surely be left behind among the countless members of the species *corpus extinctus*.

But by practicing the organized abandonment of products and services as well as its organizational models, a corporation can take the initiative and have much more control over its own destiny. For unlike the individual organism that is limited to but one lifetime in a single body, the corporate organism can transcend such limits and pass its technical knowledge from generation to generation while transforming itself in response to evolving conditions. This is the life cycle of the evolving corporation.

13

The Evolving Corporation

As the information economy continues to develop during the coming decades, recognition and response organizations will face many challenges. We are in an unprecedented situation, for humanity is now responsible for its own future and for the future of the earth itself. Among the most important issues that we will face in dealing with these responsibilities are the balance between economic growth and the restraint that will be necessary to preserve the earth, and the balance between the needs and capacities of individuals and the power of institutions. The way that we handle these issues will be significant in defining the future: The future is up to us.

We have modified our environment so radically that we must now modify ourselves in order to exist in this new environment.[1]—Norbert Wiener

The art of management is creating an organization which is able to continuously evolve.[2]—Michael Rothschild

We are not the helpless subjects of evolution—we are evolution.[3]—Erich Jantsch

The ongoing experiment called 'human evolution' was once a matter of genetic mutation and natural selection in an omnipotent natural environment, but now that humans can modify the environment on a massive scale, the environment is as subject to us as we are to it. Thus, the driving force of evolution has shifted from biology and genetics to the exponentially changing human culture.

Although we are the creators of human culture, it would be an exaggeration to say that we control it, for the truth is that we don't know what we're doing. We are simultaneously the experimenters *and* the experiment itself, a risky proposition if ever there was one.

As the work of genetic engineers moves out of laboratories and into the marketplace, the human impact on the evolutionary process will become even more pronounced, and the acceleration of change will receive yet another boost thereby sustaining the exponential trend for at least the next few decades. The complexity that we will be called upon to deal with will steadily increase simply as a consequence of the very evolution of our culture.

So, each day we set out to achieve our goals, our dreams, and our visions in a marketplace that is, for all intents and purposes, infinitely complex. In this milieu, the attempts by CEOs and senior managers to control the enterprise are doomed, for the variety of the marketplace overwhelms organizations that are tightly controlled from the top. They simply cannot respond quickly enough to changing conditions, and the pattern of declining marginal returns now prevails over all attempts to maintain control.

We are witnessing the decline of the command and control organizational model, as well as the demise of those executives who cling to it. It is because of this that so many CEOs lost their jobs in the 1990s, and also because of this that Gilbert Amelio, CEO of National Semiconductor, comments, "Give up control to get something better."[4]

A new set of organizational models is coming into focus that balance control with much greater autonomy, enabling individuals throughout the corporation to take risks, to innovate, and to respond to the new conditions that they discover in the marketplace day after day.

In this new organization, it is not people that must be managed, but *information*. Information is the difference that makes a difference in the marketplace, and it is the element that unifies the individuals of a corporation into coherence. Information is the key strategic asset, for it is transformed into the knowledge that makes distinctive products and services that achieve success in the marketplace. A new version of the ROI is increasingly important to all managerial decision making: the Return on Information.

The transformation of information into knowledge can *only* be done by individuals, working alone and working together in teams, and therefore organizations must systematically cultivate in all of their members the capacities to *learn* and to *design*, for these capacities are the methods by which information is transformed into knowledge.

Through learning and designing, individuals create the products and services that are delivered to the marketplace, and through further learning and design individuals customize them to fit the specific needs of specific customers.

Through the aggregate of these acts of adaptation, corporations evolve into greater fitness with the marketplace, which itself continues to evolve.

None of this, however, will happen by itself. It can occur only with intent, and only by design. Corporate leaders must take the initiative to question the assumptions that have dominated organizational thinking for more than 100 years, and to replace those that are obsolete (a great many) with models that can more accurately serve today's and tomorrow's realities.

FUTURE PATTERNS

Those corporations that succeed in the marketplace of the coming decades will do so by managing continually accelerating change. They will surely be well tested, for it is clear that emerging conditions will continue to bring significant challenges.

One of the most compelling of these concerns the rate of change itself. Today's exponential rate of change means that there is less and less time to respond to all manner of events, and we see it as a curve that is ascending almost vertically (Figure 13.1). Throughout society, many phenomena show the same vertical line: Population growth continues exponentially, as does the consumption of resources, the speed of computers, and the growth of databases.

The S-curve model suggests that these exponential phenomena will eventually taper off, but no ones knows when. And what then? In the meantime, how much change can society endure? How many people can the earth support before starvation or plague brings population growth to sta-

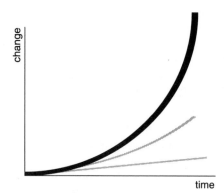

Figure 13.1 **Exponential Change**

bility? What suffering will there be if this occurs? Can the economy as we know it endure?

During the 1960s and 1970s, MIT professor Jay Forrester studied these issues using a pioneering computer modeling program that he and others developed. Many of the scenarios they developed showed explosive population growth, followed by equally steep population declines, a massive dying caused by scarcity of resources and toxic levels of pollution. Forrester's models have been disturbingly accurate over the 20 years since they were first published[5] (Figures 13.2 and 13.3). The prospects are frightening.

GROWTH OR DEVELOPMENT

While three billion humans live in relative comfort, more than two billion do not, and the gulf between the haves and the have-nots is widening. Ricardo Semler offers this prognosis:

> In a few decades all that will be left of the First World will be a few ghettos of the super-rich, islands of luxury surrounded by misery. There will be a lot of Cairo in Paris, Mexico in Colorado, and Syria in Switzerland. And as the Third

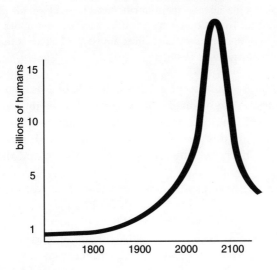

Figure 13.2 **Boom and Bust**
Jay Forrester developed a series of computer models of human society which suggested that under many different sets of conditions, the human population would increase quickly during the early 21st century, leading to a catastrophic decline thereafter as starvation and pollution combined to kill billions. In the 20 years since Forrester published his work, the trend has followed his predictions with frightening accuracy.

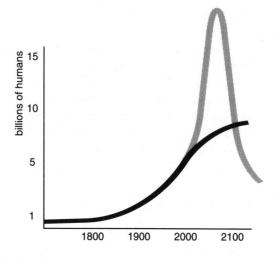

Figure 13.3 **Stabilization**
Forrester's models also showed that certain combinations of policies could lead to a stabilization of population growth, thus averting catastrophe, but these policies have not generally been followed.

> World makes it glacial movement north, it will leave places like Somalia, Bangladesh, and the Ivory Coast, which will become an even more abject Fourth World. . . . These cautionary tales illustrate what I believe is the biggest challenge any business faces: change.[6]

Human culture impacts the earth and its inhabitants on a massive scale through the aggregate of small-scale actions taken by individuals, such as the destruction of the Amazon rain forest, acid rain from industrial plants, water pollution, the destruction of ozone, and through massive one-time events such as Chernobyl, the Exxon *Valdez* oil spill, and the oil fires in Kuwait.

The Exxon *Valdez* oil spill exemplifies one of the key problems of the world which we are creating. Although 8,528 tankerloads of oil made it safely though Prince William Sound, all had the possibility of doing severe damage to the ecosystem. The 8,529th tankerload, carried by the Exxon *Valdez*, did not make it safely, and the ecosystem sustained severe damage. The possibility of this damaging event was not matched by a comparable capacity to respond when the possibility became a reality.

Unfortunately, it is true throughout human history that we have a capacity to destroy which is far greater than our capacity to create: Only nature and time can grow a tree, or create a barrel of oil or a gallon of fresh water.

The rate of change increases the frequency of significant events—and their magnitude—and moves society further from stability (Figure 13.4).

As the consequences of our actions affect ever-larger portions of our whole system, our capacity to respond to them must increase commensurably, or we risk severe and permanent damage to the earth and to our society. We are at the threshold of such damage today.

There is a key distinction that helps to frame this issue, the important distinction between *growth* and *development*. Whereas growth suggests the continued exponential expansion of consumption, development implies that we can learn to create the goods and services we want while consuming less and less per person. Clearly, the emphasis on continued growth can only assure that we accelerate our own demise, for there are absolute limits, that we will reach sooner or later.[7]

Consequently, the role of the economy in human society will necessarily be redefined in the coming decades. The economy was formerly the aggregate result of exchange between humans, and the growth of the economy meant increasing human wealth. Today, however, the growth of the economy means the destruction of the ecosystem upon which we are utterly dependent, and so the very nature of our economic system will inevitably change to take this into account. Economic activity will be redefined in terms of what is necessary to sustain life on earth, and the phrase 'economy as ecosystem' will take on another layer of meaning.[8]

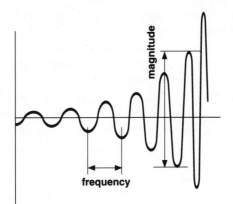

Figure 13.4 **Increasing Frequency and Magnitude**
Today's changes are happening more frequently, and many of them are also generally of greater magnitude than changes in decades and centuries passed. These are the frightening conditions in which we must manage institutions and society as a whole.

The shift from mass to intelligence exemplifies not only the response to increasing energy costs, but also the character of the economy that will inevitably develop as people come to understand the alternatives that we face ever more clearly.

In this context, the acts of learning and design will remain prominent, for these are the means by which the patterns of consumption will be shifted as a matter of individual choice, leading to an aggregate of evolution in society as a whole. Learning enables consciousness in evolution, transcending the role of chance.

INDIVIDUALS AND INSTITUTIONS

Corporations play increasingly important roles in society, for they control most of the technical information as well as the natural resources that constitutes society's wealth. More importantly, through their activities in the economy they control society's capacity to create more wealth. In response to their greater importance, they are now being called upon to provide social context and human services that were once provided by the church and the state. This trend can only continue.

Wealth-producing corporations dominate society, and the role of the nation-state is in decline. Perhaps the best example of this is in Europe, where the transnational European Community accumulates power that was once disposed only by its strongest members. This decline of the nation-state occurs simply because the Common Market is economically stronger than its separate constituents.

Corporations, nations, and national alliances are all in flux.

It seems unlikely that the actions and capabilities of an individual could play an important role in the massive changes that are churning around us all, but they do. For only individuals can comprehend information, and only individuals can comprehend the larger patterns in which its meaning achieves significance. Even more importantly, only individuals can devise appropriate responses to the new situations with which we are confronted each and every day. Because of this, the individual has come into new prominence in all organizations. As organizations depend ever more thoroughly upon the capabilities of individuals, the days are gone when masses of faceless workers toiled in anonymity. Now it is the actions of individuals that are vital to the survival of all institutions.

Thus, a second key distinction is that between *individuals* and *institutions*. Individuals are becoming more important within institutions, and commercial institutions are becoming more important within society.

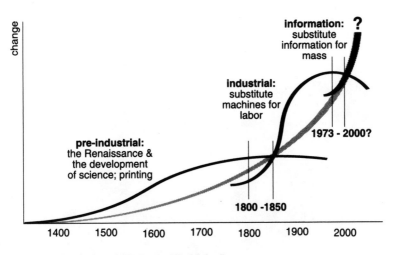

Figure 13.5   **The Future Will Be As We Make It**

KNOWLEDGE AND VISION

During the last century, corporations accumulated unprecedented power, and during the next 50 years or so, the interactions between individuals and institutions in the marketplace will determine how that power is to be used. This is an entirely new circumstance for humanity, for it means that human evolution is now entirely the responsibility of . . . humans.

In this circumstance, a third important distinction is the one between *knowledge* and *vision*. Whereas knowledge concerns the past and exists strictly as the result of what has been done, vision defines the possibilities for the future, the creation of what could be done.

It is only together that knowledge and vision compose the power to create the future in the realization of what were once only possibilities. Among individuals this is process of learning; among organizations and society as a whole, this is process of evolution. We approach it, now, with a new context and a new sense of responsibility. Due to the prevalence of exponential change we know that the future cannot be as the past was. It will be as we make it.

Acknowledgments

This book was inspired by the writing of Stafford Beer, whose *Platform for Change* profoundly outlines the challenges facing our society in these times of rapid change. My contact with Beer's work was due entirely to the kindness of Ray Smith, then an officer of Bell of Pennsylvania and now Chairman of Bell Atlantic. I spoke briefly with Ray following a seminar he presented in 1978, and a few weeks later a copy of Beer's work arrived in my mail unexpectedly, a gift from him.

Over the years, many other people have also significantly influenced the development of the ideas presented here, including the late F. Martin Brown, James L. Marriner, Dolly Stolk, Paolo Soleri, Dolores Colangelo, Jackie Krieg, the late Skip Sagar, Eric Freed, Michael Kaufman, Bryan Coffman, Robert Darling, Paul Bartoo, William Blackburn, Jim Blick, and Dwight O'Neill. Matt Taylor deserves special mention, for his own work was particularly influential in many of the areas covered in the book.

The actual writing of this book owes its start to Paul Grabhorn. Subsequently, Pascal Baudry and Christian Forthomme offered strong encouragement, without which I'm sure it would not have been written.

This work was also supported by many clients, whose willingness to explore new ways of working created opportunities through which I have learned about organization design and transformation through its practice.

Drafts of the manuscript were reviewed by Pascal Baudry, Bryan Coffman, Jeff Gill, Michael Kaufman, Elizabeth Morris, and David Semple. They each made many significant improvements to the content itself and to the clarity of the presentation, and I am grateful for their contributions. Cynthia Foo, Holly Fulton, and Luis Malonzo helped to resolve technical questions.

Matt Wagner of Waterside Productions provided timely and formative guidance, as did Jeanne Glasser of Van Nostrand Reinhold.

During the years of exploration and writing, this project received steady support from my family, particularly my parents, Langdon and Ellen Morris, my sister Nancy Morris, and Jim and Betty Davidson.

To all of those mentioned above, and those who have been omitted, my warm thanks.

Finally, I offer thanks to my wife Elizabeth, who contributed to this project in countless ways. She and I discussed these issues over many years, and many of the ideas presented here were originally hers. In addition, her skilled and patient editing has improved every page. With thanks for her abundant and tireless care and support, this book is dedicated, with love, to her.

Bibliography

Abramson, Rudy, "Poor Storage Ruining NASA Data, Report Says." *Los Angeles Times,* March 3, 1990.

Ackoff, Dr. Russell. Video recording of his presentation to the 10th annual conference of GOAL/QPC, November 8, 1993. "TQM: Creating Lasting Transformation." Metheun, MA, GOAL:QPC (Growth Opportunity Alliance of Lawrence: Quality, Productivity, Competitiveness), 1993.

Adams, James L., *Flying Buttresses, Entropy, and O-rings: The World of an Engineer.* Cambridge, MA, Harvard University Press, 1991.

Amelio, Gilbert. Remarks at The First Bionomics Conference, October 8, 1993, San Francisco, California.

Argote, Linda and Dennis Epple, "Learning Curves in Manufacturing." *Science,* Volume 247, February 23, 1990.

Bateson, Gregory, *Mind and Nature: A Necessary Unity.* New York, Bantam Books, 1979.

Beer, Stafford, *Brain of the Firm.* Chichester, John Wiley & Sons, 1981.

Beer, Stafford, *Designing Freedom.* Toronto, Canadian Broadcasting Corporation, 1974.

Beer, Stafford, *Diagnosing the System for Organizations.* Chichester, John Wiley & Sons, 1985.

Beer, Stafford, *The Heart of Enterprise.* Chichester, John Wiley & Sons, 1979.

Beer, Stafford, *Platform for Change.* Chichester, John Wiley & Sons, 1975.

Boorstin, Daniel J., *The Americans: The Democratic Experience.* New York, Vintage Books, 1973.

Braudel, Fernand, *The Wheels of Commerce: Civilization & Capitalism, 15th–18th Century.* New York, Harper & Row Publishers, 1979.

Brennan, Christine, "The Athletic Shoe Company That Won't Tread Softly." *The Washington Post National Weekly Edition,* May 31–June 6, 1993.

Brown, Warren and Swoboda, Frank, "Going After the Olds Guard." *Washington Post Weekly,* December 20–26, 1993.

Chandler, Alfred D., Jr., *Scale and Scope: The Dynamics of Industrial Capitalism.* Cambridge MA, The Belknap Press of Harvard University, 1990.

Charlton, James, *Writer's Quotation Book.* Waynscot, NY, Pushcart Press, 1980, 1985, 1991.

Clark, Don, "New Venture May Make Amdahl's Name in Software." *San Francisco Chronicle,* June 22, 1993.

Clark, Don and Ken Siegmann, "Technology Is No Longer the Friend of Dictators." *San Francisco Chronicle,* August 22, 1991.

Coffman, Bryan. Private correspondence with the author.

Cornell, Paul and Mark Baloga, "Work Evolution and the New 'Office' " in *Productivity in Knowledge-Intensive Organizations: Integrating the Physical, Social, and Informational Environments.* Working Papers of the Grand Rapids Workshop, April 8–9, 1992. H. Van Dyke Parunak, editor. Ann Arbor, MI, Industrial Technology Institute.

CRSS Architects, Inc., *Chrysler Technology Center: The Ultimate Advantage.* Published by CRSS Architects, Inc. Houston, TX, 1991.

Deming, W. Edwards, *The New Economics for Industry, Government, Education.* Cambridge, MA, Massachusetts Institute of Technology Center for Advanced Engineering Study, 1993.

Deming, W. Edwards, *Out of the Crisis.* Cambridge, MA, Massachusetts Institute of Technology Center for Advanced Engineering Study, 1985.

Doyle, Michael and David Straus, *How To Make Meetings Work.* New York, Jove Books, 1976.

Drucker, Peter, *The Age of Discontinuity.* New York, Harper & Row, Publishers, 1968, 1969.

Drucker, Peter, *Innovation & Entrepreneurship,* New York, HarperBusiness, 1985.

Drucker, Peter, *Post-Capitalist Society.* New York, HarperBusiness, 1993.

Egan, Timothy, "High Winds Hamper Oil Spill Cleanup Off Alaska." *The New York Times,* March 28, 1989.

Einstein, Albert, *Ideas and Opinions.* Avenal, NJ, Outlet Book Company, 1954.

Eldridge, Niles, *Time Frames—The Rethinking of Darwinian Evolution and the Theory of Punctuated Equilibria.* New York, Simon and Schuster, 1985.

Engelbart, Douglas C., "Toward High-Performance Organizations: A Strategic Role for Groupware." *Groupware '92 Conference Proceedings.* San Jose, Morgan Kaufman Publishers, 1992.

Feynman, Richard, *"What Do You Care What Other People Think?"* New York, W.W. Norton & Company, 1988.

Forbes Magazine. Forbes 500, April 25, 1994.

Forrester, Jay, "Counterintuitive Behavior of Social Systems." *Technology Review,* Volume 73, Number 3, January, 1971.

Friedman, Eugene, Vice President of Applied Technology, Chase Manhattan Bank. Interview with the author, June 15, 1993.

Fuller, Buckminster, *Critical Path.* New York, St. Martin's Press, 1981.

Gall, John, *Systemantics: The Underground Text of Systems Lore.* Ann Arbor, MI, The General Systemantics Press, 1986.

Gilliam, Harold, "The World's Biggest Problem." *San Francisco Chronicle,* February 16, 1992.

Halberstam, David, *The Reckoning.* New York, Avon Books, 1986.

Hammer, Michael and James Champy, *Reengineering the Corporation: A Manifesto for Business Revolution.* New York, HarperBusiness, 1993.

Hawken, Paul, *The Next Economy.* New York, Ballantine Books, 1983.

Heyne, Paul, *The Economic Way of Thinking,* Third Edition. Chicago, Science Research Associates, Inc., 1980, 1976, 1973.

Holloway, R.L., Jr, "Cranial capacity, neural reorganization, and hominid evolution: a search for more suitable parameters. *Amer. Anthropol.,* 1966, 68, 103–121. as cited in Miller, James Grier, *Living Systems*. New York, McGraw Hill, 1978. p. 467.

Inc. Magazine, "A Year-End Thought for Planners." November, 1993.

Information Week, "Executive Summary, Database Storage." April 5, 1993.

Jantsch, Erich, *The Self-Organizing Universe*. Oxford, Pergamon Press, 1980.

Jaques, Elliott, "In Praise of Hierarchy." *Harvard Business Review*, January–February 1990.

Kearns, David and David Nadler, *Prophets in the Dark: How Xerox Reinvented Itself and Beat Back the Japanese*. New York, Harper Business, 1993.

Koberg, Don & Jim Bagnall, *The Universal Traveler: A Soft-Systems Guide to Creativity, Problem-solving, & the Process of Reaching Goals*. Los Altos, CA, Crisp Publications, Inc. 1991.

Kristof, Nicholas D., "New Chinese Revolution—The Information Age." *San Francisco Chronicle*, April 12, 1993.

Kuhn, Thomas S., *The Structure of Scientific Revolutions*. Chicago, The University of Chicago Press, 1970.

Lardner, George, Jr., "The CIA Faces A New Intelligence Test." *Washington Post Weekly*, April 23–29, 1990.

Lochhead, Carolyn, "Bold Proposal by HUD On Subsidized Housing." *San Francisco Chronicle*, May 3, 1994.

Markoff, John, "Denser, Faster, Cheaper: The Microchip in the 21st Century. *The New York Times*, December 29, 1991.

Marshall, E, "Early Data: Losing Our Memory?" *Science*, Vol. 244, June 16, 1989.

McLeod, Ramon G., "Average American Family Lost 12% of Wealth From '88 to '91." *San Francisco Chronicle*, January 26, 1994.

McLuhan, Marshall, *Understanding Media: The Extensions of Man*. New York, McGraw Hill Book Company, 1964.

Meadows, Donella H., Dennis L. Meadows and Jørgen Randers, *Beyond the Limits*. Post Mills, VT, Chelsea Green Publishing Company, 1992.

Miller, James Grier, *Living Systems*. New York, McGraw Hill, 1978.

Miller, Karen Lowry, "Honda Sets Its Sights on a Different Checkered Flag." *Business Week*, August 17, 1992.

Montagu, Ashley and Floyd Matson, *The Dehumanization of Man*. New York, McGraw Hill Book Company, 1983.

Moravec, Hans, *Mind Children: The Future of Robot and Human Intelligence*. Cambridge, MA, Harvard University Press, 1988.

Morris, Langdon and Cynthia Foo with Pascal Baudry, Ph.D., *Innovation Management: The State of the Art*. Lafayette, CA, WDHB Consulting Group, 1994.

Morris, Langdon, Cynthia Foo and Christian Forthomme, *Leadership in Retail: Change Management and Customer Service Strategies*. Lafayette, CA, WDHB Consulting Group, 1994.

Nadler, David, interviewed by A.J. Vogl, " 'It Could Happen to Us.' " *Across the Board*, October, 1993.

National Aeronautics and Space Act of 1958, as Amended. Public Law 85-568, 85th Congress, H.R. 12575. July 29, 1958, Section 203. (a) (3).

Nix, Don, "Everybody Wants To Go To Heaven." Irving Music, Inc./BMI, recorded by Albert King on his albumn *Lovejoy*, December, 1970.

Norr, Henry, "Image-oriented supercomputer comes to Mac SCSI under A/UX." *MACWEEK*, November 12, 1991.

Oldenburg, Don, "Creativity From Chaos: A Free-Form Theory For Transforming the Common Meeting." *The Washington Post*, February 20, 1992.

Ornstein, Robert and Paul Ehrlich, *New World New Mind: Moving Towards Conscious Evolution*. New York, Doubleday, 1989.

Owen, Harrison, "Open Space Technology Comes of Age." *Open Space*, H.H. Owen & Company, September, 1990.

Owen, Harrison, *Open Space Technology: A User's Guide*. Potomac, MD, Abbott Publishing, 1992.

Oxford English Dictionary, 1970.

Parunak, H. Van Dyke, editor, *Productivity in Knowledge-Intensive Organizations: Integrating the Physical, Social, and Informational Environments*. Working Papers of the Grand Rapids Workshop, April 8–9, 1992. Ann Arbor, MI, Industrial Technology Institute, 1992.

Petro, Frank A., "Why Layoffs Don't Work." *San Francisco Chronicle*, March 21, 1994.

Prahalad, C.K. and Gary Hamel, "The Core Competence of the Corporation." *Harvard Business Review*, May–June 1990.

Preston, Richard, "The Mountain of Pi." *The New Yorker*, March 2, 1992.

Reich, Robert, *The Work of Nations*, New York, Vintage Books, 1991, 1992. p. 178

Richards, Evelyn, "Building Roads for the Information Age." *Washington Post Weekly*, October 2–8, 1989.

Roosevelt, Franklin D., Fireside Chat, February 23, 1942.

Rose, Colin, *Accelerated Learning*. New York, Dell Publishing Co. Inc., 1985.

Rothfeder, Jeffrey and Jim Bartimo, "How Software Is Making Food Sales a Piece of Cake." *Business Week*, July 2, 1990.

Rothschild, Michael, *Bionomics: Economy as Ecosystem*. New York, Henry Holt and Company, 1990.

Rothschild, Michael, in Frost, Bob, "The Business Digest Interview." *Pacific Bell Business Digest*, March April, 1994.

Rothschild, Michael. Remarks at The First Bionomics Conference, October 8, 1993, San Francisco, California.

Sandalow, Marc, "Bay Cities Say Drug War Failed." *San Francisco Chronicle*, May 11, 1993.

San Francisco Chronicle, "Computer Users Can Now Send E-Mail Letters to White House." June 2, 1993.

San Francisco Chronicle, "IBM Loses $8 billion, 35,000 Jobs." July 28, 1993.

San Francisco Chronicle, "IBM's Chief Lays Out Map For the Future." March 25, 1994.

San Francisco Chronicle, "Working Wives Keep America's Families Out of Red." March 14, 1994.

Schneider, Keith, "Jury Says Exxon Was Reckless in Valdez Oil Tanker Disaster." *San Francisco Chronicle*, June 14, 1994.

Schneider, Keith, "Transfer of Remaining Oil From Tanker Moves Slowly." *The New York Times*, April 2, 1989.

Schwartz, Peter, *The Art of the Long View*. New York, Doubleday Currency, 1991.

Semler, Ricardo, "Managing Without Managers." *Harvard Business Review*, September–October 1989.

Semler, Ricardo, *Maverick*. New York, Warner Books, 1993.

Senge, Peter, *The 5th Discipline: The Art & Practice of the Learning Organization*. New York, Doubleday Currency, 1990.

Shabecoff, Philip, "Largest U.S. Tanker Spill Spews 270,000 Barrels of Oil Off Alaska." *The New York Times*, March 25, 1989.

Siegmann, Ken, "Apple Troubles Send Stock Sliding 23%." *San Francisco Chronicle*, July 17, 1993.

Siegmann, Ken, "Canon Drops Deal to Buy Next Inc.'s Hardware Unit." *San Francisco Chronicle*, April 8, 1993.

Siegmann, Ken, "Failure to Evolve Staggers Big Blue." *San Francisco Chronicle*, December 16, 1992.

Siegmann, Ken, "Hewlett-Packard Shifts Direction: The high-tech giant hopes to benefit by merging technologies." *San Francisco Chronicle*, January 24, 1994.

Siegmann, Ken, "Red Ink Flowing at Apple." *San Francisco Chronicle*, July 16, 1993.

Steelcase Inc., Grand Rapids, MI, *Hybritech Incorporated Case Study*. 1994. Comments by Jim Killion, Ph.D., senior research scientist of Hybritech.

Stewart, Thomas A., "Managing in a Wired Company." *Fortune*, July 11, 1994.

Tainter, Joseph A., *The Collapse of Complex Societies*. Cambridge, Press Syndicate of the University of Cambridge, 1988.

Tichy, Noel M. and Stratford Sherman, *Control Your Destiny or Someone Else Will*. New York, Currency Doubleday, 1993.

Waldrop, M. Mitchell, *Complexity: The Emerging Science at the Edge of Order and Chaos*. New York, Touchstone, 1992.

Watterson, Bill, "Calvin and Hobbes." October 11, 1993.

Webster's New Universal Unabriged Dictionary, Second Edition.

Wheatley, Margaret, *Leadership and the New Science*. San Francisco, Berrett-Kohler Publishers, Inc., 1992.

Whiting, Rick, "A clash of giants shakes the low-end workstation market." *Electronic Business*, April 27, 1992.

Wiener, Norbert, *The Human Use of Human Beings: Cybernetics and Society*. New York, Avon Books, 1967.

Woodruff, David, "Saturn: GM Finally Has a Real Winner. But Success Is Bringing a Fresh Batch of Problems." *Business Week*, August 17, 1992.

Yeats, William Butler, "The Second Coming," *The Poems of W. B. Yeats*. New York, Macmillan, 1983.

Yergin, Daniel, *The Prize: The Epic Quest for Oil, Money & Power*. New York, Touchstone, 1991, 1992.

Notes

INTRODUCTION

1 Nadler, David interviewed by A.J. Vogl, " 'It Could Happen to Us.' " *Across the Board*, October 1993.

2 McLeod, Ramon G., "Average American Family Lost 12% of Wealth From '88 to '91." *San Francisco Chronicle*, January 26, 1994.

3 *San Francisco Chronicle*, "Working Wives Keep America's Families Out of Red." March 14, 1994.

4 *Forbes* Magazine. Forbes 500, April 25, 1994. p. 199.

5 Drucker, Peter, *Post-Capitalist Society*. New York, HarperBusiness, 1993. p. x.

6 This phenomenon is referred to as 'cost-push inflation.' Because oil is so fundamental to our economy, one could argue that dollars should be denominated in oil rather than gold, as was the case for the decades prior to 1973. Thus, the nominal cost of oil is probably a more accurate reflection of economic reality than its inflation-adjusted cost. Economist Paul Heyne comments, "The Fed promoted inflation in response to OPEC's price increases; but it did so in an effort to counter the reduced output and employment caused by OPEC's unexpected success in cartelization." Heyne, Paul, *The Economic Way of Thinking*. Chicago, Science Research Associates, Inc., 1980, 1976, 1973. p. 461.

7 Tichy, Noel, and Stratford Sherman, *Control Your Destiny or Someone Else Will*. New York, Currency Doubleday, 1993. p. 241.

8 Hawken, Paul, *The Next Economy*. New York, Ballantine Books, 1983.

9 Tainter, Joseph A., *The Collapse of Complex Societies*. Cambridge, Press Syndicate of the University of Cambridge, 1988. p. 1.

10 Ibid. p. 195.

11 Rothschild, Michael, *Bionomics: Economy as Ecosystem*. New York, Henry Holt & Company, 1990.

12 See Senge, Peter, *The 5th Discipline: The Art & Practice of the Learning Organization*. New York, Doubleday Currency, 1990. p. 21.

13 Gall, John, *Systemantics: The Underground Text of Systems Lore*. Ann Arbor, MI, The General Systemantics Press, 1986. p. 35.

14 Ibid. p. 36: "The Germans later re-mounted them facing westward toward France, thus demonstrating that they, too, could be Fully Prepared for the Past."

15 Waldrop, M. Mitchell, *Complexity: The Emerging Science at the Edge of Order and Chaos*. New York, Touchstone, 1992. p. 359. Copyright © 1992 by M. Mitchell

Waldrop. Reprinted by permission of Simon & Schuster, Inc. and Sterling Lord
Literistic, Inc.

PART ONE MODELS: The 21st Century Organization

1 Senge, Peter, *The Fifth Discipline: The Art & Practice of the Learning Organization.*
   New York, Currency Doubleday, 1990. p. 241.

CHAPTER 1 Structure Becomes Process

1 Amelio, Gilbert. Remarks at The First Bionomics Conference, October 8, 1993,
   San Francisco, California.
2 Drucker, Peter, *Innovation & Entrepreneurship.* New York, HarperBusiness, 1985.
   p. 4.
3 Tichy, Noel M. and Stratford Sherman, *Control Your Destiny or Someone Else Will.*
   New York, Currency Doubleday, 1993. p. 38.
4 Ibid. p. 6.
5 "IBM Loses $8 billion, 35,000 Jobs." *San Francisco Chronicle,* July 28, 1993.
6 Waldrop, M. Mitchell, *Complexity: The Emerging Science at the Edge of Order and
   Chaos.* New York, Touchstone, 1992. p 327. Copyright © 1992 by M. Mitchell
   Waldrop. Reprinted by permission of Simon & Schuster, Inc., and Sterling Lord
   Literistic, Inc.
7 Ibid. p. 329.
8 Ibid. p. 12.
9 Ibid. p. 11.
10 Jantsch, Erich, *The Self-Organizing Universe.* Oxford, Pergamon Press, 1980. p. 6.
11 Drucker, Peter, *Innovation & Entrepreneurship.* New York, HarperBusiness, 1985.
   p. 4.
12 Amelio, Gilbert. Remarks at The First Bionomics Conference, October 8, 1993,
   San Francisco, California.
13 Tichy, Noel M. and Stratford Sherman, *Control Your Destiny or Someone Else Will.*
   New York, Currency Doubleday, 1993. p. 204.

CHAPTER 2 Beyond Hierarchy

1 Semler, Ricardo, *Maverick.* New York, Warner Books, 1993. p. 283.
2 Tichy, Noel M. and Stratford Sherman, *Control Your Destiny or Someone Else Will.*
   New York, Currency Doubleday, 1993. p. 21.
3 *Webster's New Universal Unabridged Dictionary,* Second Edition.
4 Chandler, Alfred D., Jr., *Scale and Scope: The Dynamics of Industrial Capitalism.*
   Cambridge, MA, The Belknap Press of Harvard University, 1990. p. 54.
5 Yergin, Daniel, *The Prize: The Epic Quest for Oil, Money & Power.* New York, Touchstone, 1991, 1992. p. 35–40.
6 Semler, Ricardo, "Managing Without Managers." *Harvard Business Review,* September–October 1989.

7 Deming, W. Edwards, *The New Economics for Industry, Government, Education.* Cambridge, MA, Massachusetts Institute of Technology Center for Advanced Engineering Study, 1993. p. 50.

8 Ibid. p. 62.

9 Ibid. p. 51.

10 Waldrop, M. Mitchell, *Complexity: The Emerging Science at the Edge of Order and Chaos.* New York, Touchstone, 1992. p. 91. Copyright © 1992 by M. Mitchell Waldrop. Reprinted by permission of Simon & Schuster, Inc. and Sterling Lord Literistic, Inc.

11 Morris, Langdon and Cynthia Foo with Pascal Baudry, Ph.D., *Innovation Management: The State of the Art.* Lafayette, CA, WDHB Consulting Group, 1994. p. A-7.

12 Rothschild, Michael, *Bionomics: Economy as Ecosystem.* New York, Henry Holt and Company, 1990. p. xi.

13 Rothschild, Michael, in Frost, Bob, "The Business Digest Interview." *Pacific Bell Business Digest,* March–April, 1994. p. 12.

14 Beer, Stafford, *Brain of the Firm.* Chichester, John Wiley & Sons, 1981.

15 Beer, Stafford, *The Heart of Enterprise.* Chichester, John Wiley & Sons, 1979.

16 Beer, Stafford, *Diagnosing the System for Organizations.* Chichester, John Wiley & Sons, 1985.

17 A very comprehensive approach to these issues is presented in Miller, James Grier, *Living Systems.* New York, McGraw Hill, 1978. Miller identifies 19 critical subsystems of a living system and shows in detail how they process matter, energy, and information to constitute the process of life.

18 Bateson, Gregory, *Mind and Nature: A Necessary Unity.* New York, Bantam Books, 1979. See particularly Chapter IV, Criterion 6, p. 127. Bateson refers to Bertrand Russell and Alfred North Whitehead's concept of 'logical types' as the mathematical corollary of the ideas discussed here.

19 Prahalad, C. K. and Gary Hamel, "The Core Competence of the Corporation." *Harvard Business Review,* May–June 1990.

20 Ibid.

CHAPTER 3 Recognition and Response

1 Jantsch, Erich, *The Self-Organizing Universe.* Oxford, Pergamon Press, 1980. p. 8.

2 Rothschild, Michael, *Bionomics: Economy as Ecosystem.* New York, Henry Holt and Company, 1990.

3 Jaques, Elliott, "In Praise of Hierarchy." *Harvard Business Review,* January–February 1990. p. 131.

4 Beer, Stafford, *Diagnosing the System for Organizations.* Chichester, John Wiley & Sons, 1985. p. 66.

5 Hammer, Michael and James Champy, *Reengineering the Corporation: A Manifesto for Business Revolution.* New York, HarperBusiness, 1993.

6 Drucker, Peter, *Innovation & Entrepreneurship.* New York, HarperBusiness, 1985. p. 151.

PART TWO THEORY: Patterns of Change

1 Michael Rothschild interviewed by Bob Frost in *Pacific Bell Business Digest*, March/April 1994. p. 13.

CHAPTER 4 The Rate of Change

1 Siegmann, Ken, "Failure to Evolve Staggers Big Blue." *San Francisco Chronicle*, December 16, 1992. p. C1.
2 Much of this loss is attributable to a change in accounting rules that required all American companies to set aside money for retiree health benefits, which caused many companies to report losses for 1992. Nevertheless, if IBM had been doing well, the accounting change would have had little impact.
3 *San Francisco Chronicle*, "IBM Loses $8 Billion, 35,000 Jobs." July 28, 1993.
4 Senge, Peter, *The 5th Discipline: The Art & Practice of the Learning Organization.* New York, Doubleday Currency, 1990. p. 21.
5 Markoff, John, "Denser, Faster, Cheaper: The Microchip in the 21st Century." *The New York Times*, December 29, 1991. p. F5.
6 Moravec, Hans, *Mind Children: The Future of Robot and Human Intelligence.* Cambridge, MA, Harvard University Press, 1988. p. 68.
7 Siegmann, Ken, "Failure to Evolve Staggers Big Blue." *San Francisco Chronicle*, December 16, 1992. p. C1.
8 Markoff, John, "Denser, Faster, Cheaper: The Microchip in the 21st Century." *The New York Times*, December 29, 1991.
9 Whiting, Rick, "A clash of giants shakes the low-end workstation market." *Electronic Business*, April 27, 1992. Data from Dataquest, Inc.
10 Senge, Peter, *The 5th Discipline: The Art & Practice of the Learning Organization.* New York, Doubleday Currency, 1990.
"The fixation on events" is one of seven learning disabilities.
"today, the primary threats to our survival, both of our organizations and our societies, come not from sudden events but from slow, gradual processes." [Author's italics.] p. 22.
11 Tainter, Joseph A., *The Collapse of Complex Societies.* Cambridge, Press Syndicate of the University of Cambridge, 1988.
12 Moravec, Hans, *Mind Children: The Future of Robot and Human Intelligence.* Cambridge, MA, Harvard University Press, 1988.
"new products . . . are designed with the trend in mind. Established manufacturers design and price products to stay on the curve, to maximize profit; new companies aim above the curve, to gain a competitive edge." p. 68.
13 Siegmann, Ken, "Failure to Evolve Staggers Big Blue." *San Francisco Chronicle*, December 16, 1992. p. C1.
14 McLuhan, Marshall, *Understanding Media: The Extensions of Man.* New York, McGraw Hill, 1964.
15 Braudel, Fernand, *The Wheels of Commerce: Civilization & Capitalism, 15th–18th Century.* New York, Harper & Row, 1979. p. 572.
16 Meadows, Donella H., Dennis L. Meadows, and Jørgen Randers, *Beyond the Limits.* Post Mills, VT, Chelsea Green Publishing Company, 1992. p. 18.

17 Gilliam, Harold, "The World's Biggest Problem." *San Francisco Chronicle*, February 16, 1992.
"The Population Reference Bureau of Washington, D.C., tells us that it required 99 per cent of the human race's time on this planet to reach a global population of 1 billion by 1800. Thanks to the industrial revolution, it took only 130 years to reach the second billion in 1930. The third billion came in 30 years, in 1960, and the fourth in 15 years, by 1975. The fifth billion came 12 years later in 1987, and the sixth is due by 1998, six years from now. . . . How long this kind of growth can continue is best left to your imagination."

18 Ibid.

19 Senge, Peter, *The 5th Discipline*. New York, Doubleday Currency, 1990. p. 22.

20 Forrester, Jay, "Counterintuitive Behavior of Social Systems." *Technology Review*, Volume 73, Number 3, January, 1971. p. 1.

21 Ornstein, Robert and Paul Ehrlich, *New World New Mind: Moving Towards Conscious Evolution*. New York, Doubleday, 1989. p. 2.

22 Beer, Stafford, *Brain of the Firm*. Chichester, John Wiley & Sons, 1981. See particularly Chapter 1.

23 Lardner, George, Jr., "The CIA Faces A New Intelligence Test." *Washington Post Weekly*, April 23–29, 1990.

CHAPTER 5   The Flow of Information

1 *Information Week*, "Executive Summary, Database Storage." April 5, 1993. p. 8.

2 Lochhead, Carolyn, "Bold Proposal by HUD On Subsidized Housing." *San Francisco Chronicle*, May 3, 1994.
"In a major reassessment of public housing, U.S. Housing Secretary Henry Cisneros yesterday released a plan to demolish urban highrise projects. . . ."

3 Tichy, Noel M. and Stratford Sherman, *Control Your Destiny or Someone Else Will*. New York, Currency Doubleday, 1993. p. 242.

4 Brennan, Christine, "The Athletic Shoe Company That Won't Tread Softly." *Washington Post Weekly*, May 31–June 6, 1993.
Nike Chairman Phil Knight: "I just hope we continue to make some mistakes. If we're not making mistakes, we're not trying enough new things." p. 20.

5 Tichy, Noel M. and Stratford Sherman, *Control Your Destiny or Someone Else Will*. New York, Currency Doubleday, 1993. See chapter 2.

6 National Aeronautics and Space Act of 1958, as Amended. Public Law 85–568, 85th Congress, H.R. 12575. July 29, 1958, Section 203. (a) (3).

7 Feynman, Richard, *"What Do You Care What Other People Think?"* New York, W.W. Norton & Company, 1988. See Part 2, pp. 113–237.

8 Adams, James L., *Flying Buttresses, Entropy, and O-rings: The World of an Engineer*. Cambridge, MA, Harvard University Press, 1991. p. 171.

9 Gall, John, *Systemantics: The Underground Text of Systems Lore*. Ann Arbor, MI, The General Systemantics Press, 1986.
"[Garbage is] a product of a System, for which no immediate use is apparent. The point to remember is that ONE SYSTEM'S GARBAGE IS ANOTHER SYSTEM'S PRECIOUS RAW MATERIAL." p. 217.

10 Richards, Evelyn, "Building Roads for the Information Age." *Washington Post Weekly,* October 2–8, 1989.

11 Abramson, Rudy, "Poor Storage Ruining NASA Data, Report Says." *Los Angeles Times,* March 3, 1990. p. A18.

12 Marshall, E., "Early Data: Losing Our Memory?" *Science,* Vol 244, June 16, 1989. p. 1250.

"90% of the data collected before 1979 are now inaccessible. The reason: the data tapes were recorded on old Xerox computers which can no longer be operated. In addition, the satellite location and timing data were recorded on a kind of video tape that no longer exists."

13 Clark, Don, "New Venture May Make Amdahl's Name in Software." *San Francisco Chronicle,* June 22, 1993.

"Big corporate computer users face a problem as intractable as the federal budget deficit. Their programming departments are months or years behind schedule in developing new software to make their businesses run more efficiently."

14 *San Francisco Chronicle,* "Computer Users Can Now Send E-Mail Letters to White House." June 2, 1993. p. A4.

15 Moravec, Hans, *Mind Children: The Future of Robot and Human Intelligence.* Cambridge, MA, Harvard University Press, 1988. p. 69.

16 Rothschild, Michael, *Bionomics: Economy as Ecosystem.* New York, Henry Holt and Company, 1990. p. 99.

17 Charlton, James, *Writer's Quotation Book.* Waynscot, NY, Pushcart Press, 1980, 1985, 1991. p. 16.

18 Beer, Stafford, *The Heart of Enterprise.* Chichester, John Wiley & Sons, 1979. p. 283.

19 Bateson, Gregory, *Mind and Nature: A Necessary Unity.* New York, Bantam Books, 1979. p. 110.

20 Deming, Edwards W., *The New Economics for Industry, Government, Education.* Cambridge, MA, Massachusetts Institute of Technology, Center for Advanced Engineering Study, 1993. p. 105, 109.

21 Drucker, Peter, *The Age of Discontinuity.* New York, Harper Torchbooks, 1968, 1969. p. 269.

22 Ackoff, Dr. Russell. Video recording of his presentation to the 10th annual conference of GOAL/QPC, November 8, 1993. TQM: Creating Lasting Transformation. Metheun, MA, GOAL:QPC (Growth Opportunity Alliance of Lawrence: Quality, Productivity, Competitiveness), 1993. Ackoff attributes the distinction between doing things right and doing the right thing to Peter Drucker.

23 Beer, Stafford, *Diagnosing the System for Organizations.* Chichester, John Wiley & Sons, 1982. p. 22.

24 Einstein, Albert, *The World as I See It.* Secaucus, NJ, Citadel Press, 1979.

25 Gall, John, *Systemantics: The Underground Text of Systems Lore.* Ann Arbor, MI, The General Systemantics Press, 1986. p. 158.

26 Ibid. p. 141.

27 Senge, Peter, *The 5th Discipline: The Art & Practice of the Learning Organization.* New York, Doubleday Currency, 1990.

28 Halberstam, David, *The Reckoning.* New York, Avon Books, 1986.

29 Yergin, Daniel, *The Prize: The Epic Quest for Oil, Money & Power*. New York, Touchstone, 1991, 1992. See also Schwartz, Peter, *The Art of the Long View*. New York, Doubleday Currency, 1991.

30 Schneider, Keith, "Transfer of Remaining Oil From Tanker Moves Slowly." *The New York Times*, April 2, 1989.

31 Egan, Timothy, "High Winds Hamper Oil Spill Cleanup Off Alaska." *The New York Times*, March 28, 1989.

32 Forrester, Jay, "Counterintuitive Behavior of Social Systems." *Technology Review*, Volume 73, Number 3, January 1971.

33 For example, Wheatley, Margaret, *Leadership and the New Science*. San Francisco, Berrett-Kohler Publishers, 1992.

34 Sandalow, Marc, "Bay Cities Say Drug War Failed." *San Francisco Chronicle*, May 11, 1993.
    "The mayors and police chiefs of the Bay Area's three largest cities declared the nation's war on drugs a failure and called for a new anti-drug strategy that emphasizes prevention rather than law enforcement."

35 Drucker, Peter, *Innovation & Entrepreneurship*. New York, HarperBusiness, 1985. See chapter 3.

36 Gall, John, *Systemantics: The Underground Text of Systems Lore*. Ann Arbor, MI, The General Systemantics Press, 1986.
    ". . . every Bug, no matter how humble, always gives us at least one important piece of information; namely, it tells us one more way in which our System can fail. Since success is largely a matter of Avoiding the Most Likely Ways to Fail, and since every Bug advances us significantly along that path, we may harken back to the advice given in the Preface and urge the following Policy: Cherish Your Bugs. Study Them." p. 85.

37 Deming, W. Edwards, *Out of the Crisis*. Cambridge, MA, Massachusetts Institute of Technology, 1985.

38 Yeats, William Butler, "The Second Coming." *The Poems of W. B. Yeats*. New York, Macmillan, 1983.

CHAPTER 6   Individuals and Institutions

1 Siegmann, Ken, "Canon Drops Deal to Buy Next Inc.'s Hardware Unit." *San Francisco Chronicle*, April 8, 1993. p. D1.

2 Rothschild, Michael, *Bionomics: Economy as Ecosystem*. New York, Henry Holt and Company, 1990. p. xiii.

3 Ibid.

4 Drucker, Peter, *Post-Capitalist Society*. New York, HarperBusiness, 1993.

5 Rothschild, Michael, *Bionomics: Economy as Ecosystem*. New York, Henry Holt & Company, 1990. p. 166, 180. Rothschild cites Dutton, John M. and Anne Thomas, "Treating Progress Functions as a Managerial Opportunity," *Academy of Management Review* (1984), p. 238.

6 Prahalad, C.K. and Gary Hamel, "The Core Competence of the Corporation." *Harvard Business Review*, May–June 1990. p. 81.

7 Boorstin, Daniel J., *The Americans: The Democratic Experience*. New York, Vintage Books, 1973. p. 413–419.

8   Drucker, Peter, *Post-Capitalist Society*. New York, HarperBusiness, 1993. p. 46, 210.

9   Drucker, Peter, *The Age of Discontinuity*. New York, Harper & Row, 1968, 1969. ". . . what we call profits are simply costs of the future that we cannot yet allocate. . . . It is clear that we need revenue to cover the risks of investing in growth. These revenues can come only out of current production, just as the revenues to cover the costs of doing business today—the accountant's costs—can only come out of current production." p. 147.

10 Watterson, Bill, "Calvin and Hobbes." October 11, 1993.
    Calvin: "Nowadays, ads don't just sell a product. They sell an attitude! Look at this one! Here's a cool guy saying nobody tells him what to do. He does whatever he wants and he buys this product as a reflection of that independence.
    Hobbes: "So basically, this maverick is urging everyone to express his individuality through conformity in brand-name selection.
    Calvin: "Well, it sounded more defiant the way he said it."

11 *Oxford English Dictionary*, 1970.

12 Semler, Ricardo, "Managing Without Managers." *Harvard Business Review*, September–October 1989. p. 79.

13 Tichy, Noel M. and Stratford Sherman, *Control Your Destiny or Someone Else Will*. New York, Currency Doubleday, 1993. p. 33.

14 Ibid. p. 32.

15 Ibid. p. 6.

16 Ibid. p. 103.

17 Gall, John, *Systemantics: The Underground Text of Systems Lore*. Ann Arbor, MI, The General Systemantics Press, 1986. p. 47.

18 Godwin, Pamela, senior vice president, Direct Response Group, as quoted in Hammer, Michael and James Champy, *Reengineering the Corporation*. New York, HarperBusiness, 1993. p. 187.

19 Andy Ludwick, CEO of SynOptics Communications, as quoted in Stewart, Thomas A., "Managing in a Wired Company." *Fortune*, July 11, 1994.

20 *Inc.* Magazine, "A Year-End Thought for Planners." November 1993. p. 12. Reprinted with permission of *Inc.* Magazine. Copyright 1993 by Goldhirsh Group, Inc., 38 Commercial Wharf, Boston, MA 02110.

21 Tichy, Noel M. and Stratford Sherman, *Control Your Destiny or Someone Else Will*. New York, Currency Doubleday, 1993. p. 32.

22 Montagu, Ashley and Floyd Matson, *The Dehumanization of Man*. New York, McGraw Hill, 1983.

23 Miller, James Grier, *Living Systems*. New York, McGraw Hill, 1978. p. 392.

24 Holloway, R.L., Jr., "Cranial capacity, neural reorganization, and hominid evolution: a search for more suitable parameters." *American Anthropology*, 1966, 68, 103–121. As cited in Miller, James Grier, *Living Systems*. New York, McGraw Hill, 1978. p. 467.

CHAPTER 7   The Design Process

1   Tichy, Noel M. and Stratford Sherman, *Control Your Destiny or Someone Else Will*. New York, Currency Doubleday, 1993. p. 245.

2 Deming, W. Edwards, *The New Economics for Industry, Government, Education.* Cambridge, MA, Massachusetts Institute of Technology Center for Advanced Engineering Study, 1993.

3 This model of the design process is adapted from a guidebook to creativity and problem solving called *The Universal Traveler,* by design professors Don Koberg and Jim Bagnall. Many of the refinements to Koberg and Bagnall's model that are reflected here were developed by management consultant Matt Taylor (unpublished). Koberg, Don & Jim Bagnall, *The Universal Traveler: a Soft-Systems Guide to Creativity, Problem-solving, & the Process of Reaching Goals.* Los Altos, CA, Crisp Publications, Inc. 1991.

4 Drucker, Peter, *Post-Capitalist Society.* New York, HarperBusiness, 1993. p. 193.

5 Siegmann, Ken, "Red Ink Flowing at Apple." *San Francisco Chronicle,* July 16, 1993.

6 Siegmann, Ken, "Apple Troubles Send Stock Sliding 23%." *San Francisco Chronicle,* July 17, 1993.

PART THREE PRACTICE: Knowledge Infrastructure

1 Drucker, Peter, *Post-Capitalist Society.* New York, Harper Business, 1993. p. 39.

2 For example, Dr. Douglas Engelbart, whose work is described in Chapter 8.

3 Parunak, H. Van Dyke, editor, *Productivity in Knowledge-Intensive Organizations: Integrating the Physical, Social, and Informational Environments.* Working Papers of the Grand Rapids Workshop, April 8–9, 1992. Ann Arbor, MI, Industrial Technology Institute, 1992.

CHAPTER 8 Information and Communication

1 Senge, Peter, *The 5th Discipline: The Art & Practice of the Learning Organization.* New York, Doubleday Currency, 1990. p. 226.

2 Shabecoff, Philip, "Largest U.S. Tanker Spill Spews 270,000 Barrels of Oil Off Alaska." *The New York Times,* March 25, 1989.

3 Schneider, Keith, "Jury Says Exxon Was Reckless in Valdez Oil Tanker Disaster." *San Francisco Chronicle,* June 14, 1994.

4 Rothfeder, Jeffrey and Jim Bartimo, "How Software Is Making Food Sales a Piece of Cake." *Business Week,* July 2, 1990. p. 54.

5 Friedman, Eugene, Vice President of Applied Technology, Chase Manhattan Bank, interview with the author, June 15, 1993.

6 Rothfeder, Jeffrey and Jim Bartimo, "How Software Is Making Food Sales a Piece of Cake." *Business Week,* July 2, 1990. p. 54.

7 Engelbart, Douglas C., "Toward High-Performance Organizations: A Strategic Role for Groupware." *Groupware '92 Conference Proceedings.* San Jose, Morgan Kaufman Publishers, 1992.

8 Hammer, Michael and James Champy, *Reengineering the Corporation: A Manifesto for Business Revolution.* New York, HarperBusiness, 1993. p. 60.

9 Beer, Stafford, *Diagnosing the System for Organizations.* Chichester, John Wiley & Sons, 1982.

10 Beer describes his work in considerable detail in his *Brain of the Firm* (Chichester, John Wiley & Sons, 1981) and *Platform for Change* (Chichester, John Wiley & Sons, 1975). The latter also has photographs. It should be noted that the book that you are now reading is a result of work inspired in large part by Beer's work. Please see the Acknowledgments for more detail.

11 Moravec, Hans, *Mind Children: The Future of Robot and Human Intelligence*. Cambridge, MA, Harvard University Press, 1988. p. 68.

12 Norr, Henry, "Image-oriented supercomputer comes to Mac SCSI under A/UX." *MACWEEK*, November 12, 1991, p. 102.

13 Preston, Richard, "The Mountain of Pi." *The New Yorker*, March 2, 1992. p. 52.

CHAPTER 9   Collaboration

1 Senge, Peter, *The 5th Discipline: The Art & Practice of the Learning Organization*. New York, Doubleday Currency, 1990. p. 9.

2 Rothschild, Michael, *Bionomics: Economy as Ecosystem*. New York, Henry Holt and Company, 1990. p. 185.

3 Drucker, Peter, *Post-Capitalist Society*. New York, HarperBusiness, 1993. p. 193.

4 Semler, Ricardo, "Managing Without Managers." *Harvard Business Review*, September–October 1989.

5 Drucker, Peter, *Post-Capitalist Society*. New York, HarperBusiness, 1993. p. 193.

6 Doyle, Michael and David Straus, *How To Make Meetings Work*. New York, Jove Books, 1976. p. 9.

7 Ibid. p. 19.

8 Tichy, Noel M. and Stratford Sherman, *Control Your Destiny or Someone Else Will*. New York, Currency Doubleday, 1993. p. 248.

9 Ibid. pp. 200, 201.

10 Rose, Colin, *Accelerated Learning*. New York, Dell Publishing Co. Inc., 1985.

11 Senge, Peter, *The 5th Discipline: The Art & Practice of the Learning Organization*. New York, Doubleday Currency, 1990. p. 313.

12 Hammer , Michael and James Champy, *Reengineering the Corporation: A Manifesto for Business Revolution*. New York, HarperBusiness, 1993. p. 11.

13 Ibid. p 32.

14 Ibid. p. 3.

15 Oldenburg, Don, "Creativity From Chaos: A Free-Form Theory For Transforming the Common Meeting." *The Washington Post*, February 20, 1992.

16 Owen, Harrison, "Open Space Technology Comes of Age." *Open Space*, H.H. Owen & Company, September, 1990.

17 Owen, Harrison, *Open Space Technology: A User's Guide*. Potomac, MD, Abbott Publishing, 1992. p. 18.

18 Ibid. p. 68.

19 Oldenburg, Don, "Creativity From Chaos: A Free-Form Theory For Transforming the Common Meeting." *The Washington Post*, February 20, 1992.

20 Owen, Harrison, *Open Space Technology: A User's Guide*. Potomac, MD, Abbott Publishing, 1992. p. 12.

21 Owen, Harrison, "Open Space Technology Comes of Age." *Open Space*, H.H. Owen & Company, September, 1990.

CHAPTER 10   Places for Learning

1 CRSS Architects, Inc., *Chrysler Technology Center: The Ultimate Advantage*. Published by CRSS Architects, Inc., Houston, TX, 1991.

2 Hammer , Michael and James Champy, *Reengineering the Corporation: A Manifesto for Business Revolution*. New York, HarperBusiness, 1993. p. 194. Regis Feltz, describing work at Bell Atlantic.

3 Rothschild, Michael. Remarks at The First Bionomics Conference, October 8, 1993, San Francisco, California.

4 Argote, Linda and Dennis Epple, "Learning Curves in Manufacturing." *Science*, Volume 247, February 23, 1990. p. 920.

5 Tichy, Noel M. and Stratford Sherman, *Control Your Destiny or Someone Else Will.* New York, Currency Doubleday, 1993. p. 18. Unfortunately, these figures do not seem to have been adjusted for inflation.

6 Drucker, Peter, *The Age of Discontinuity.* New York, Harper & Row, Publishers, 1968, 1969.

7 Drucker, Peter, *Post-Capitalist Society.* New York, HarperBusiness, 1993. p. 39.

8 Reich, Robert, *The Work of Nations.* New York, Vintage Books, 1991, 1992. p. 178.

9 Morris, Langdon and Cynthia Foo with Pascal Baudry, Ph.D., *Innovation Management: The State of the Art.* Lafayette, CA, WDHB Consulting Group, 1994. Interview with William Miller, January 12, 1994.

10 Drucker, Peter, *Post-Capitalist Society.* New York, HarperBusiness, 1993.

11 Semler, Ricardo, *Maverick.* New York, Warner Books, 1993. p. 297.

12 Hammer , Michael and James Champy, *Reengineering the Corporation: A Manifesto for Business Revolution.* New York, HarperBusiness, 1993. p. 112.

13 Coffman, Bryan, private correspondence with the author, 1994.

14 Beer, Stafford, *Platform for Change.* Chichester, John Wiley & Sons, 1975.

15 Beer, Stafford, *Brain of the Firm.* Chichester, John Wiley & Sons, 1981.

16 Ibid. p. 194.

17 Steelcase Inc., Grand Rapids, MI. *Hybritech Incorporated Case Study.* 1994. Comments by Jim Killion, Ph.D., senior research scientist of Hybritech.

18 Cornell, Paul and Mark Baloga "Work Evolution and the New 'Office' " in *Productivity in Knowledge-Intensive Organizations: Integrating the Physical, Social, and Informational Environments;* Working Papers of the Grand Rapids Workshop, April 8–9, 1992. H. Van Dyke Parunak, editor. Ann Arbor, MI, Industrial Technology Institute.

PART FOUR   PRACTICE: Transformation

1 Tichy, Noel M. and Stratford Sherman, *Control Your Destiny or Someone Else Will.* New York, Currency Doubleday, 1993. p. 245.

CHAPTER 11   Transformation by Design

1 Roosevelt, Franklin D., Fireside Chat, February 23, 1942.

2 Kearns, David and David Nadler, *Prophets in the Dark: How Xerox Reinvented Itself and Beat Back the Japanese.* New York, HarperBusiness, 1993. p. 287.

3 Senge, Peter, *The Fifth Discipline: The Art & Practice of The Learning Organization.* New York, Doubleday Currency, 1990. pp. 241, 242.

4 Morris, Langdon, Cynthia Foo and Christian Forthomme, *Leadership in Retail: Change Management and Customer Service Strategies.* Lafayette, CA, WDHB Consulting Group, 1994. Interview with Gerardo Ruiz, Public Relations Coordinator, Wal-Mart, March 19, 1994.

5 Morris, Langdon, Cynthia Foo and Christian Forthomme, *Leadership in Retail: Change Management and Customer Service Strategies.* Lafayette, CA, WDHB Consulting Group, 1994. Interview with a Nordstrom Regional Buyer, March 20, 1994.

6 Godwin, Pamela in Hammer, Michael and James Champy, *Reengineering the Corporation: A Manifesto for Business Revolution.* New York, HarperBusiness, 1993. p. 186.

7 Gall, John, *Systemantics: The Underground Text of Systems Lore.* Ann Arbor, MI, The General Systemantics Press, 1986. p. 157.

8 Prahalad, C.K. and Gary Hamel, "The Core Competence of the Corporation." *Harvard Business Review,* May–June 1990.

9 Miller, Karen Lowry, "Honda Sets Its Sights on a Different Checkered Flag." *Business Week,* August 17, 1992.

10 Siegmann, Ken, "Hewlett-Packard Shifts Direction: The high-tech giant hopes to benefit by merging technologies." *San Francisco Chronicle,* January 24, 1994.

11 Hammer, Michael, and James Champy, *Reengineering the Corporation: A Manifesto for Business Revolution.* New York, Harper Business, 1993. p. 196.

12 Fuller, Buckminster, *Critical Path.* New York, St. Martin's Press, 1981.

CHAPTER 12 Transformation Strategies

1 Nix, Don, "Everybody Wants To Go To Heaven," Irving Music, Inc./BMI, recorded by Albert King on his album "Lovejoy," December, 1970.

2 Tichy, Noel M. and Stratford Sherman, *Control Your Destiny or Someone Else Will.* New York, Currency Doubleday, 1993. p. 71.

3 Kearns, David and David Nadler, *Prophets in the Dark: How Xerox Reinvented Itself and Beat Back the Japanese.* New York, HarperBusiness, 1993. p. 281.

4 Hammer, Michael and James Champy, *Reengineering the Corporation: A Manifesto for Business Revolution.* New York, HarperBusiness, 1993. p. 200.

5 Drucker, Peter, *Innovation & Entrepreneurship,* New York, HarperBusiness, 1985. pp. 220–224.

6 *San Francisco Chronicle,* "IBM's Chief Lays Out Map For the Future." March 25, 1994.

7 Semler, Ricardo, *Maverick.* New York, Warner Books, 1993. pp.1–7, 58.

8 Hammer, Michael and James Champy, *Reengineering the Corporation: A Manifesto for Business Revolution.* New York, HarperBusiness, 1993. p. 71.

9 Kearns, David and David Nadler, *Prophets in the Dark: How Xerox Reinvented Itself and Beat Back the Japanese.* New York, HarperCollins, 1992. p. 268.

10 Ibid. pp. 134, 258.

11 Ibid. p. 246.

12 Tichy, Noel M. and Stratford Sherman, *Control Your Destiny or Someone Else Will.* New York, Currency Doubleday, 1993. p. 5.

13 Ibid. p. 71.

14 Ibid. pp. 200, 201.

15 It is largely because of the negative political consequences of filmed news reports from the Vietnam war that TV coverage of the Gulf was heavily edited prior to being broadcast.

16 Clark, Don and Ken Siegmann, "Technology Is No Longer the Friend of Dictators." *San Francisco Chronicle,* August 22, 1991.

17 Kristof, Nicholas D., "New Chinese Revolution—The Information Age." *San Francisco Chronicle,* April 12, 1993.

18 Brown, Warren and Frank Swoboda, "Going After the Olds Guard." *Washington Post Weekly,* December 20–26, 1993. p. 19.

19 Petro, Frank A., "Why Layoffs Don't Work." *San Francisco Chronicle,* March 21, 1994.

20 Woodruff, David, "Saturn: GM Finally Has a Real Winner. But Success Is Bringing a Fresh Batch of Problems." *Business Week,* August 17, 1992.

21 Kuhn, Thomas S., *The Structure of Scientific Revolutions.* Chicago, The University of Chicago Press, 1970. pp. 148–150.

22 See Rothschild, Michael. *Bionomics: Economy as Ecosystem.* New York, Henry Holt and Company, 1990. Chapter 5, "Life's Pulse." Rothschild cites the theory of punctuated equilibrium developed by Niles Eldridge and Stephen Jay Gould documented in Eldridge, Niles, *Time Frames—The Rethinking of Darwinian Evolution and the Theory of Punctuated Equilibria.* New York, Simon and Schuster, 1985.

CHAPTER 13　The Evolving Corporation

1 Wiener, Norbert, *The Human Use of Human Beings: Cybernetics and Society.* New York, Avon Books, 1967. p. 66.

2 Rothschild, Michael interviewed in Frost, Bob, "The Business Digest Interview." *Pacific Bell Business Digest,* March/April 1994.

3 Jantsch, Erich, *The Self-Organizing Universe.* Oxford, Pergamon Press, 1980. p. 8.

4 Amelio, Gilbert. Remarks at The First Bionomics Conference, October 8, 1993, San Francisco, California.

5 Forrester, Jay, "Counterintuitive Behavior of Social Systems." *Technology Review,* Volume 73, Number 3, January, 1971.

6 Semler, Ricardo, *Maverick.* New York, Warner Books, 1993. p. 287.

7 Meadows, Donella H., Dennis L. Meadows and Jørgen Randers, *Beyond the Limits.* Post Mills, VT, Chelsea Green Publishing Company, 1992.

8 Rothschild, Michael, *Bionomics: Economy as Ecosystem.* New York, Henry Holt and Company, 1990.

Index

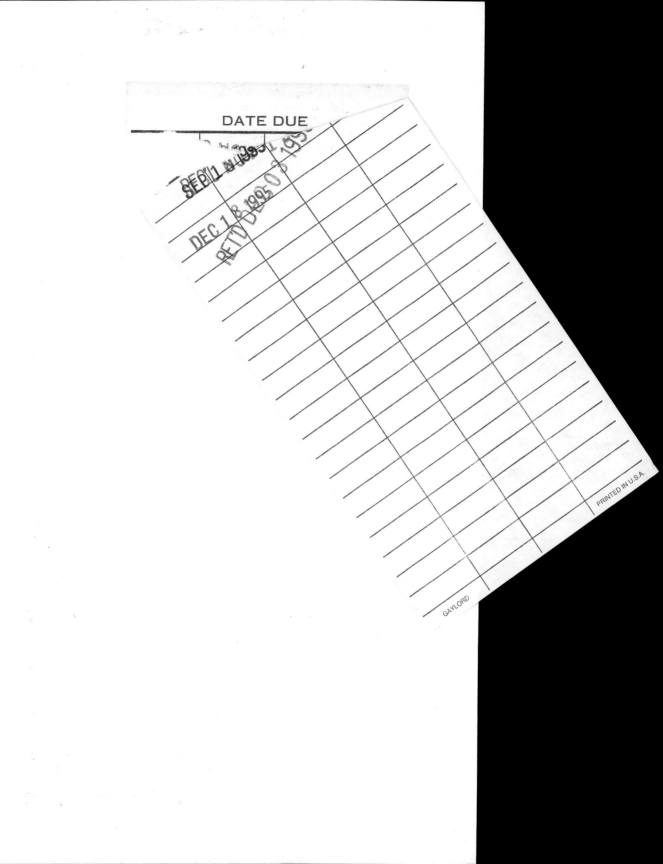

DATE DUE

SEP 11 1993

DEC 1 8 1995

PRINTED IN U.S.A.

GAYLORD